Christian Missionaries
and the Creation
of Northern Rhodesia,
1880-1924

Christian Missionaries

and the Creation of

Northern Rhodesia

1880-1924

by Robert I. Rotberg

PRINCETON, NEW JERSEY

1965 · PRINCETON UNIVERSITY PRESS

For

Rebecca Twiga Hellicar

Preface

THE activities of Christian missionaries, particularly during the colonial interlude, were of outstanding importance in the emergence of modern tropical Africa. The missionaries purveyed the ideas of the West and were responsible both for the earliest articulation of these new concepts and for their careful introduction into indigenous circles. They necessarily became agents of many types of social, economic, and political change. As such, the missionaries exercised, individually and collectively, a powerful influence, both directly and indirectly, over scattered villages and, in time, whole tribes. They prepared young Africans to appreciate the advantages of Western life and encouraged them to benefit from the temporal and spiritual concepts that were part of its foundation. The stations subsequently became the training grounds of indigenous leadership and, at the same time, the centers of anti-European disaffection.

It is this difficult dialogue between tutelage and incipient nationalism that is at the heart of any assessment of the role of Christian missionaries in African history. This book is an attempt to provide a case study of the contribution made by Christian missions to the formation of Northern Rhodesia.

Since I have tried to treat them elsewhere, this book does not discuss separatist churches and their role in Rhodesian history. For want of data, this study also fails adequately to reflect African opinion of the day about missionaries in general and the missionary occupation of Northern Rhodesia in particular. I chose to conclude my study in 1924, at which time Northern Rhodesia ceased to be run by the British South Africa Company and became a British Protectorate governed by the Colonial Office.

Northern Rhodesia has since announced its intention to become the Republic of Zambia. Nevertheless, for reasons of historical accuracy, I retain the name "Northern Rhodesia" in the title and throughout the text.

In accordance with current usage, I have refrained from using many of the common Bantu pronominal concords.

My debts are many and real. Professors Stephen K. Bailey, Cyril Black, and Paul Bohannan encouraged me to turn my attention to Africa and its history. At the University of Oxford, Professor Kenneth Kirkwood permitted many impositions upon his time and kindly read and criticized the thesis on which the present study is based. Mr. E. T. Williams, the Warden of Rhodes House, also criticized my first drafts and, in innumerable ways, contributed to making this book, and the research upon which it was based, possible. Mrs. E. M. Chilver, then the Director of the Institute of Commonwealth Studies at the University of Oxford, encouraged and facilitated my work at a time when optimism seemed in short supply. Mr. George Bennett, Dr. A. F. Madden, Professor Roland Oliver, and Professor George Shepperson all read the thesis and gave me the benefit of their thoughts. In addition, Professor Shepperson kindly read and criticized the final draft of the present book with his usual perspicacity. Professors Elizabeth Colson and Jeffrey Butler, and Mr. C. M. N. White, also read and suggested improvements to different drafts. At various times, Professor Max Gluckman, Dr. Richard Gray, and Dr. William Watson graciously permitted me to benefit from their own research experiences in Rhodesia and with mission sources.

The directors and staffs of a number of missionary societies and secular archives in Britain and several African countries all opened their doors and furnished assistance in a munificent manner. Miss Irene M. Fletcher has with great skill and wisdom introduced a generation of scholars and embryo-scholars to the widespread activities of the London Missionary Society. Both she and Canon John Kingsnorth, the General Secretary of the Universities' Mission to Central Africa, willingly read the final draft of this book with fine eyes for detail. The Rev. Mr. Neil Bernard, the Africa Secretary of the Church of Scotland Foreign Mission Committee, and the administrators of the other societies, all helped to provide the information included in Appendix III.

The Colonial Office Social Science Research Council, the Rockefeller Foundation, the Beit Trust, and the Rhodes Trust all generously supported the research in Northern Rhodesia on which this book primarily rests. I am also grateful to Mr. Henry A. Fosbrooke and the staff of the Rhodes-Livingstone Institute for providing me with a hospitable base from which to carry out my research. Drs. Raymond J. Apthorpe, W. John Argyle, and David Bettison, my sometime colleagues at the Institute, kindly permitted me to benefit from their own experiences and to learn as much from them as I could absorb.

Sir Glyn Jones, the then Northern Rhodesian Secretary for Native Affairs (later the Governor-General of Malawi), granted me access to district records and enlisted the cooperation of his administrative officers. During the course of my travels many of these officers and their wives gave me the benefit of their counsel on divers subjects and provided a high standard of hospitality. In this connection, I cannot refrain from mentioning Messrs. H. R. Beck, Gervas Clay (who kindly introduced me to the Litunga and the Mulena Mukwae of Barotseland and to the glories of Bulozi), G. G. Davies, D. P. Rees, Roy Stokes, and John Waddington. Two education officers, Messrs. David Bell and Kenneth Balcomb, likewise permitted me to share their houses as well as their tents.

The missionaries of Northern Rhodesia welcomed me personally and spared no effort to further my research. The Superiors of the various Roman Catholic mission orders graciously made records and other facilities available. The Anglican Bishop of Northern Rhodesia, the Rt. Rev. Oliver Green-Wilkinson, now the Archbishop of Central Africa, encouraged my work at an early stage and allowed me to use the records of his diocese. I can hardly mention all of the numerable missionaries who made my long stay in their adopted country both physically easier and intellectually enjoyable. Nevertheless, I wish particularly to remember Canon John Houghton, Canon A. G. Rodgers, Rev. M. A. Prokoph, S.J., Mr. Bernard Jenkin, the Rev. Mr. John Shaw, Dr. James T. Worsfold, Mr. William Lammond, the Rev. Mr. Robert Foster, Rev. Killian Flynn (O.F.M. Cap.), Mr. Frank Hodgson, the Rev. Dr. J. E. Parry, and the Rev. Mr. J. P. Burger, then the Field President of the Paris Missionary Society, all of whom kindly went far out of their way to help me on myriad occasions. For permission to read in and quote from their diaries, correspondence, and papers, I am also indebted to the persons and organizations listed in Appendix IV.

During my days in Northern Rhodesia I was also blessed with the invaluable assistance and the warm companionship of Messrs. M. Rodgers Mumbi, Simon Katilungu (with whom I had many memorable adventures in Bembaland), Humphrey Maunga, James C. Chinjavata, Edward Mbewe, Leshomwa Muuka, Roger M. S. Ng'ombe, Basil Mweene, and Benson Kakoma.

Professor and Mrs. Peter McEwan, Mr. and Mrs. Peter Stutley, and Mr. Roy M. Hofheinz Jr. contributed far more than they realized at the time to the book as it eventually emerged. Miss Linda Harsh arranged to have the final draft of this book typed and Mrs. Mary Hodgdon helped me ready it for the press. Mr. Robert Sutcliffe generously helped me to compile the original, longer, bibliography. Joanna, my wife, drew the maps. In her usual perceptive way, she also read and criticized constructively successive drafts. She added to them constantly and this book itself remains as much hers as mine.

R. I. R.

4 August 1964

Contents

Contents

Illustrations

Christian Missionaries
and the Creation
of Northern Rhodesia,
1880-1924

Chapter I. The Occupation of
Northern Rhodesia

FOR David Livingstone, "the end of the geographical feat [was] the beginning of the missionary enterprise."[1] His patient explorations kindled a renewed Western interest in the heart of Africa and encouraged other Britons to concern themselves with the welfare of "darkest Africa." Although he was anticipated in his discoveries by a number of Portuguese entrepreneurs, his example alone opened up Central Africa and made its rapid occupation by missionaries of many denominations possible. In some way each denomination sought to emulate him, and to minister to the benighted millions of Central Africa in his name.

Livingstone went to work in a Scottish cotton mill at the age of ten, and later studied medicine in Glasgow. He joined the London Missionary Society (an undenominational foundation that later developed strong ties to the Congregational Church), hoping to be sent to China, but the first Opium War intervened, and he was instead persuaded to join the experienced Robert Moffat at the Kuruman station in Bechuanaland. Before too long, Livingstone had begun to prospect for sites for a new mission station beyond Kuruman.

In 1849, after marrying Moffat's daughter and establishing his own stations, Livingstone guided the first successful European crossing of the Kalahari desert to

[1] Quoted in George Seaver, *David Livingstone: His Life and Letters* (London, 1957), 267.

Lake Ngami. Later, in order to provide a new outlet for evangelical enterprise, he followed up the visit to Lake Ngami with journeys across the desert toward the Chobe and Zambezi Rivers. Upon reaching the Zambezi at Old Sesheke in August 1851, he anticipated that the river might provide him with an easy road into the heart of Africa—with its unevangelized millions—that was not dependent upon the dangerous route across the Kalahari desert. For the first time, he also came into contact with the slave trade. Together, apparent evangelical opportunity and the horrors of the slave trade provided the tasks to which he devoted the remainder of his life. He wrote: "You will see . . . what an immense region God in His Providence has opened up. If we can enter in and form a settlement we shall be able in the course of a very few years to put a stop to the slave trade in that quarter. . . . Providence seems to call me to regions beyond."[2]

Livingstone became obsessed with a desire to open up the interior of tropical Africa to new forms of commerce and Christianity in order to end the slave trade, foster missionary endeavor, and destroy ignorance, poverty, and isolation—all obstacles to the "civilization" of Africa. Between 1853 and 1856 he therefore investigated the "unknown" regions of Central Africa. From Linyanti, the Kololo center on the Chobe, Livingstone in 1853 travelled up the Zambezi River at the head of a small company of Africans. This, his first visit to Barotseland, in many ways prepared the way for its later settlement by British and French Protestant missionaries. Wherever his party went, it was greeted hospitably: "The people of every village treated us most liberally, presenting,

[2] *Ibid.*, 144.

4

besides oxen, butter, milk, and meal, more than we could stow away in our canoes. The cows in this valley are now yielding . . . more milk than the people can use, and both men and women present butter in such quantity, that I shall be able to refresh my [Kololo] men as we move along."[3]

They continued north, across Lunda country—to which Plymouth Brethren were later to take the Gospel—and in early 1854 traversed Portuguese territory to Luanda, on the Atlantic Ocean. After a much needed rest, Livingstone turned once again towards the Zambezi River. In September 1855, after another trek across Barotseland, he reached Linyanti, where he had originally embarked upon his explorations nearly two years before.

Within a few months Livingstone completed his pioneer examination of the heart of Africa. Travelling down the Zambezi River, he experienced the thrill of the falls that he named Victoria, after the Queen of England. Then, avoiding the warlike Ila, he crossed the Tonga plateau and eventually followed the course of the Zambezi River to Tete and Quelimane, in Moçambique. He arrived at the Indian Ocean in May 1856, having taken twenty months to negotiate the African continent from west to east. Six months later, after the news of his travels had preceded him home, Livingstone arrived in London to receive Britain's highest honors and to set in motion a series of events that in time resulted in the rapid growth of missionary enterprise in the parts of Central Africa that he had explored.

Livingstone completely captured the public sympathy. When he appealed for religious reinforcements and for a full-scale attack upon the slave trade, all Britain lis-

[3] David Livingstone, *Missionary Travels and Researches in South Africa* (London, 1857), 246.

tened. The famous speech at Cambridge epitomized his appeal: "I know that in a few years I shall be cut off in that country which is now open; do not let it be shut again. I go back to Africa to try to make an open path for Christianity. Do you carry out the work which I have begun. I leave it to you."[4] This speech, and others like it, contributed to the formation of the Universities' Mission to Central Africa (an Anglican foundation) and, in time, to the direction of a number of Scottish, English, and French missionary bodies towards the tribal areas of what became Northern Rhodesia. But, before they were able to take up his challenge, Livingstone returned again to Central Africa.

At the head of an expedition sponsored by the British government, the Scottish explorer sought ways whereby Christianity and commerce could most expeditiously be introduced into the heart of Africa. An attempt to ascend the Zambezi River by ship proved abortive, and Livingstone therefore concentrated his efforts upon what became Nyasaland. In 1859 he became the first European to describe Lakes Chilwa and Nyasa. During the course of the next four years, he and his white companions came intimately to know much of what is now the Shire Highlands and the environs of Lake Nyasa. They assisted an ill-fated expedition to establish a Universities' Mission station in the Highlands and contributed measurably to a growing British interest in the Nyasa region before the expedition's recall in 1863.[5]

4 William Monk, ed., *Dr. Livingstone's Cambridge Lectures* (London, 1860), 168.

5 See David and Charles Livingstone, *Narrative of an Expedition to the Zambesi and its Tributaries* (New York, 1866); Owen Chadwick, *Mackenzie's Grave* (London, 1959); Reginald Coupland, *Kirk on the Zambesi* (Oxford, 1928).

In 1866 Livingstone again reached Zanzibar on his way to trans-Zambezia. This time he was even more determined than before to seek further information about the slave trade and to obtain as thorough an understanding as possible of the configuration of the major watersheds of Central Africa. Although John Hanning Speke and Samuel White Baker had, by this time, seen the "main" sources of the Nile River, Livingstone was not yet persuaded that its "true" origins had been found. He speculated that Lake Nyasa might flow north into Lake Tanganyika, which again might be linked to Lake Albert, and thence to the Nile. He also hoped to find the source of the Congo River, which in turn, he thought, might prove to be the "true" source of the Nile itself. He reasoned that if the Congo began in a series of "fountains"—as Africans said that it did—then these might also be the "fountains" from which Herodotus had said that the Nile flowed.[6]

Livingstone's last desperate quest propelled him first from Zanzibar to Lakes Nyasa and Tanganyika. Growing steadily weaker in body and more obsessed in mind, he turned to the west, where he "discovered" Lake Mweru (previously reached by a Lusitanian doctor in 1798) and Lake Bangweulu in 1867/1868. Between 1868 and 1870 he investigated the river system that flowed north from Mweru and, in 1871, he was "found" by Henry Morton Stanley at Ujiji. Together they dispelled Livingstone's pet theory about the interconnection of Lake Tanganyika and the Nile system. But this information in turn strengthened Livingstone's belief that Lake Mweru and some branches of the Congo River system fed the Nile. After Stanley had returned to Europe and America,

[6] Herodotus, II, 28.

7

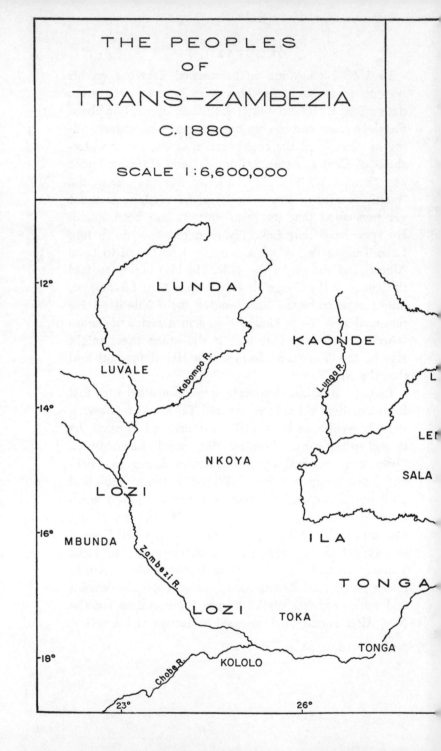

THE PEOPLES
OF
TRANS—ZAMBEZIA
C. 1880

SCALE 1:6,600,000

LUNDA

KAONDE

LUVALE

Kabompo R.

Lunga R.

-12°

-14°

NKOYA

LOZI

LEI

SALA

-16°

MBUNDA

Zambezi R.

ILA

TONGA

-18°

LOZI

TOKA

TONGA

Choba R.

KOLOLO

23°

26°

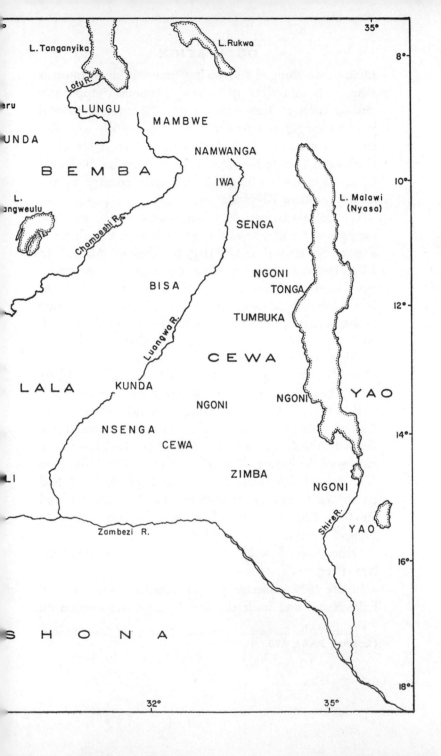

Livingstone plunged for the last time southwest towards Bangweulu and Katanga, where "fountains" supposedly gushed forth to form the Congo. For another painful year he sought the fountains; sick physically and discouraged mentally, he nevertheless continued his quest until 1873. During the first week of May he died near Chief Chitambo's village, in the Lala country of the future Northern Rhodesia.

The circumstances of Livingstone's death, and the example of his life, proved a bright beacon that directed a new evangelical outpouring to "darkest Africa." In 1874, but a few weeks after the explorer's ceremonious burial in Westminster Abbey, the influential Dr. James Stewart, of Scotland and the Lovedale Institute in South Africa, proposed that the Free Church of Scotland establish a mission in Africa that would carry Livingstone's name and be a living memorial to his ideals. Stewart suggested that "Livingstonia" should be established "in a carefully selected and commanding spot in Central Africa," and that it should be "an institution at once industrial and educational, to teach the truths of the Gospel and the arts of civilised life to the natives of the country."[7] By the end of 1874 both the Free Church and the Established Church of Scotland had committed themselves to memorial missions; Stewart and Sir John Kirk, who had both travelled extensively in Central Africa, recommended that the two Scottish churches should send their missionaries to the Lake Nyasa regions.

In late 1875 a mission party reached the south end of Lake Nyasa and built the first Livingstonia mission on

[7] James Wells, *Stewart of Lovedale: The Life of James Stewart* (London, 1908), 125.

an uncomfortably hot, isolated promontory near Cape Maclear.[8] A year later the Established Church—whose emissary had disliked all of the possible lakeshore sites—dispatched a new group of men to found a station at a place in the Shire Highlands to which they gave the name Blantyre, after the Scottish town of Livingstone's birth.

At Livingstonia the Free Church opened a school where the rudiments of reading and writing were taught and parts of the New Testament committed to memory. Dr. Robert Laws, the moving spirit of the mission, also began a medical practice there that was to draw Africans of different tribes to the small Scottish outpost. At Blantyre, however, the staff of the Established Church was slow to teach or to minister to the medical needs of the predominantly Muslim Yao among whom its members had settled. During 1879 they instead took the law into their own hands; they charged, tried, and imprisoned Africans accused of murder or theft, flogged many of the accused until they were on the verge of death, and, in at least one instance, ordered the execution of an African without a thorough investigation into the circumstances of his misdemeanor.[9] When these incidents were disclosed in 1880, the Foreign Mission Committee of the Established Church ordered its Blantyre staff to abandon the exercise of all civil jurisdiction and, later, to concentrate upon the education of Africans for useful trades.

[8] See E. D. Young, *Nyassa: A Journal of Adventure* (London, 1877); Robert Laws, *Reminiscences of Livingstonia* (Edinburgh, 1934), 15-23; W. P. Livingstone, *Laws of Livingstonia* (London, 1923), 72-104.

[9] Alexander John Hanna, *The Beginnings of Nyasaland and North-Eastern Rhodesia, 1859-95* (Oxford, 1956), 29-32.

Laws and the Free Church had meanwhile decided to move Livingstonia to a site less remote from the people of Central Africa. In 1881 the mission was therefore transferred to Bandawe, on the western shore of Lake Nyasa, and a second, permanent Livingstonia—from which Northeastern Rhodesia was later evangelized—was founded, in 1894, farther north along the shore of the lake. At Bandawe and Livingstonia, Laws and his devoted colleagues established prosperous educational and medical centers and the beginnings of an indigenous church. Their success reassured the other missionary societies which soon established stations nearby, inside the borders of the future Northern Rhodesia, and provided an example that they each tried, somewhat vainly, to imitate in the years to come.

Frederick Stanley Arnot, a playmate of Livingstone's children, was the first Christian missionary to settle within the borders of the future Northern Rhodesia. Long before Cecil John Rhodes had even begun to think constructively about the wild lands beyond the Zambezi River, Arnot made a youthful decision to follow in the footsteps of his Lanarkshire playmates' father. At the same time, his family became committed to the spreading religious movement whose followers were collectively styled Plymouth Brethren. Young Arnot assisted his father's evangelical efforts on behalf of the Brethren and became a firm believer in their fundamentalist creed. To earn his livelihood, he labored in the local shipbuilding yard, and worked in a linen warehouse in Glasgow; he also prepared himself for future journeys in Africa by learning to take cross-country walks by compass, to make shoes, to tailor cloth, to repair watches, and to work metal as a blacksmith and wood as a joiner. Shortly after

his twenty-third birthday he finally left Glasgow, with
Brethren blessings, for Africa. He intended to establish
mission stations somewhere along the Upper Zambezi
River or on the high land to the north of the river. Afterwards, he expected to summon reinforcements to continue
the cause proclaimed so boldly by Livingstone, his child-
hood hero.

The sect that Arnot represented was born in England
and Ireland in 1830.[10] Never an organized society, its
members—the Plymouth Brethren—were persons who
held common views about the literal nature of the Bible
and personal salvation without sacraments. Their bond
was a common antipathy towards established religion,
and an abhorrence of any ordained or central leadership.

The founders of the Brethren movement had independ-
ently become disenchanted with the ways of the English
Church. Anthony Norris Groves thought that one need
not be especially ordained to celebrate communion.
Edward Cronin resented the need to belong to a particular local congregation in order to receive communion.
John Gifford Bellett wanted to break bread for himself
on the Lord's Day. In general, the early Brethren were
unaware of any Scriptural justification for a large body
of commonly accepted religious ritual. Like other reform-
ing Christian leaders, they wanted to return to the
"original" teachings of the New Testament.

Arnot was the first to carry the Brethren doctrines to
Africa. Nonetheless, when he arrived at Durban in 1882,
fresh from the long sea-voyage from Glasgow, he had
few specific ideas about the future of his particular

[10] For studies of the Brethren, see David J. Beattie, *Brethren*
(Kilmarnock, 1939); William Blair Neatby, *A History of the
Plymouth Brethren* (London, 1901).

13

missionary endeavor. All he knew was that he wanted, somehow, to find a good site north of the Zambezi River where the establishment of a mission station would prove possible. He planned initially to begin proselytizing among the Tonga and Toka tribesmen near the Victoria Falls.[11] But a short visit to Shoshong, the Ngwato capital in Bechuanaland, where he learned that the permission of Lewanika, the Lozi chief, would be necessary before he could settle among the Tonga, encouraged him to go to Barotseland instead.[12]

Except for the five winter months of 1883, Arnot lived in Lealui, the Lozi capital, from October 1882 until May 1884.[13] He participated in all of its activities and tried earnestly to preach the Brethren Gospel and to ingratiate himself to his tribal hosts. He practiced elementary medicine and studied the local customs. Of these, his opinion was in the British missionary tradition: "The depth of [the Lozi] heathendom seems unfathomable; it is a nation of secret bloodshed, superstition, and enchantments."[14] Moreover, the Lozi, wrote Arnot: "are clever at . . . deceit in all its imaginable forms. Never can you trust one word they say, from the king to the beggar—but indeed they are all beggars, and mean. I have often longed just to see in one a glance of truth or

[11] The hunter and explorer Frederick Courteney Selous persuaded Arnot to settle among the Tonga. Selous, said Arnot, termed the Tonga "the best disposed tribe of Kaffirs [he had] met with." *The Missionary Echo* (February 1882), 20-29.

[12] There is some evidence that Arnot also went to Barotseland in order to prevent a party from the Society of Jesus from establishing stations there. See, especially, Arnot's letter of 18 March 1882, *The Missionary Echo* (June 1882), 86-87.

[13] Arnot spent the five winter months trying to obtain supplies at Pandamatenga, in Bechuanaland.

[14] *The Missionary Echo* (March 1883), 40-41.

spark of honesty."[15] Arnot therefore opened a school where he could teach boys "of sin, death and judgment, and of God's love in the gift of His Son." The students were told of the world in which they lived—"which is the white man's world."[16] But this first British instructor in Barotseland unfortunately had an impossible task. He found that it was hopelessly difficult to obtain or to retain pupils, and when a few would come to his school, it was only with supreme effort that Arnot could interest them. Finally, after fits and starts, the school was abandoned a few months after it had begun. Not until 1887 was it reopened by the Huguenot missionary, François Coillard.

Evangelically, Arnot met with little success. Nonetheless, he urged the chief to eliminate witchcraft and trials by ordeal, to eschew sacrifices to idols, and to forbid adultery and polygyny. He even attempted to convert Lewanika, mistakenly interpreting the chief's tolerance for genuine encouragement. At one point the Scottish missionary was confident enough to preach the parable of Nebuchadrezzar to Lewanika—"the kingdom has departed from you, and you shall be driven from among men, and your dwelling shall be with the beasts of the field, and you shall be made to eat grass like an ox"— and to suffer his resultant rage gladly. But Lewanika's only reaction was to seek to marry the missionary to one of the chief's own nieces. In all, Arnot accomplished little of lasting value in Barotseland beyond encouraging Lewanika to consolidate an embryonic alliance with Kgama, the Ngwato chief—an alliance that led ultimately

[15] A letter from Arnot, dated 1 February 1884, *The Missionary Echo* (January 1884), 13-16.
[16] A letter from Arnot, dated 18 October 1882, *The Missionary Echo* (April 1883), 52-54.

to the Lochner treaty and the white settlement of Northern Rhodesia.

By the beginning of 1884, at about the time when Coillard was planning to lead a Paris Missionary Society expedition to Barotseland, Arnot finally lost confidence in his own endeavor. He had made few converts and was having little effect upon the activities of those around him. Moreover, Lewanika refused to allow him to seek more fruitful evangelical fields among vassal tribes of the Lozi. For Arnot there was small hope, and little Christian joy in Lealui. A civil war was also brewing (it took place between September and December 1884). Arnot therefore availed himself of the first opportunity to leave Lealui for the west coast of Africa. In May 1884 he crossed Angola with António Francisco Ferreira da Silva Porto, the Lusitanian trader, and settled for a time in Benguela. Years later, this journey, which followed Livingstone's route of 1854, was recognized as the beginning of widespread Brethren enterprise in Africa as well as the end of the group's first excursion into Northern Rhodesia. Brethren missions subsequently were established in Angola, from Benguela to Kalunda, in Katanga, and across Northern Rhodesia from Kaleñe Hill to Johnston Falls.

After Arnot's solo venture, the first organized Christian body to begin settled activity within the borders of modern Northern Rhodesia[17] was the London Missionary Society. In 1875, eighty years after it had been founded,

[17] But see Lewis H. Gann, *The Birth of a Plural Society* (Manchester, 1958), 22-23; Hanna, *op.cit.*, 46. For the early history of the London Missionary Society, see Richard Lovett, *The History of the London Missionary Society* (London, 1899), 2 v.; Norman Goodall, *A History of the London Missionary Society* (London, 1954).

1. Paramount Chief Lewanika, Litunga of Barotseland. The photograph was taken in 1902, when Lewanika was on his way to England for the coronation of King Edward VII

2. Members of the first Paris Missionary Society to settle in Barotseland. Front row (l. to r.) George Middleton, the wife of Levi, Ma-Ruthi, Isaiah, and William Waddell. Second row: Levi, Mlle. Elise Coillard, and Mme. Christina Coillard. Standing: François Coillard and Dorwald Jeanmairet. The

the Society received funds with which to send a Livingstone Memorial Mission to Lake Tanganyika.[18] It dispatched a pioneer expedition overland from Bagamoyo to Ujiji, on the eastern shore of the lake, and later established missions at Urambo, among the Nyamwezi, and at Ujiji itself. But many of the early missionaries died, the overland transport route through hostile country proved difficult and dangerous, Ujiji was abandoned as a station because of the antagonism of the Arab slave-traders (Kavala Island, near the western shore of Lake Tanganyika, became the mission's main center), and, in 1880, the Society proposed to utilize the somewhat safer route to Lake Tanganyika that proceeded *via* the Zambezi River and Lake Nyasa.

Captain Edward Coode Hore, the London Missionary Society's leading mariner, in 1880 explored the southern shores of Lake Tanganyika in order to find a transshipment port and an evangelical center between Lake Nyasa and Kavala Island. At the mouth of the Lofu (also Lufubu or Saisi) River, where it cut through a rich and narrow valley to empty into the southern reaches of Lake Tanganyika, Hore found villages and port facilities that favorably impressed him. He wrote quickly to a colleague at Zanzibar: "I shall recommend this place on the River Lofu as the most excellent site for our southern station. There are many villages . . . and pleasant, peace-

---

[18] The money was given by Robert Arthington, an industrialist of Leeds known as "the miser philanthropist." He personally was animated in his liberal contributions to missionary causes by the conviction that the Second Advent of Christ awaited only the preaching of the Gospel in all parts of the world. He gave the London Missionary Society a second benefaction in 1900 and supported the activities of the Baptist Missionary Society in the Congo. For his life, see A. M. Chirgwin, *Arthington's Million* (London, 1935).

ful people."[19] In 1883, after the directors in London had consented to open another Central African station, Hore returned to the Lofu estuary and established his Society's first mission to the people of the future Northern Rhodesia.

Between 1883 and 1885 Hore and others sent out by the London Missionary Society made the southern end of Lake Tanganyika, with stations at Lofu and Niamkolo, their parish. Their primary objective was the assembling of the *Good News*, an iron steamship originally constructed in Scotland and then taken apart, plate by plate and rivet by rivet, and sent in numbered sections by sea to the mouth of the Zambezi River. There the African Lakes Company shipped the sections by river boat up the Zambezi and Shire Rivers, overland to Lake Nyasa, by ship to Karonga, and then overland, along the Stevenson Road, to Lake Tanganyika. From October 1883, when the first fifty-four sections of the *Good News* arrived at the Lofu station, to March 1885, when sufficient plates were available to launch it, the missionaries spent their days wondering at the inefficiency of the African Lakes Company and, in their spare time, telling Africans "what we were sent here to tell them about."[20] They failed to evangelize successfully, and this inability to reach the Lungu people of the lakeshore with the Christian Gospel finally impelled the missionaries to withdraw from the southern end of Lake Tanganyika and, with the exception of occasional visits to Niamkolo,

[19] London Missionary Society archives (hereinafter, LMS), Hore to Whitehouse, 12 April 1880, box Central Africa (CA) iii/1/d. For a somewhat later description of the estuary, see Roland Oliver, *Sir Harry Johnston and the Scramble for Africa* (London, 1957), 167-168.

[20] LMS, Roxburgh to Thompson, 31 October 1884, CA v/5/c.

temporarily to concentrate their efforts upon Kavala Island.

The London Missionary Society returned permanently to the southern end of Lake Tanganyika only in September 1887. At Fwambo, among the Mambwe people who inhabited the high plateaux overlooking the lake, the Society established a station that was to be the sole manifestation of the British presence between Lakes Nyasa and Tanganyika until 1891. As such, the early construction of an inland base permitted the Society to acquire a firm evangelical hold on some of the peoples of the plateaux. At the same time, Fwambo was intentionally designed to serve as a secure base from which the missionaries could spread the Gospel throughout what was to become Northeastern Rhodesia. It was independent of Kavala Island and the other Tanganyika bases and it constituted an implicit recognition that the Society's original attempt to spread the Gospel from a fleet of ships had been ill-adapted to the needs and realities of Africa. Just as the dispatch of the *Good News* marked the beginning of the end of the very policy that it was meant to serve, so the establishment of Fwambo accelerated this end.[21]

By the time that the London missionaries had finally selected Fwambo as the site of their first Rhodesian station, the Paris Missionary Society had already succeeded Arnot in Barotseland. This Society, founded in 1828, entered Basutoland in 1833 and subsequently played a substantial role in bringing the mountainous enclave within the Western orbit. Foremost among the missionaries there was François Coillard (1834-1904), a Huguenot pastor of strong evangelical beliefs and great

---

[21] Cf. Hanna, *op.cit.*, 46.

moral courage who had joined the society in response to the inspiration of Robert Moffat.[22] Between 1858 and 1884 he was intimately associated with the vicissitudes of the Suto nation at the Leribé station. Throughout this period, wars with Boers, temporary exile in Natal and Bechuanaland, and the trying pioneer life to which he was subjected prepared him for the often more difficult, and spiritually less immediately rewarding, attempt to bring the Gospel to Barotseland.

The direction of the Paris missionaries to Barotseland came after the failure of two expeditions to the Shona, or Banyai, in what became Southern Rhodesia. In 1876 a small party of Suto evangelists and a French missionary were prevented by the Republican government from travelling through the Transvaal to the country of the Banyai. In 1877 the Basuto Church Synod placed Coillard in charge of a second party of evangelists and missionaries. This party successfully negotiated the Transvaal, but was molested by the Shona and held captive for three months by Lobengula, chief of the Ndebele. The Shona were vassals of the Ndebele, who justifiably feared that white interlopers would work to destroy their hold over the Shona. "Where," the Ndebele asked, "shall we go raiding if the Banyai have missionaries?"[23] The expulsion of the missionaries from Ndebeleland followed, and Coillard and his Christian party were directed to Shoshong, where Kgama, the Ngwato chief, received them

[22] For Coillard's life, see Catherine Winkworth Mackintosh, *Coillard of the Zambesi* (London, 1907).

[23] Quoted in *ibid.*, 264. See also the Coillard Papers: Coillard to Smith, 5 March 1878, folios 412-419, in National Archives of Rhodesia, Salisbury; François Coillard, "Voyage au pays des Banyais et au Zambèse," *Bulletin de la Société de Géographie* (November 1880), 385-401.

warmly. He listened to an account of their experiences with the Ndebele, and advised Coillard to forget the Shona, and instead to open a station in Barotseland. This was a logical step: the Lozi people spoke a language similar to Sesuto, and the Lozi had, for a time, been ruled by Kololo tribesmen of the same Zulu diaspora from whence the Suto themselves had come.

Coillard reached the Zambezi River in August 1878, and quickly announced his arrival, and his desire to open a mission station, in a message sent to Lewanika in Lealui. But this was an unfavorable moment to enter Barotseland. The chief was still involved in a violent internal conflict for the Lozi throne and the kingdom had not recovered from the long years of internecine strife. Lewanika therefore was at that moment unwilling to allow the missionaries to establish themselves in his country. In November he said that they must go away. The chief hoped, however, that they would return for good in April, at the conclusion of the next rainy season.

Seven years later, after Lewanika had rebuffed a mission from the Society of Jesus,[24] and after Arnot had departed, Coillard finally returned to begin his long and devoted stay among the Lozi. In the interim he had tried to raise funds in Europe for the new mission to Barotseland and had thereafter patiently continued his work at Leribé until 1884, when £5,000, sufficient finance for

[24] This was the Jesuit mission of 1882-1884, which had an unhappy time in Barotseland. In 1879-1880 an earlier Jesuit party attempted to establish a station among the Tonga of the Zambezi valley. For one version of these events, see J. P. O'Reilly, "A History of the Zambesi Mission" (unpublished typescript) and the extensive correspondence contained in the Campion Papers (located at the headquarters of the Society of Jesus in Salisbury, Southern Rhodesia) and in the *Zambesi Mission Record* (May 1898, and February and July 1899).

the proposed expedition, was at last obtained. Later that year he left Leribé once again for the Zambezi. At Shoshong, on his way to the Zambezi, he found that a letter from Lewanika to Kgama (written by Arnot) awaited him. It promised the Paris missionaries a warm welcome: "The one we are looking for is M. Coillard, and I ask you [Kgama], as a favour, to help him that he may come here as quickly as possible."[25] By the time that Coillard reached the Zambezi, however, the civil war that Arnot had feared had engulfed Barotseland. Lewanika was in exile; Coillard was nevertheless well received when he reached Lealui in January 1885. In September of the same year, the Paris missionaries opened their first station in Barotseland, at Sesheke on the Zambezi River. Eight months later, after Lewanika had recaptured the throne and had urged Coillard to make a new home closer to Lealui, the Huguenot leader selected a site about four hours away from Lealui by canoe. Sefula, as this second station was known, remained Coillard's home until 1892, when he opened a third station practically in the capital itself.

Coillard and his fellow Paris missionaries slowly wrung a grudging acceptance from the Lozi chiefs. Patiently Coillard attempted to introduce Western ideas and morality into Lozi life. In the school at Sefula he taught children of the royal family and of the principal chiefs. He became a doctor to the people of Barotseland. He preached against witchcraft and sorcery, and urged the ruling hierarchy to end indiscriminate manslaughter. He also encouraged Lewanika to rear cattle productively, to grow wheat, and to eat bananas, previously regarded as "medicine" rather than as food. Other missionaries showed

[25] Quoted in Mackintosh, *op.cit.*, 314.

the Lozi how to drain the marshy parts of *Bulozi* and to make canals. By 1890 their position was relatively secure; indeed, Coillard himself occupied a position of some prominence in the kingdom.

For the wider history of Northern Rhodesia, Coillard's most significant and far-reaching accomplishment was the signing away in 1890 of a large measure of Lozi sovereignty. He was instrumental in persuading Lewanika to request the protection of Queen Victoria of England and, later, to accept a treaty giving Rhodes' British South Africa Company virtually a free hand in what became Northwestern Rhodesia. Rhodes, who had obtained a British charter for the Company in 1889, thought that Barotseland and its environs were rich in minerals. He wanted to acquire control of this area without resort to bloodshed, and without giving offence to the armies of Lewanika.[26] Coillard, of whose influence in Barotseland Rhodes was fully informed, was therefore urged to obtain a plea for British protection from Lewanika. The French missionary, who was married to a Scot, undertook this errand willingly; he believed that a settled government would prevent further tribal unrest in Barotseland and would make for an ordered and regular development of Lewanika's domain. He wrote: "I have no doubt that for the nation this will prove the one plank of safety. The Barotsi are incapable of governing, and, left to themselves, they would before long have annihilated each other."[27] He also assumed that it would end his own fears of Portuguese claims from the west, or of German

[26] Cawston Papers: Cawston to Rhodes, 14 March 1890; Cawston to Sir Robert Herbert and Sir Philip Currie, 3 April 1890, Rhodes House. See also Coillard Papers: Harris to Lochner, 5 July 1890; CT 1/4/5: Hepburn to Coillard, 23 November 1889; in National Archives, Salisbury.

[27] Quoted in Mackintosh, *op.cit.*, 380.

23

encroachment from the southwest (the Anglo-German omnibus treaty of 1890 had given German Southwest Africa a window—the Caprivi strip—on the Zambezi River). Moreover, he was able to assure Lewanika that British protection would prevent another civil war and would keep the Ndebele from attacking. In these regards Coillard was fortunately supported by Kgama, upon whose advice Lewanika had previously relied. "I have the people of the great Queen with me," Kgama told Lewanika, "and I am glad to have them. I live in peace with them, and I have no fear of the Matabele [Ndebele] or the Boers any longer attacking me. . . ."[28]

Frank Elliot Lochner arrived in Barotseland in June 1890, in order to obtain Lewanika's signature to an elaborate treaty drafted by the Company. But the chief was in no hurry to sign away his prerogatives, and the negotiations, delayed as much by Lochner's lack of tact as by Lewanika's caution, occupied the course of many weeks. The *kuta* (court of councillors) wanted sufficient time to subject the treaty to thorough scrutiny, while Lochner, naturally in haste, sought to avoid the elaborate protocol by which the Lozi court protected itself.

Coillard, according to Lochner and the missionary himself, did everything within his power to contribute to the success of Lochner's mission. He encouraged Lewanika to consider the treaty quickly, and restrained Lochner when the latter sought to avoid due ceremony or when it seemed that he might commit disastrous social blunders. Throughout this period, Coillard and his fellow Paris missionaries evidently thought that the provisions of the Company's treaty would prove beneficial to Barotseland.

[28] Quoted in *ibid.*, 382. See also Coillard to Sir Sidney Shippard, 8 January 1889, in *Africa South*, 372, no. 120 (encl.).

As finally signed by Lewanika and the *kuta*, it gave protection and an annual subsidy to the Lozi. In return, the Company acquired exclusive rights of settlement, mineral exploitation and, ultimately, control of all of Northwestern Rhodesia.[29] The treaty also provided, erroneously, the basis for the Company's claim to the rich Copperbelt of Northern Rhodesia. Had the missionaries opposed the signing of the treaty, the annexation of Barotseland might well have been delayed. But without Coillard's intercession and his active furthering of Rhodes's scheme, the assumption of British rule in Northwestern Rhodesia would probably have come about less peacefully, and with far more deleterious consequences.

Whatever the Lozi may have felt at the time, within six months Lewanika and the *kuta* regretted putting their signatures to the treaty. They were understandably aggrieved when they discovered that a Company's document, not that of Queen Victoria, had been signed. Their indignation was hardly muted when they learned that a gift of elephant tusks, destined explicitly for Queen Victoria's drawing room, had instead found its way to the walls of the British South Africa Company's boardroom in St. Swithin's Lane, London.[30]

The Lozi felt that their country had been unfairly seized by a commercial group under the pretext of British protection. They had been prepared to become vassals of a great white queen, but the interposition of the Company had denied them such an opportunity. Not unexpectedly, Coillard was regarded as a traitor, and

[29] A copy of the treaty is printed in *Africa South*, 414, no. 245 (encl.). Although it was never ratified by the British government, its provisions were largely contained and extended in the Anglo-Lozi agreements of 1900 and 1909.

[30] See James Johnston, *Reality Versus Romance in South Central Africa* (London, 1893), 30-39.

members of his society suffered indignities and occasional physical harm as a result of their role in helping to secure the treaty. In addition, a new missionary group which had recently arrived from England—the Primitive Methodists—were for three years confined to the Zambezi frontier of Barotseland.

The Primitive Methodist church was formed in 1811 by a schism in the orthodox Wesleyan Methodist church.[31] Primitive Methodism was strongest in the Midland industrial towns, and tended to be radical in its views towards church and governmental authority and literal in its interpretation of Scripture and its view of the role of the church in public life. Often called "Ranters," the Primitive Methodists were "led by rough, uneducated men, who made their appeal to the poor." Like the medieval friars, their "preachers . . . were to be found tramping through the country districts preaching, in face of much persecution, a gospel of simple Christianity."[32]

The first Primitive Methodist preachers became estranged from their orthodox forbears by pursuing a policy of extreme revivalism among the poor people of the industrial slums. Fired by a vision of a New Jerusalem and by an expectation of an imminent day of judgment, they sought to counter social evils, to preach the Gospel in factories and market places, and, eventually, to found

[31] For the origins of Primitive Methodism, see John Petty, *The History of the Primitive Methodist Connexion from its Origin to the Conference in 1859* (London, 1860); R. F. Wearmouth, *Methodism and the Working Class Movements of England, 1800-1850* (London, 1937); L. F. Church, *The Early Methodist People* (London, 1948).

[32] Montague Fordham, *A Short History of English Rural Life from the Anglo-Saxon Invasion to the Present Time* (London, 1916), 153-154. See also J. L. and Barbara Hammond, *The Town Laborer, 1760-1832* (London, 1949), II, 105-106; George Eliot, *Felix Holt* (London, 1866), 42.

missions in southern Africa and along the shores of the Bight of Benin. Those who acted most decisively in these matters had been trained to speak and to pray in the little societies and class-meetings founded by their fathers a generation or two before. But they were not necessarily well adapted to conditions in Africa.

In 1888, after sixteen years in the Cape Colony, the leaders of the missionary society of the Primitive Methodist church decided that it should open up a new evangelical sphere in order to avoid a competitive race with other missionary bodies for the souls of Xosa-speaking peoples.[33] Coillard, an acquaintance of the Methodists in the Cape Colony, suggested that they would find their earnest quest for new religious opportunity satisfied if they settled on the eastern marches of Barotscland among the war-like Ila, or Mashukulumbwe, vassals of the Lozi whom Livingstone had carefully avoided. Such a challenge appealed to the Primitive Methodists, and in 1889 their first missionary volunteers sailed to Central Africa from Southampton.

The Mashukulumbwe were notorious in tales of the time. In 1885 Dr. and Frau Emil Holub and Oswald Sollner, all Bohemian adventurers, entered Mashukulumbwe-land despite strong warnings given to them by the trader George Westbeech. Sollner was killed and the Holubs were forced to flee. As Westbeech later wrote: "I'm very, very sorry for him, but especially so for his poor wife, though we can only be surprised at their miraculous escape, for a miracle it is. He had to take to shooting in

[33] John Smith, the leading figure in this attempt to find a new sphere north of the Zambezi, had been among the original Primitive Methodist pioneers at Aliwal North. His son, Edwin Williams Smith, later joined the Primitive Methodists in Mashukulumbwe-land.

27

self-defence and shot three niggers which had the effect of making them cautious and so escaped. . . . The Dr. and his poor wife have not even a blanket to cover them and no change of clothing, and they and their two surviving servants have not a complete pair of boots amongst them, the males are compelled to wear native sandals and are terribly footsore and blistered. . . . Had the Dr. not taken to shooting they would all excepting Mrs. H. have been murdered, and she to a white woman would have had a fate worse than death, for she would have been the slave of the one who captured her and entirely at his will."[34]

Three years later Frederick Courteney Selous, an experienced hunter and explorer who had earlier befriended Arnot, was chased from the same country after twelve of his carriers had been killed.[35] But the Primitive Methodists, who heard the relevant details from Selous' own lips, were not deterred. They reasoned that it was their duty to attempt to transform such blatantly unregenerate natures by the introduction of the Christian Gospel and Western civilization.

The Primitive Methodist party reached the banks of the Zambezi, after a memorable trek across the Kalahari desert in September 1890. They could not have come to Barotseland at a time more unfavorable for the success of their mission. A few months before, Lewanika had signed the Lochner treaty. In its aftermath, he refused to allow the new missionaries to proceed to Mashuku-

[34] The diary of George Westbeech, typescript, 38. See also Emil Holub, *Von der Capstadt ins Land der Maschukulumbe* (Wien, 1890), II, 196-225; John R. Shaw, "The History of Nanzhila" (unpublished typescript).

[35] Frederick Courteney Selous, *Travel and Adventure in South-East Africa* (London, 1893), 216-220.

lumbweland. He refused to permit them even to sound out the feelings of the Ila chiefs resident at Lealui in November and December 1890. For three years, in fact, the Primitive Methodist party was immured in Kazungula, on the southernmost boundary of the Lozi kingdom. On a number of occasions Lewanika offered various explanations to the missionaries, but even Coillard was unable to ascertain precisely why they were denied permission to evangelize in the interior. Initially, Lewanika was evidently suspicious of their intentions; he did not want to be deceived a second time by Europeans. Then he relented, and said that the mission party could settle among the Lozi, but never among a subject people like the Ila. But the Methodists were unwilling to bargain. They were also reluctant to give the paramount chief a cash payment, and they refused to promise that they would recruit mechanics and traders, in lieu of missionaries, when reinforcing their own ranks. The Primitive Methodists furthermore had a penchant for the unfortunate blunder at the wrong time. Whenever negotiations with Lewanika took a favorable turn, some member of the mission party would transgress Lozi custom or otherwise anger the Lozi aristocracy. Henry Buckenham, its leader, appropriated Lozi cattle without realizing that all cattle were the property of the chief; Arthur Baldwin and Frederick Ward, Buckenham's younger companions, unwittingly trespassed on the grounds of the Mulena Mukwae's hunting camp and were accused of sorcery.[36] As Coillard finally wrote to Buckenham: "I think it my duty to warn

[36] The details are contained in Baldwin Papers: Baldwin to his mother, 23 April and 6 June 1891, and in his journal for the same period, Methodist Missionary Society archives (hereinafter, MMS). The Mulena Mukwae was the second chief of Barotseland; she ruled Lewanika's southern dominions.

you that our position here in this land and yours especially has become . . . very critical. . . . I deeply regret that at such a time you should have had such rows with your boys, for that does not improve the situation. . . . I beseech you, be careful, do not yield to provocation for your sake and for *ours* too. You have fallen already in many snares unaware. . . ."[37]

Had the Primitive Methodists been of less determined stock, they would surely have returned home to England in disgust. Instead, they endured the disease and discomfort of Kazungula and waited, with ever-diminishing hope, for Lewanika to change his mind and to "give them the road" to the interior. A contemporary observer, in somewhat faint praise, noted: "One cannot but admire their heroism and self-sacrifice; and as they are determined to wait at all costs rather than face the criticisms of the society at home with a report of failure, let us hope the king may yet relent and give them the road."[38]

As late as December 1892 Lewanika told the missionaries that they were not wanted and that they "had better go back." But it seems that, during most of this period, the chief was playing for time; he was attempting to consolidate his own position in the face of concerted opposition from within a *kuta* that had expressed itself firmly against any new concessions to white men, particularly missionaries. The Lochner experience had doubtless made them wary of men who "pretended" to speak of God. Eventually, Lewanika may have overcome opposition within the *kuta*. A letter from Kgama may also have encouraged him to let the missionaries go. Or perhaps he

[37] Coillard Papers: Coillard to Buckenham, 3 March 1893, folios 1129-1131.
[38] Johnston, *op.cit.*, 162.

simply wearied of the Primitive Methodists' continued entreaties. At last, in May 1893, they were allowed to enter Mashukulumbweland. The interior of Northwestern Rhodesia was thus opened up to missionaries, and to the administrators and traders who were to follow.

Shortly before Christmas 1892 the badly equipped Primitive Methodist party arrived in what they erroneously took to be the heart of Mashukulumbweland. On the road from Kazungula, the missionaries had crossed seventeen rivers and innumerable stretches of Kalahari sand with their sickly oxen. When they finally reached N'goma, they stopped and rejoiced to find themselves among the people whom they had come so far to serve. But these first villages, where the inhabitants were only part-Ila, were mere outposts on the western edge of the center of Ila population. Thankful to have removed themselves from Kazungula, Buckenham and Baldwin chose to establish their first stations near N'goma. In later years, however, other missionaries were wont to attribute the failings of Primitive Methodism in Northern Rhodesia to the disastrous experiences of the pioneer party. Its choice of a first site, and the subsequent selection of a second, were both unfortunate in terms of evangelical opportunity and of geographical environment.

In Northeastern Rhodesia, the sphere of the London Missionary Society had meanwhile expanded west and south from the original stations at Fwambo and Niamkolo. The society sought to increase its influence over the Mambwe, Lungu, Bemba, and Lunda tribesmen, to prevent the Roman Catholic White Fathers from encroaching upon its evangelical "preserve," and, at the same time, to retain the southern end of Lake Tanganyika and the still unadministered plateaux of Northeastern Rhodesia in British hands. Both Captain Hore and Alfred James Swann, his fellow missionary-mariner, were fervid British imperialists in an imperialist age. They therefore used every opportunity afforded them by their evangelical pursuits to further the territorial ambitions of the British South Africa Company and the British Foreign Office. Indeed, Swann believed that he was "the only person who could have attempted to secure for Britain what they had a perfect right to. . . ."[39] On several occasions, despite the studied disapproval of his directors in London, Swann negotiated with the Arab slave traders of Ujiji on behalf of Henry Hamilton (later Sir Harry) Johnston, the Queen's Commissioner and Consul-General in British Central Africa. Swann served as a go-between for many of the more prominent Lake Tanganyika ivory and slave merchants and, as he appropriately wrote: "Britain owe[d] her success to the missionaries as far as this lake [Tanganyika] is concerned. . . ."[40]

In the early 1890's, before Johnston's administration had even been nominally extended to the southern end of Lake Tanganyika, the London Missionary Society sought to ensure that the paramountcy of Britain was never jeopardized or questioned seriously in Northeastern Rhodesia. Its missionaries, worried about the territorial ambitions of Germany and King Léopold, and fearful of the designs of the White Fathers, appealed to Johnston for guarantees of British protection and, occasionally, took the law into their own hands in order to buttress their own, and Britain's, position locally. In 1891, for example, the missionaries helped members of the local branch of the Af-

[39] LMS: Swann to Thompson, 30 January 1891, CA viii/3/c.
[40] LMS: Swann to Thompson, 20 January 1890, CA viii/1/a. See also Hanna, op.cit., 161-166.

rican Lakes Company, a Scottish trading concern, to depose Tafuna, a Lungu chief who was unwilling to obey
periodic demands by the missionaries and the company
for free labor and for signs of respect. The missionaries
and the traders therefore destroyed two of Tafuna's villages, captured the chief, and sent him to jail in Blantyre.[41] To the subsequent displeasure of the Society's
board of directors, the missionaries smugly congratulated
themselves upon a job well done. They reported that they
had at last assured the hegemony of the mission and of
Britain at the southern end of Lake Tanganyika.

The White Fathers nonetheless began to encroach
upon the London Missionary Society "preserve" towards
the end of 1891. This Roman Catholic order, founded in
1868 by Cardinal Lavigerie, had been active in German
East Africa—particularly along the northern shores of
Lake Tanganyika—since 1878.[42] Its missionaries moved
south, towards the high plateaux of Northeastern Rhodesia, and in 1891 established a station in the country of
the Mambwe, comparatively close to Fwambo. Four years
later, the Order prepared to abandon Mambwe, and
opened Kayambi, on the borders of the country of the
warring Bemba. The White Fathers thereafter began to
learn Cibemba in preparation for a full-scale attempt to
transform Bembaland into a Roman Catholic enclave.

The time to establish themselves in Bembaland came
in 1898. Bishop Joseph Dupont, an opportunist who believed that control over the Bemba would give his church

[41] Foreign Office Papers (hereinafter, FO) 84/2115: Buchanan
to the Foreign Office, 10 June 1891. See also LMS: Jones to
Thompson, 13 April 1891, CA viii/3/a; Mather to Thompson, 7
October 1893, CA ix/1/c.

[42] Roland Oliver, *The Missionary Factor in East Africa* (London, 1952), 48, 165.

incalculable advantages in the race for African souls, in that year attempted to save the life of Mwamba, a very important Bemba chief. Earlier in 1897 Bishop Dupont had visited Mwamba and had sought to open a mission station. Rebuffed then, the Bishop periodically distributed lavish presents to influential Bemba and ministered generally to the sick. The Bemba grew to appreciate him and his fellow White Fathers and, in 1898, naturally summoned him to Mwamba's deathbed in the vain hope that he could alleviate the chief's suffering or in some way prolong his life. Perhaps by the use of drugs, Bishop Dupont made the last weeks of Mwamba's life more comfortable. At the same time, the Bishop attempted to ensure that his presence by Mwamba's side would lead the White Fathers naturally to a prominent place in future Bemba affairs.[43]

Before the chief's death, Bishop Dupont induced, or purported to induce, Mwamba to nominate the missionary as heir and successor to the tribal stool. After the chief's death, the Bishop proclaimed himself chief: "I am Mwamba's heir . . . and all [the] people want me to be their chief."[44] The new "chief" attempted to consolidate

[43] The discussion of Bishop Dupont's part in the subjugation of Bembaland is derived from correspondence contained in Foreign Office papers or in the Public Records of Southern Rhodesia. The White Fathers were unwilling to make available the Chilubula and Kayambi mission diaries, which might have shed further information of importance upon this incident. The published sources include Henri Pineau, *Évêque-Roi des Brigands, Mgr. Dupont* (Quebec, 1949), based upon Dupont's own account; Glenn D. Kittler, *The White Fathers* (London, 1957), 275-284, which is somewhat romantic; Cullen Gouldsbury and Hubert Sheane, *The Great Plateau of Northern Rhodesia* (London, 1911), 240-242, which is somewhat misleading.

[44] London Office papers (hereinafter LO) 5/4/13: Dupont to Law (n.d., but 20 October 1898); Mackinnon to Codrington, 31 December 1898, National Archives, Salisbury.

his rights of succession to the chieftaincy by persuading a number of local Bemba to ratify what the Bishop said was the "will" made by Mwamba. He also asked them to append their signatures to a rather legalistic document of cession. The French text was explained in Swahili and Cibemba to those who signed: "We the undersigned ministers and officers of the King do hereby make known to all those whom it may concern that Mwamba . . . on his own initiative and by the wish of his people had called His Lordship Monseigneur Joseph Dupont, Bishop of Thibar. . . . This same Mwamba in full possession of his faculties and liberty, in public and before us present, on the 12th day of October 1898, has appointed . . . Dupont, the forementioned, as his successor and heir and has given him the whole of his country with the rights of the soil, all his goods movable and immovable, real and personal . . . both the right of sovereignty over the whole country and territory and the special protection of his women and children."[45]

The Bishop also is supposed to have tried to bribe two European rubber traders to affix their own signatures to the document of cession; instead they discussed his claims with officials of the British South Africa Company.[46] Nonetheless, when called to account by Robert Codrington, the Company's administrator of Northeastern Rhodesia, Bishop Dupont claimed that his only object in seeking to assume sovereignty over Mwamba's people was to acquire a grant for a station in the Bemba heartland. Even so, Codrington disabused Dupont of his chiefly pretensions, while allowing him to obtain a favor-

[45] LO 5/4/13: Codrington to the Administrator (Salisbury), 6 March 1899.
[46] *Ibid.*, enclosing the declaration of John Campbell Hunter, dated 16 January 1899.

able position near Mwamba's village for the propagation of his faith.

The Bishop's intervention in the affairs of the Bemba, no matter how narrow the motive, helped to prevent bloodshed after the death of Mwamba and precipitated the assumption of British sovereignty for the first time over the central plateaux of Northeastern Rhodesia. Codrington personally nominated Mwamba's successor and told Kalongjofu, the new chief, "exactly what would be required of him in his position of chief, and directed him to enter on his inheritance without committing the barbarities customary to his tribe."[47] Bishop Dupont's singular attempt to rule Mwamba's chiefdom had, in sum, greatly facilitated the consolidation of British rule in Northeastern Rhodesia.

Only in 1901 was the British South Africa Company able to begin administering all of Northern Rhodesia in an orthodox colonial manner. By that date, two other missionary societies had sent their representatives to join those of the London, Paris, Primitive Methodist, and White Fathers organizations. Both the Dutch Reformed Church of the Orange Free State and the Livingstonia (Free Church of Scotland) missions each established one station before 1901 and later expanded their operations to encompass a chain of missions on either side of the Luangwa River—the Scots on the north, the Afrikaners on the south. Each entered Northern Rhodesia from Nyasaland, where each had been established for a number of years. In 1895 the Scots had gone north from the second Livingstonia station to construct a station called Mwenzo, near the Fife boma in Namwanga country.

[47] FO 2/248: Codrington to the Administrator (Salisbury), 15 June 1899.

Later, after British forces had subdued Chief Mpeseni's Ngoni warriors in 1898, the Afrikaner missionaries quickly entered his country, founding Magwero mission.

In 1901 the occupation of Northern Rhodesia drew to a close. The various missionary societies had begun to consolidate their individual spheres of influence and to attach a network of village churches and schools to their first stations. Together with the administrators of the British South Africa Company, they had attempted to introduce the rudiments of Western civilization into Northern Rhodesia and to prepare Africans for the parts that they would play in an increasingly more European-dominated society. Just as the missionaries opened up a hitherto unknown land and assisted the Company's attempt to make it British, so they were conscious agents of social change. Without the energies of men like Baldwin, Coillard, Dupont, Hore, and Swann, the joining of two dissimilar cultures would have proved much more painful than it was.

Chapter II. The Introduction
of Western Ideas: A New Dialogue

REDERICK STANLEY ARNOT, Northern Rhodesia's first missionary, described mightily the "awful heathenism" by which he was surrounded. In his eyes, Barotseland was a vast den of sin; examples of African depravity were everywhere. For François Coillard, who followed Arnot into Barotseland, the Lozi were, without exception, "utter heathen." They wallowed in an "unfathomable abyss of corruption and degradation, of which [he had] found a parallel no where in heathen Africa." In 1891 Coillard included this typical observation in a long letter to his supporters in Europe: "The Barotse are treacherous and suspicious—no savages' feet are swifter than theirs to shed blood. The least provocation, the most groundless suspicion, envy, jealousy, and vengeance justify the most atrocious crimes."[1]

Likewise, after their first expressions of pleasure at finding a people who smelted iron into hoes and were "rather superior," members of the London Missionary Society vied with each other in their condemnation of the "cowardly, lazy, thieving, and depraved" Mambwe among whom they had settled.[2] The Primitive Methodists were similarly disheartened by the tribesmen whom they had come so far to serve. These missionaries wrote of the "purely heathen" Mashukulumbwe who were, "like all

[1] Coillard Papers: Coillard to friends, 6 April 1891, folios 71-87, National Archives of Rhodesia, Salisbury.
[2] LMS: Jones to Thompson, 13 April 1891, CA viii/1/c.

38

heathens, filthy." The Mashukulumbwe were "truly wild and savage . . . a dirty nation of liars." At the same time, they were "just average heathen . . . good tempered, lazy, lousy, lying, thievish. . . ." In fact, Mashukulumbweland was "the kind of place where a man might go about at first fearing he wouldn't live six months and after that period fear he wouldn't die."[3]

Missionaries were not slow to damn the habits, the customs, and the beliefs of the indigenous peoples of what later became Northern Rhodesia. In their own eyes, and in the eyes of their committees at home, they had, after all, gone to Central Africa to offer a backward people the benefits of a European Christian civilization. Indeed, their supporters thought that the task was one of monistic simplicity. In 1889, for example, the secretary of the London Missionary Society urged his workers in the field to provide concrete evidence of their daily battles against "darkest heathendom": "We long to know that our Central Africa Mission has become a real mission of Christian teaching and Christian inspiration to the natives among whom you . . . are settled. . . . We . . . do long to hear . . . that earnest, daily, settled work is going on . . . the work of telling the glad tidings."[4] Those white men who pursued the missionary calling in early Northern Rhodesia therefore set about swiftly to destroy inimical practices; they preached a new doctrine of sin, taught Africans to read in order that they might appreciate the wisdom of the Scriptures, and sought by example, practice, and occasional coercion to encourage the necessary reforms.

[3] Lea Papers: Mrs. Henry Buckenham to Lea, 12 November 1894, MMS. See the similar description in Emil Holub, *Seven Years in South Africa* (London, 1881), II, 258-259.
[4] LMS: Thompson to Jones, 22 February 1889, CA xxii.

With the worthy obsession of the earlier Evangelicals, the first missionaries to Northern Rhodesia preached a straightforward doctrine of salvation and social change. They translated the "glad tidings" imperfectly into the relevant local languages according to the individual affiliations of the divers missionary pioneers. Yet, in addition to advocating spiritual rebirth, they demanded of Africans some visible signs of change. In the first instance, the missionaries demanded that women should wrap skins or calico around their waists and drape "something substantial" across their breasts. They wanted women to be less ostentatious about feeding their babies. Men, already accustomed to gird their loins, were encouraged to wear clothing of a Western kind. Indeed, missionaries rejoiced when a few Africans began "to respect themselves by pulling on Sunday clothes."[5] Some, perhaps beguiled, wrote home in triumph when the need to don Western attire was for the first time accepted by a nucleus of the indigenous population. In 1891 a London missionary was pleased to report: "All [my] servants are already neatly dressed and have assumed a civilized appearance."[6]

It proved more difficult to alter a wide range of indigenous customs than to change African sartorial habits. In a description of the Ila that, in evangelical eyes, generally applied to peoples throughout Central Africa, an experienced missionary wrote: "[The Ila] are a people whose national business is polygamy, their national pasttime beer drinking, and their national sport fornication."[7]

[5] Chapman Papers: Chapman to Pickett, 14 September 1906, MMS.

[6] LMS: Hemans to Thompson, 11 July 1891, CA vii/4/a.

[7] Chapman Papers: Chapman to Guttery, 23 August 1911, MMS.

All aspects of traditional African marriage were prohibited by the missionaries: polygyny, bride wealth, and a host of associated practices were roundly condemned. Persons who practiced adultery and pre-marital intercourse were punished severely, usually by flogging. All except the White Fathers tried to eliminate beer brewing and drinking; acts of drunkenness were dealt with harshly. Tribal dancing and singing, which generally offended missionaries and their wives, were prohibited. To the missionaries, drumming and other traditional ways of expressing joy seemed sinful, and were eschewed within the precincts of the mission stations. In all, the missions advocated austerity, and expected the Africans whom they protected and employed—the first converts particularly—to deport themselves in a manner befitting newly made Christians.[8]

Africans were not only unwilling to discard their tribal ways, but they were also generally reluctant to listen to the Gospel. Often the mere gathering of an audience proved impossible, and the missionaries, unlike their brethren in other parts of Africa, were unable to achieve startling initial successes. For whatever reason, therefore, the early years of missionary activity in Northern Rhodesia were largely unproductive. One pioneer lamented: "I have no thrilling Christian adventure to narrate; I have no trophies of the Cross to point you to; no illustration of the power of Divine Grace to draw. We have not had the joy of seeing starving multitudes crying for the bread of life, nor of hearing the cry of repentance. . . . Ours has been pioneer work, we have been opening a road. . . ."[9]

[8] For a further discussion, see Chapter Seven.
[9] Arthur Baldwin, quoted in the Primitive Methodist Missionary Society, *Fifty-Third Annual Report* (London, 1896), xv.

The first few converts were all in some way dependent upon Christian action for security or for advancement outside the normal tribal arrangements. Some had been rescued from slavery and introduced into the missionary household as servants. "Kalulu," for example, was redeemed from slave-traders, attached to one of the earliest London missionaries, and finally baptised in 1891. Africans who had freely accepted employment on a mission station were also numbered among the few early converts. One missionary employed a builders' assistant: "As we worked together I would take occasion to implant some scripture truths into his mind."[10] And for tribal misfits, cast out of their own environment, the missions provided a useful alternative.[11] Indeed, to receive the full bounty of the missionaries—their calico, their protection and, in time, their educational training—the ceremony of baptism was necessary. On the whole, however, this combination of forces was insufficient to provide the nucleus of a large indigenous church before 1900. Each of the pioneer missions was disheartened by its inability to make numerous and lasting conversions. The Primitive Methodists, for example, waited thirteen years to make their first convert. Moreover, he, and five other students who followed him, soon lapsed into apostasy, and the Primitive Methodists were compelled to wait patiently until a new group of catechumens could be prepared slowly for baptism. For all missions, these were the barren, pioneer years.

The "starving multitudes" cried not for the Gospel, but

[10] LMS: Hemans to Thompson, 19 April 1892, CA viii/5/b.
[11] This also was the Bechuanaland experience, according to Professor I. Schapera, *in litt.* (10 February 1960). For an excellent fictional portrayal of the similar Nigerian experience, see Chinua Achebe, *Things Fall Apart* (New York, 1959), 155-165.

for powder, guns, cloth, and technical assistance. As an indirect means of spreading the Gospel, missionaries opened schools and urged young men and boys to enroll in large numbers. Initially, however, Africans did not desire a Western education; true utilitarians all, they were reluctant to read or to write without clearly seeing the need or the use of such education. Moreover, the concept of sitting or squatting in the hot sun in order to listen to a foreign tutor was generally thought by Africans to be wasteful of time and essentially frivolous. Frederick Stanley Arnot, François Coillard, the London missionaries, the Primitive Methodists, and the White Fathers all found the gathering and instruction of Africans an almost impossible task. To overcome this reluctance, some tried to use coercion and others offered financial and material blandishments along lines later described by a missionary pioneer: "As for the school, for the first year or two the only way we could get pupils was to hire them to work about the place and then give them an hour each day in the schoolroom. . . ."[12]

Still Africans resisted the missionaries. But, ultimately, a few began occasionally to attend the early schools. In 1887 Coillard gave lessons "under the scanty shade of a hollow tree" to twenty youths, most of whom were royalty or their slaves.[13] The learning process proved haltingly slow, however; the pupils shared four books (written in Sesuto) and six slates, and were uninterested in learning how to read. They cared more for mischief; Coillard described their village as a "den of thieves and the hot bed of the grossest, shameless immorality. . . ." Furthermore,

[12] John M. Springer, *The Heart of Central Africa* (Cincinnati, 1909), 38.
[13] François Coillard, *On the Threshold of Central Africa* (London, 1902), 286.

43

the pupils "impudently rode [the mission] donkeys to death in broad daylight, stole cloth, food, tools, everything . . . even . . . barometers."[14] Nevertheless, Coillard was patient. By 1891 he was teaching 185 Africans at Sefula, Louis Jalla taught 20 at Kazungula, and Auguste Goy instructed 15 at Sesheke.[15]

Other societies were less successful. The London missionaries, for example, tried impatiently from 1887 to 1891 to gather sufficient students to start a school. Finally, in 1892, a missionary from Jamaica began a school at Niamkolo, the lakeshore mission station. Thirty-one pupils received three hours of daily instruction. Flat stones from Lake Tanganyika were used in place of slates. The emphasis of the lessons was upon the memorization of the English alphabet, English script, and Biblical stories but, for the missionaries, the results were discouraging. After three months only six students appeared for the one hour of instruction that was given each day. "Progress," wrote another missionary, "was painfully slow."[16] The Primitive Methodists likewise had little success with their early attempts to educate the Ila. They opened a school in 1895 where 25 men were taught to sing, to sew, and to memorize selected Scriptures. The mission fed them, clothed them, and, indeed, disciplined them: After two men stole vegetables from a mission garden, the missionary Arthur Baldwin whipped them and denied them supper. He explained: "My concern [was] not so much to make scholars of them, but to

[14] Coillard Papers: Coillard to friends, 6 April 1891, folios 71-87, National Archives, Salisbury.

[15] Coillard Papers: Report of the Fourth Conference of the Paris Evangelical Mission, at Kazungula, 16-22 July 1891, folios 139-155, National Archives, Salisbury.

[16] LMS: David Jones to Thompson, 5 July 1892, CA viii/6/a.

teach them truth and righteousness. . . ."[17] Within a few months, perhaps as a result of Baldwin's heavy hand, the Primitive Methodist classroom had been deserted. Not until 1900 were the missionaries in a position to open a permanent school.

In their various ways, the missions to Northern Rhodesia struggled to teach Africans to read and write their own or other indigenous languages and to acquaint them with the message of the Bible. The missionary motives were mixed and, in time, often contradictory. On the one hand, education—for its own sake—was a long-term investment in the youth of Central Africa. However elementary its level, the missionaries thought that it would help Africans to become better citizens of the new colony and, therefore, better Christians. On the other, the missionaries also felt they could not expect "mere heathens" to understand the Gospel if they were unable to read the Scriptures for themselves. The great pressure to introduce the arts of reading and writing thus came from two sources. At the same time, a number of missionaries felt that the inculcation of good manners, simple trade skills, and memorized Biblical knowledge was sufficient. This point of view and, indeed, the divergent motives that originally encouraged missionary societies to educate Africans, were neatly summarized in a letter from the secretary of the London Missionary Society to one of his younger appointees to Northern Rhodesia: "It is most important that the converts should learn to read in order that they may attain to a fuller knowledge of the Scriptures, when the Scriptures can be provided for them, but I think it is even more important

[17] Baldwin Papers: Baldwin to his mother, Whit Monday, 1895, MMS.

that they should learn to live self-respecting, progressive Christian lives. The mission that turns out good carpenters and blacksmiths does more among such people as you have . . . than that which turns out good readers and writers."[18]

The early schools were simple affairs. "A fence of grass, six feet high, surrounding some big tree . . . a few poles laid across short forked sticks for seats, and a mass of wriggling, chocolate brown, youthful humanity . . ." constituted a typical classroom sight.[19] There students traced letters of the Roman alphabet in the sand, recited its components phonetically, and slowly graduated to the learning of whole syllables. Once syllables were satisfactorily mastered, the missionary teacher wrote passages from the Bible—usually translations from the Gospel according to Mark and John—upon pieces of calico and enjoined his pupils to memorize the gobbets faithfully. He taught them to count, and to learn sums by rote. These first students, destined to be in the vanguard of the struggle to bring Christianity to Northern Rhodesia, also learned to sing religious hymns (by the tonic solfa method) and to participate in the life of the missionary church. In order to play a larger part in the activity of the mission stations, they also learned to thatch houses, to sew, to wash and to iron European clothes, and to cook in the European manner. In time, they became the evangelists, the teachers, and the station *capitãos* of the indigenous church.

From their first days in Northern Rhodesia, the need for translations of Scripture, hymns, and other instructional

[18] LMS: Thompson to May, 2 June 1900, CA xxix, 47.
[19] William Lammond, letter of 22 April 1920, in *The Echoes of Service* (August 1920), 185-186.

matter was evident to those missionaries responsible for training the leaders of the indigenous church. The task of translation was complicated by the multiplicity of languages within the country—thirty is the usual estimate among a population that then numbered about 1,500,000 people. All were unwritten, and only the peoples of the far west and the far east spoke languages similar to those for which grammars and dictionaries had already been compiled elsewhere. Most of the pioneer missionaries were therefore destined to spend months, if not years, understanding only little of what went on around them. Obviously, until they could learn the language sufficiently to communicate intelligibly, their influence would prove less than optimal. A large portion of missionary time and energy—both during and after the pioneer period—thus went into language study and translation.

The introduction of a *lingua franca* would have assisted both the efforts of the missionaries and the development of the country as a whole. Swahili, a Bantu language similar in structure but not in grammatical complexity to Northern Rhodesia's many variations on the same constructional theme, might well have provided the necessary linguistic medium. Harry Johnston, when he was Commissioner of British Central Africa, recommended its adoption by the London missionaries as a language of instruction. But the missionaries rejected this suggestion on innumerable occasions. Swahili—the language of the Muslim slave-traders of East Africa—was "infected with Islam" and was to them unsuitable as a language for Christian instruction.[20] Furthermore, even if the mission-

[20] LMS: Thompson to Jones, 18 May 1888, CA xxi, 217-218. See also Foreign Office 2/68: Marshall to Johnston, 7 August 1894, PRO.

aries of Northeastern Rhodesia had suggested the introduction of Swahili as a *lingua franca* in order to provide a common Christian tongue and in order to release missionaries of every denomination from the need to translate and study local languages, the missionaries of Northwestern Rhodesia would have suggested Sesuto, the Christian language of Barotseland and Mashukulumbweland until the end of World War I, as a more suitable alternative. English was a third possibility, but most missionaries for a long time believed that the teaching of English in rural schools would encourage their students to seek employment in the towns, and that it would hasten the emancipation of a "bad class" of "cheeky" Africans.[21] This understandable preference to teach Africans in their own language (although both the Paris missionaries and the Primitive Methodists used Sesuto instead of Silozi and Cila respectively) thus plunged the missionaries of every denomination into the deep waters of such linguistic seas as Cilungu, Cibemba, Citonga, and Kikaonde.

The efforts of the more linguistically talented missionaries contributed measurably to the effectiveness of the particular Christian endeavor and to Western knowledge of the peoples of Northern Rhodesia. With the help and encouragement of both the British and Foreign Bible Society and the Religious Tract Society, they gradually produced a number of valuable dictionaries, grammars, and translations.[22] As early as 1895 the London missionary David Jones translated *Aesop's Fables* into Cimam-

[21] For a further discussion of this point, see Chapter Six.

[22] For details and statistics, see C. P. Groves, *The Planting of Christianity in Africa* (London, 1958), IV, 357-373. See also Clement Doke, "The Linguistic Work and Mss. of R. D. MacMinn," *African Studies*, XVIII (1959), 180-189.

The ruins of the first permanent church erected in Northern Rhodesia by the London Missionary Society, 1895

KHAMKOLO CHURCH

THIS BUILDING IS DANGEROUS.
PERSONS APPROACHING IT
DO SO AT THEIR OWN RISK

bwe and began to translate the Gospel of Mark. Others throughout the territory followed suit, and reduced the languages of their own areas to writing. The most significant work was that contributed by the Primitive Methodist Edwin Williams Smith (later a charter member of the International African Institute). In 1899, before he had even set foot north of the Zambezi River, he had made known his determination to master Cila, the language of the Ila people among whom his society had chosen to work. He later wrote that he felt a "divine duty" to give the New Testament to the Ila people in their own language: "It was that which led me to Africa and carried me . . . these many years. . . ."[23] By 1903, after devoting nearly all of his spare time since 1901 to the study of Cila, he had prepared a reader and a translation of a number of Psalms. In 1906 he published his *Handbook of the Ila Language* and began to translate the Scriptures. His work, in addition to providing the basis for linguistic endeavor within his own region, became the model for those other missionaries who later tried elsewhere in Northern Rhodesia to discover the structure and organization of Bantu languages.

Parallel to their evangelical, educational, and linguistic endeavors, the pioneer missionaries to Northern Rhodesia were continuously concerned physically with the task of adapting the exigencies of an African environment to their own standards of comfort and well-being. The location of the mission station was itself important, and a cause of frequent activity. High ground, away from the torpor and the miasma of the low-lying riverain and lakeshore regions, was naturally preferred. But the estab-

[23] Smith Papers: Smith to the General Missionary Council of the Primitive Methodist Connexion, 6 February 1913, MMS.

lishment of stations in such ideal sites often separated missionaries from their supply of water and from the African population. The annals of all of the missionary societies of Northern Rhodesia therefore contain detailed stories of innumerable attempts to transfer or otherwise to improve upon the location of the original or subsequent stations.

The avoidance of miasma was always an important consideration; before 1905 the missionaries to Northern Rhodesia, like their colleagues elsewhere, were convinced that the fevers and ague from which they suffered were transmitted, if not caused, by the dank noxious gases that rose out of the swamps and the river valleys. Unaware of the role of the mosquito and the tsetse fly, they naturally blamed overeating, dense fogs, and the richness of the long grass of the plateaux for all of their own illnesses and the fatalities of their livestock. Despite David Livingstone's successful demonstration of its use, there was also little acceptance of the prophylactic function of quinine in the suppression of malaria.[24] No matter how carefully they situated their stations and their houses, missionaries therefore frequently suffered from remittent malaria and died from blackwater fever, its acute stage. They were afflicted with yaws and suffered the agonies of typhus and typhoid in addition to playing host to a number of injurious parasites. Before white men in Northern Rhodesia learned to take preventive medicine, to use mosquito nets, and to avoid areas seriously infected

[24] In 1899 Dr. C. W. Daniels, of the British Malaria Commission, for the first time surmised that the anopheles mosquito carried a malaria parasite. His discovery was neither confirmed nor accepted until after 1905. See also Philip D. Curtin, "'The White Man's Grave': Image and Reality, 1780-1850," *The Journal of British Studies*, I (November 1961), 94-110.

with disease, many missionaries were invalided home and the health of their more fortunate compatriots remained a source of continued anxiety.

Proper housing was essential if the missionaries were to stay healthy. The first mud and thatch houses were followed by better dwellings, schools, and offices of sun-dried or burnt brick. Whatever their denomination or previous training, pioneer missionaries probably spent more than half of their days engaged in the continuous struggle to keep their stations habitable. Indeed, the records of those missionaries who settled in Northern Rhodesia read like those of a number of managers of brickworks in Britain or America. Few weeks passed in a diary, or in the calendar of letters to relatives and officials, without some specific mention of the making of bricks. Each station had its own kiln, with the products of which missionaries tried, often unsuccessfully, to compete with the destructive instincts of African termites.

For some of their building needs, and for many of their material comforts, the rather isolated Central African missionaries were dependent upon long and complicated supply lines. (In 1880 the London missionaries even attempted unsuccessfully to maintain contact with Zanzibar by means of a flight of homing pigeons.) Unable to become self-sufficient, they imported clothing and calico —for African wages—from Zanzibar and South Africa. Sugar, tea, flour, and other necessities were shipped from Europe to the African coasts and thence overland along historic trade routes into the interior. Initially, the missionaries hoped that they might negotiate these routes with ox-drawn caravans, but the ravages of the tsetse fly limited the movement of draught animals and reasserted the white man's dependence upon Africans for the

51

carriage of Europe's bag and baggage. A large proportion of each missionary month was therefore spent in the recruitment of carriers for long and short journeys, and in the organization of resupplying expeditions to the coast or, later when it became possible, to the nearest railhead. The railway from South Africa reached Broken Hill in 1906 and helped somewhat to alleviate the isolation to which most missionaries had become accustomed. In fact, the coming of the train and the automobile measurably eased the burdens of pioneer life, but on their stations, and in the enjoyment of material comforts, the missionaries remained thankful for the strenuous labor of Africans.

Missionaries were no different from other Europeans resident in tropical Africa. They required domestic servants in the house, workers to maintain their stations, and numerous porters to carry themselves, their wives, and their luggage while touring areas distant from the station. Unfortunately, Africans were willing only infrequently to work freely for the missionaries. In the early years they resisted the missions' rewards of calico and beads and their methods of coercion. No matter how forcefully the missionaries advocated the Gospel of "Christian work" and discussed the "dignity of honest toil," their efforts to gather a willing cadre of energetic workers proved vain. A Primitive Methodist missionary explained to his friends in London that "the dignity and necessity of labour [was] the hardest lesson the African [had] to learn."[25] Only after the territorial government had, to some extent at missionary instigation, begun to collect taxes were Africans willing in sufficient number to ac-

[25] Chapman Papers: Chapman to Pickett, 19 November 1903, MMS.

cept the employment offered them by the missionaries. In this way, too, the missionaries helped to introduce Africans to the economic and entrepreneurial expectations of the Western world.

The missionaries helped to shape their environment in innumerable other ways, and in so doing introduced Africans to a whole range of Western concepts and techniques. The missionaries naturally sought to better their physical surroundings and tried, the White Fathers more than others, to make themselves at least partially self-sufficient. The construction of roads, bridges, and canals, was an early and, from their own point of view, necessary contribution to the infrastructure of Northern Rhodesia. They also introduced new foods into the indigenous diet: although one missionary attempted unsuccessfully to grow wheat and another failed to make cotton an economic crop, melons, oranges, tangerines, coffee, bananas, thyme, and barley all were diffused from missionary to indigenous gardens throughout the territory.

Without really being able to do otherwise, the missionaries became increasingly enmeshed in a secular web of their own creation. The need to maintain an ever larger and more costly station or group of stations became to some extent obsessive. The Protestants, with their families, were apt to succumb to the ease of a settled station life, and to rationalize more intensely about the necessary inevitability of such a situation. The White Fathers, unencumbered by family responsibilities and assisted by lay brothers, were to a greater extent freed from such ties. They were able to live more easily off the land and thereby to acquaint themselves more widely with African rural problems. At the same time, the missionaries naturally remained preoccupied with their own existence and standards of life. In the short as well as the long run, this preoccupation tended to minimize contact between missionaries and Africans, to increase their shared sense of social distance, and to enhance the missionaries' feeling of racial superiority.

Chapter III. Christian Authority
and Secular Power

T HE Christian pioneers, whether Roman Catholic or Protestant, in time transformed their elaborate stations into cultural oases in the vast material desert of Northern Rhodesia. They constructed large houses and churches, small schools, and primitive hospitals. They planted gardens, devised systems of irrigation, and built aqueducts in order to distribute the water from springs, streams, or wells. To maintain such increasingly elaborate edifices they employed numerous Africans in various capacities. In some degree, each of the missions, enmeshed as it was in an extensive secular network of its own creation, came easily to exert a measure of temporal influence over the stations and in the surrounding hinterland for which each individually came to feel responsible.

Of the pioneer missionary bodies, none exercised control over Africans more completely than the London Missionary Society. Its representatives in Northern Rhodesia, despite the notoriety of a similar assumption of temporal authority at Blantyre in 1879, gradually turned a fortuitous assertion of theocratic prerogatives into a system of governmental authority. At and in the vicinity of its stations near Lake Tanganyika, the word of the missionaries became law for Africans who were in any way subject to their influence. And like the men of Blantyre, the London missionaries enforced their own laws vigorously, according to a Western conception of right and wrong. They regulated life within the mission precincts with as sure and as hard a hand as a medieval lord his demesne.[1]

Of all the missions to Northern Rhodesia, only the London Society carried the rule of Africans to its logical conclusion. In the absence of a substitutable secular authority, each of the others likewise ruled Africans; they too recognized the truth of an early missionary aphorism: "Many a little Protestant Pope in the lonely bush is forced by his self-imposed isolation to be prophet, priest, and king rolled into one—really a very big duck, he, in his own private pond."[2] But none were as systematic as the London missionaries; none were as successful or as wholeheartedly committed to the exercise of temporal power. Their experience thus stands as a particularly dramatic example of the impact of missionaries upon the Africans of Northern Rhodesia.

Unusual circumstances encouraged the London missionaries to govern Africans who resided in the vicinity of the first stations. In 1887 David Jones, a Welsh Congregationalist, established the Fwambo station and speedily realized that the local Mambwe and Lungu population wanted him to protect them from slave-raiders. Long preyed upon by Bemba and Arab war-parties, the Mambwe and Lungu were accustomed to live within sturdy stockades for security.[3] They welcomed Jones, but refused

---

[1] For the East African comparison, see Roland Oliver, *The Missionary Factor in East Africa* (London, 1952), 51-52. Additional references will be found in Robert I. Rotberg, "Missionaries as Chiefs and Entrepreneurs: Northern Rhodesia 1882-1924," *Boston University Papers in African History* (Boston, 1964), I, 195-216.

[2] Daniel Crawford, *Thinking Black: Twenty-Two Years Without a Break in the Long Grass of Central Africa* (London, 1913), 324-325.

[3] See Lionel Decle, *Three Years in Savage Africa* (London, 1898), 296.

to work for the mission, or to listen to his version of the Gospel, until he had constructed proper fortifications and had demonstrated a capacity to resist the Bemba and Arab incursions. Jones and the other London missionaries were, however, reluctant to involve themselves in African wars. They were therefore shunned at Fwambo and at Niamkolo—labor was scarce and the churches and schools remained empty—until the missionaries belatedly built stockades around both of the stations in 1890. Once the stockades were constructed, Mambwe and Lungu families built their homes on mission land, and looked to the missionaries for protection. In their turn, the missionaries, like the medieval lords, exacted a price in return for their protection: they demanded that Africans should discard their tribal ways and instead should conform to Christian practices.

Long before the directors of the London Missionary Society fully comprehended the extent to which their representatives exercised temporal power, the missionaries had become the unquestioned rulers of a large part of Northeastern Rhodesia. They had protected Africans. Gradually—perhaps without any realization of what they were doing—they transformed an *ad hoc* means of protection into a system of total control. They felt impelled to settle conflicts that arose between Africans living on their land—conflicts that would ordinarily have been settled within the indigenous jural context. Soon they found themselves promulgating laws and judging and sentencing offenders. They had interfered with the traditional system, and they consequently appointed new subordinate African authorities or headmen. They also appointed maintenance men, road sweepers, and refuse collectors. In sum, they came to govern absolutely.

In the years before there was any other real white government in Northeastern Rhodesia, the London missionaries were, in their own and in African eyes, the dominant secular power. They consolidated their local influence. They compelled the Mambwe and Lungu who had chosen to settle in villages within the mission precincts to attend church at specified times and to send their children regularly to school. For example, when David Jones moved the Fwambo station to nearby Kawimbe in 1891, he insisted that all those Mambwe who wanted to move with him must first promise faithfully to participate in the Sunday worship and to work "cheerfully" on behalf of the mission.[4] If they refused, physical sanctions were imposed. Subsequently, when the supply of labor became comparatively abundant, the missionaries gave jobs only to loyal Africans who resided within the mission villages. Indeed, in 1898, after the threat of Bemba raids had been eliminated, employment opportunities seem to have provided the primary incentive for the continued residence of Africans within the villages controlled by the London missionaries.

By the middle of the 1890's, the London missionaries agreed that only by virtue of their rather peculiar control over certain African villages were they able to assert a religious influence. Beyond the confines of their dependent villages, Africans generally refused to listen to the Christian message. The missionaries thus concluded that they must concentrate upon their captive African audiences until the day when Africans who were not in any way beholden to them would come willingly to church

[4] Jones to Thompson, 16 September 1891, CA viii/4/b. (Unless stated otherwise, all references in this chapter are from the archives of the London Missionary Society.)

and school. For that reason, and in order to command the physical assistance of Africans when needed, the London missionaries became convinced that they must continue to rule and, if possible, to extend their system of mission villages. In letters to their directors in London, they candidly justified their own exercise of secular authority: ". . . we cannot depend on gathering the people together for the purpose of telling them our message or of getting the children into our schools. If we lose control of our villages we may lose our people and the work of years would be undone."[5] Members of other denominations would also have agreed with the additional claims made by another London missionary: "Without full control of the villages the children would not come to school; the people would not attend Sunday services; the villages would be thoroughly corrupted; missionaries would often be, as in the early days, without servants; if called upon hurriedly to go on a journey it would be impossible to get men [as carriers]; in cases of emergency . . . it would be impossible to get them [to help]. . . ."[6]

Within their domain, the London missionaries promulgated a vast number of stringent regulations. Villages were to be kept clean; no villagers were to use the village enclosure, or their own huts, or the huts of others, for "improper purposes." No loaded guns were permitted. Guns were not to be fired within the villages. All children were to attend school. Everyone was ordered to take part in Christian worship on Sundays and on holidays.[7] Breaches of these regulations were punishable by flog-

[5] May to Thompson, 9 November 1898, CA x/2/a.
[6] Hemans to Thompson, 2 November 1898, CA x/2/b.
[7] Minutes of the Tanganyika District Committee, 12-22 October 1898, CA x/2/a.

ging, by work on the roads without pay, or by the forfeit of hoes and spears. The crimes of drunkenness, adultery, theft, blackmail, administration of the poison ordeal, attempted murder, and murder were all similarly punishable by floggings or by fines. These punishments were mandatory, and were carried out without a trial whenever Africans were caught *in corpus delicto* or whenever they freely confessed to their crimes. But when an accused refused readily to admit to a misdeed, missionaries transformed their verandahs into courtrooms and acted as prosecutor, defence attorney, judge, and jury all at once. They rendered decisions quickly and, if necessary, often administered the resultant punishments themselves. London missionaries in that way became "Protestant Popes"; they *were* the government.

The London missionaries, like white men elsewhere in Africa, frequently used force to maintain their theocratic law. A favorite instrument by which they made known their disapproval was the *cikoti*, a long whip made of cured hippopotamus hide. With it, Africans were freely flogged on almost any pretext. In 1888 David Jones explained that "anyone [who knows] the African's character knows that he must be well looked after or he will take all sorts of advantages. . . ."[8] In 1898 a new missionary, astonished by the behavior of his more experienced colleagues, reported home that at one of the London stations there were "half a dozen long strips of thick hippo-hide hanging from a tree, with heavy weights, being cured for the abominable practice in the hands of the missionaries of the London Missionary Society, of horsewhipping the natives, in accordance with the necessity of their

[8] David Jones to Thompson, 26 February 1888, CA vii/3/c.

positions. . . ."[9] Beatings and thrashings were common-
place. But the missionaries acted without malice. They
merely behaved as white men throughout tropical Africa
often did when they were confronted with what they
called "outright disobedience," "simple malfeasance," or
"irresponsibility" on the part of weaker and essentially
"subject" people. An early Rhodesian administrator once
tried similarly to explain the reason why he had flogged
an elderly African: "In punishing him I was not acting as
a government official, but simply as a white man who had
to establish and sustain the prestige of his race among a
wild community. . . ."[10]

In many parts of Northern Rhodesia, missionaries
usurped the prerogatives of the indigenous chiefs. As
the missionaries were able to extend the limits of their
effective power, so they destroyed tribal authority and,
even before there was any effective administration by
the British South Africa Company, they had persuaded
Africans to respect the power that they wielded and to
regard white men in general as superior. Occasionally,
the indigenous authorities attempted to prevent the col-
lapse of their own sources of power. In the sphere of the
London Missionary Society, such challenges were coun-
tered energetically. Tafuna, the Lungu chief, was defeated and imprisoned when he opposed the missionaries
in 1891.[11] In 1895, near the Kambole mission station,
two chiefs tried to persuade their former subjects to
forsake the mission by confiscating the people's supply
of grain. But the London missionaries speedily reacted
to such a threat: they sent several men to retrieve the

[9] Purves, in Mackay to Thompson, 6 August 1898, CA x/2/c.
[10] Gielgud to Codrington, 21 November 1900, in A/3/8/1, the
Lusaka archives.
[11] See above, 33.

61

grain. When the men reached the village to which the grain had been taken, the gate of its stockade was "shut in their faces." "They were defied." The missionaries therefore armed their retainers, stormed the stockade, "got the goods away," and flogged the recalcitrant chiefs.[12] In general, the London missionaries applauded such demonstrations of their authority. They rarely concerned themselves with the diminution of the power of the African chiefs; indeed, even those who were concerned usually applauded the demise of the chiefs, or persuaded themselves that the risks that might result from a lessening of indigenous authority were adequately compensated for by the importance of the labors carried on for and by the mission within its special station villages. "Work carried on in native villages," they assured their directors, "is not to be compared with the work prosecuted in our own."[13]

By 1898 the London missionaries had developed a mode of secular rule that far exceeded, in geographical spread and duration of time, any theocracies that had existed previously in Central Africa. Individual missionaries had successfully suspended the teleological ethic and had unwittingly condoned the excesses endemic in a system of Christian authoritarianism. Only infrequently, one of their own, perhaps a brash youth fresh from an English seminary, challenged the system. In 1894, for example, Adam Purves, a young missionary artisan, disputed the right of one of his colleagues "to act as Law Maker and Judge without appeal."[14] But he, like others, was overruled by the yearly conference of local mission-

[12] Nutt to Thompson, 25 July 1895, CA ix/3/c.
[13] Ibid.
[14] Purves to Thompson, 2 October 1894, CA ix/2/e.

aries. Finally, in late 1898, an older missionary, who had been transferred from a London Missionary Society station on Madagascar, denounced the evils of temporal rule, and his fellow missionaries who perpetrated these evils, in a long letter to the directors of the Society. It deserves partial quotation:

"The frequent administration of corporal punishment by the missionary often exercise[d] a most baneful influence upon his personal character and tend[ed] largely to prevent the spiritual progress of the mission. First, the missionary as chief appears to [be] a mistake because of the moral influence of the position of the man himself; secondly, it creates friction between members on a station, and thirdly the fact of having a merely nominal head or chief makes it difficult or even impossible for the natives to understand that the companions of the missionary in charge, whoever he may be, are other than his headmen. . . .

"The fact of having as a missionary society to take magisterial charge of a station, is . . . not conducive to a right understanding on the part of the natives of our real intentions regarding them, if they are at all able to understand these beneficent intentions, or are taught them, they are in this mission at any rate able to be immediately nullified by the necessity of our having to inflict punishment. In fact instead of being regarded as the white men who carry to them the good tidings of God's love . . . we are known and feared . . . and the spiritual side of the work seems almost necessarily quite subordinate to the material."[15]

The other missionaries attempted to justify their belief in the system of temporal control. They demonstrated

[15] Mackay to Thompson, 6 August 1898, CA x/2/c.

that the system of mission-controlled villages had largely been responsible for the physical development of the mission, for well-filled classes, a large congregation, and a certain degree of financial solvency. They also tried to explain away the excessive punishments of which they personally were accused. John May averred that he had whipped Africans on only a few occasions. Once, when the night watchmen had been caught smoking in defiance of standing instructions, they received "a well-deserved" beating for "such flagrant disobedience" and "never tried the same thing again." Again, on the day of an important funeral, he had ordered that no guns were to be discharged. But the orders "expressly given," were "expressly disobeyed," and May thrashed the various offenders. On another occasion, he whipped a suspected murderer before the case had been tried.[16] Percy Jones (no relation to David Jones) wrote that he had administered the *cikoti* only in circumstances where it appeared to him to be absolutely necessary. He beat a man and a woman accused of adultery. He flogged a drunk, thrashed a man who had injured a boy, whipped a man who had used another African's hut as a privy, punished a man who had fired a gun with intent to wound, and soundly beat a man for "repeated disobedience."[17] Purves, who had evidently come latterly to accept the missionary's role as a "lawgiver and judge," was said to have forced into the water boys who were unable to swim, to have flogged a man who would not give him a gun, and to have used a cricket bat to punish a man who had displeased him in the course of an athletic event.[18]

[16] May to Thompson, 9 November 1898, CA x/4/c.
[17] Percy Jones to Thompson, 27 October 1898, CA x/4/c.
[18] Hemans to Thompson, 5 June 1899; Mackay to Thompson, 6 July 1899, both in CA x/3/d.

When the directors of the London Missionary Society at last understood the extent to which they were compromised by the exercise of temporal rule in Northern Rhodesia, they roundly condemned it. "The Society's missionaries," they said, "are not in future to take any responsibility in passing sentences or administering punishment."[19] By this time, the British South Africa Company had posted an administrator to the area. The directors presumed that he would be willing to govern their domain and that his presence would thereby obviate the need for the further demonstration by missionaries of secular power. The directors made their wishes known: "As soon as there is a fixed and responsible authority in the government of a country, the religious teachers ought not to have anything further to do with the administration of justice."[20] But the representatives of the British South Africa Company were not particularly anxious to deprive the London missionaries of their accustomed secular prerogatives. And the missionaries themselves continued to make laws and to administer punishment to transgressors. Indeed, Percy Jones preferred to deal with suspected adulterers himself, rather than to trust them to the tortuous proceedings of British colonial law. His reason was somewhat convoluted in expression: "In a country . . . where so-called magistrates can carry out any course which seems to suit their nature, it behoves the missionaries, as the only friends the hapless native has, to stand up against cruelty, adultery, injustice, and murder."[21] He flogged the adulterers himself.

[19] Thompson to May, 24 December 1898, CA xxvii, 102-104.
[20] Thompson to Mackay, 17 February 1899, CA xxviii, 168.
[21] Percy Jones to Thompson, 28 May 1899, CA x/3/b.

A few years later, another missionary confessed that he had flogged his houseboy, "but this is my own business."[22] Even as late as 1905, Robert Laws, the venerable Presbyterian missionary, reported to the directors of the London Missionary Society that their representatives in Northern Rhodesia were still exercising temporal authority and using the *cikoti*. He urged the directors to propel this misplaced zeal down more desirable channels.[23] Once again the secretary of the Society made it perfectly clear that missionaries were not to usurp the rightful functions of the secular arm: "Under no circumstances is flogging to be resorted to by the Society's missionaries as punishment of *adult* natives, and . . . it is not advisable that a missionary should, in any case, take the law into his own hands by inflicting penalties. . . ."[24]

Slowly, in the years after 1906, the London missionaries relaxed their attempt simultaneously to rule Africans and to spread the "glad tidings" of Christian joy. Excesses tended to be more infrequent, and younger missionaries were loath to continue practices that had been condemned repeatedly by their directors. The administration was also more zealous in protecting its own right to govern. Moreover, Africans had discovered a new mobility; the London missionaries no longer remained the sole source of protection, employment, and Western advancement.

[22] Wareham to Thompson, 4 January 1905.

[23] Laws to Thompson, 29 May 1905.

[24] Thompson to McFarlane, 7 April 1906, CA xxxiii, 486; Wilfred McFarlane, *in litt.* (21 April 1960). But see Oliver, *op.cit.*, 59; A. J. Hanna, *The Beginnings of North-Eastern Rhodesia and Nyasaland* (Oxford, 1956), 50.

Chapter IV. Reinforcements: The
Strengthening of Western Influence

N THE early years of the present century—
after the Christian pioneers had begun to
meet with some evangelical success and the
British South Africa Company had likewise
begun to govern effectively—a number of
new missionary organizations contributed to the variety
of religious choice that was offered to the indigenous
population of Northern Rhodesia. Each new missionary
body had previously established itself in South Africa,
Southern Rhodesia, or Nyasaland. Individually, at various
times before Northern Rhodesia became an Imperial
Protectorate in 1924, each sought to convert the Africans
within its borders who had hitherto been "untouched"
by the Scriptures. The missions gradually covered the
country, occupying its remote regions and leaving no
tribe without at least an introduction to the teachings
of the Gospel. There was abundant room for the establishment of stations in Northern Rhodesia, but the new
societies nevertheless often competed with the old for
African souls and clashed vigorously in order to acquire
the exclusive privilege of introducing their individual
brands of religious belief. In time, too, each of the missionary groups contributed uniquely to the secular and
spiritual development of modern Northern Rhodesia.

The Plymouth Brethren was the first missionary organization to be represented in Northern Rhodesia during the second wave of evangelical enthusiasm. Since
the days of Frederick Stanley Arnot, its African pioneer,

67

no Brethren had again settled within the confines of Northern Rhodesia. Several had trekked across its plateaux and had visited its chiefs; indeed, some of the Brethren had built stations on its very borders. But, until 1901, they devoted themselves exclusively to the evangelization of the peoples of nearby Angola and the Congo. They had been particularly active in the Katanga, or Garenganze, region of the Congo since 1886, when Arnot had settled in Bunkeya, near the great chief Msiri. Later, after the emissaries of King Léopold of the Belgians had killed Msiri and had occupied Katanga in 1891, the Brethren were free to open new stations east of Bunkeya, along the borders of Northern Rhodesia.[1] From that time, and particularly after Daniel Crawford, a vigorous Scot, had established a station in 1893 on the Congo side of Lake Mweru, the Brethren had contemplated the subsequent opening of similar missions in Northern Rhodesia. "At last," wrote Crawford in 1893, "we can throw our nets across the Luapula."[2]

The Brethren wanted particularly to work among the Lunda tribesmen who owed allegiance to Chief Mwata Kazembe. In the years after 1893, they therefore ventured among the African peoples who lived between Lakes Mweru and Bangweulu; Crawford visited Kazembe on a number of occasions, each time finding him unreceptive to the proposal that missionaries should settle permanently within his kingdom. Mrs. Crawford has left a graphic description of one of these early meetings:

"On the other bank Kazembe soon appeared, carried by

[1] For the Katanga experience, see Robert I. Rotberg, "Plymouth Brethren and the Occupation of Katanga," *The Journal of African History*, v (1964), 285-297.

[2] Daniel Crawford, diary, 1 January 1893, in *Echoes of Service* (October 1893), 239.

some sixty men, on a marvellous throne, made chiefly of skins. He wore a becoming head-gear, a crown of cowries.

"Round his neck were numberless chains of beads of every description. A loose jacket of bright colours covered the upper part of his body, while the lower was hidden by several rugs. Well, there he sat in state, staring at each of us in turn."[3]

Kazembe distrusted whites generally, perhaps because of the fate that had befallen his neighbor Msiri, and he rightly feared that the establishment of mission stations would presage the conquest of his country by the British South Africa Company. Despite the chief's objections, however, the Brethren in 1897 opened a station at the Johnston Falls on the Luapula River.[4] Kazembe, who could command an army of 5,000 warriors, immediately threatened to destroy the mission and its missionaries, and the Brethren withdrew with alacrity. During the next two years, they frequently urged the Company to depose Kazembe, in order that they might spread the Gospel in safety. Finally, as a result of Brethren entreaties and its own strategic considerations, the Company prepared to humble the Lunda chief. In 1899 Mrs. Crawford was therefore able to send a cheery forecast home to her supporters: "Poor old Kazembe! This month he is to be subdued. . . . I hear he has been sending cheeky messages to [the Company's representative at] Kalunguizi."[5]

[3] Grace Crawford, diary, 14 June 1897, *Echoes* (October 1897), 365-366.
[4] Alfred Sharpe named the falls on the Luapula River after Harry Johnston. Foreign Office 2/54: Sharpe to Johnston, 17 December 1892.
[5] Grace Crawford, letter, 1 October 1899, *Echoes* (February 1900), 47.

Kazembe had consistently refused to recognize the Company's hegemony over the Luapula region. He had demonstrated his unwillingness to treat with British representatives. Furthermore, the Company accused him of sheltering "malcontents and bad characters in his town," of preventing legitimate trade, and of "declaring war" by "killing natives friendly" to the Company. He supposedly had also "received European traders in a hostile manner."[6] Alfred Sharpe, then Commissioner of British Central Africa, and Robert Codrington, the Administrator of Northeastern Rhodesia, assembled an army of about 200 African troops from Nyasaland, equipped them with machine guns, and marched toward Kazembe's fortified village. Despite a telegraphed plea from the Foreign Office urging him to avoid military action, Sharpe was prepared to strike "the final blow for order in Northeast Rhodesia." He later explained: "I assembled [the army] . . . [and] informed Kazembe of the foolishness of his actions and that I did not want to use force. . . . He was told to destroy his stockade. . . . He replied that he was ready for war. Further negotiations were useless."[7] The British troops prepared to invade his village. Before any shots were fired, however, Kazembe abandoned the defence of his capital and fled into the Congo.[8] An administrative post was estab-

[6] FO 2/210: Hubert Harrington to Codrington, 6 August 1899; FO 2/388: Codrington to Chief Secretary (Salisbury), 19 September 1899.

[7] FO 2/210: Sharpe to Foreign Office, 29 December 1899.

[8] Details of the attack on Kazembe are found in FO 2/210, FO 2/211, FO 2/248, FO 2/388, LO 5/4/13, and in *Echoes* for 1899 and 1900. J. Slaski, *Peoples of the Lower Luapula Valley* (London, 1950), 81, seems remiss in his account of the affair. W. Vernon Brelsford, *The Tribes of Northern Rhodesia* (Lusaka, 1957), 37, erroneously places these events in 1901.

lished near his village and the Brethren were at long last able to cast their evangelical nets across the Luapula. The Brethren were also instrumental in arranging for Kazembe's safe return home and in 1901 they permanently re-occupied their station at Johnston Falls. Additional stations were later established in the Luapula valley, and on the shores of Lake Bangweulu.

One by one, the "untouched" areas of Northern Rhodesia were occupied. In 1905 the Society of Jesus and the Seventh-day Adventist Church augmented their work in Southern Rhodesia by starting stations near one another, north of the Zambezi River among the people later known as the Plateau Tonga. Cecil Rhodes and Robert Coryndon, the first Administrator of North-western Rhodesia, had encouraged the Jesuits to settle among the Tonga and had indeed granted the mission 10,000 acres of good land. In return, the Company expected the missionaries to teach the Tonga modern methods of agriculture. Eventually, the Jesuits selected land near the railway, only to find that the Adventists, an American Sabbatarian movement, coveted roughly the same site for its proposed station. The Jesuits staked their claim first and obtained the better site, both missions thereafter competing continually with each other for the religious allegiance of the Tonga.[9]

They were soon joined on the plateau between the Kafue and Zambezi Rivers by the Brethren-in-Christ, an American fundamentalist sect with strong roots in the Dutch and German settlements of Pennsylvania and Indiana. This church had already been active near

[9] The early activities of the Society of Jesus in Northern Rhodesia are particularly well documented in the archives of Campion House, Salisbury, Southern Rhodesia. For its role in vocational education, see also Chapter Six.

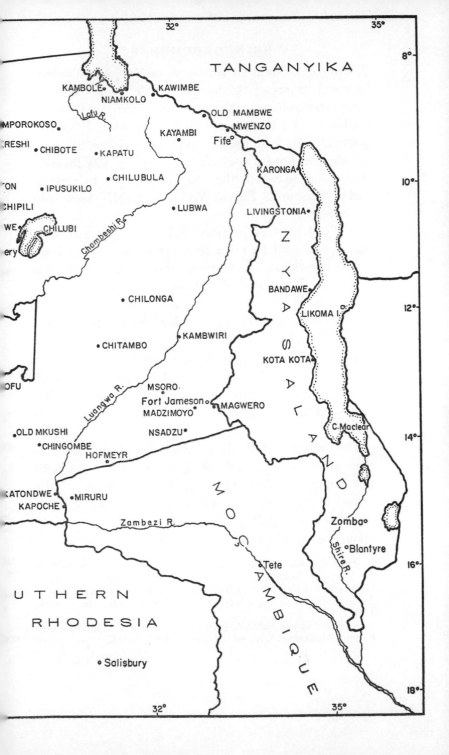

Bulawayo, in Southern Rhodesia; in Northern Rhodesia its members proselytized among both the Ila and the Tonga, competing on the one hand with the Primitive Methodists, on the other with the Jesuits and the Adventists.[10] For their part, the Primitive Methodists were not slow to heed the challenge posed by this invasion of a region in which they had long hoped to exercise exclusive control. Edwin Williams Smith's view was eloquent.

"I dread lest this [mission] field, so long regarded as our own, should be filled by other societies. . . . I am not so bigoted . . . as to resent their coming, but I am jealous of the honour of our own church, and anxious for her to hold this country. . . .

"For all these years we have had the country to ourselves. [Soon] . . . there will be . . . at least four other churches. They will quickly seize upon the best places . . . and we shall be shut out. That the Lord's work should be done by any church . . . is . . . joy . . . but [better it be my own that is] the dominant church [here]."[11]

The Primitive Methodists quickly opened up new stations among the Ila and among the Gwembe Tonga of the Zambezi Valley. As a direct consequence of the arrival of the Jesuits, they also crossed the Kafue River to bring the Gospel to the Sala and Lenje peoples. "I know our people would be sorry to hear," one of the

[10] For the Brethren-in-Christ, see the mission records held at the church's headquarters in Bulawayo. See also H. Frances Davidson, *South and South-Central Africa* (Elgin, Ill., 1915); Anna R. Engle, et al., *There Is No Difference* (Nappanee, Ind., 1950).

[11] Smith Papers: Smith to Pickett, 10 September 1906; Smith to General Missionary Council, 15 March 1908, MMS.

responsible missionaries wrote, "that owing to our lethargic policy the opportunity had been embraced by Jesuit fathers."[12] After World War I the Wesleyan Methodist Missionary Society (united in 1932 with the Primitive Methodists as the Methodist Missionary Society) established an important station among another branch of the Lenje people. Like the Jesuits, they also catered for the Soli. In 1923 the Church of Christ, another fundamentalist denomination with supporters in America, Britain, and the Antipodes, settled north of the Victoria Falls among the Tonga and the Toka.

Another vast, but thinly populated, area of Northern Rhodesia had been left untouched by the missionary pioneers. This was the region between the upper reaches of both the Kafue and the Zambezi Rivers, north of Mashukulumbweland, and south of the Congo. Within it, roughly from east to west, lived the Lamba, the Kaonde, the Ndembu or Western Lunda, and the Luvale. The Lamba were the first to witness the arrival of European missionaries. In 1905 two members of the Nyasa Industrial Mission traversed much of Northeastern Rhodesia and selected a site, near what later became the Copperbelt, for their first station in Northern Rhodesia. (Eight years later Arnot persuaded the South African Baptist Missionary Society to assume responsibility for this station after its original support had been withdrawn.)[13] In 1906 a second branch of the Plymouth Brethren began to transfer itself from Angola to the country of the Lunda and the Luvale. In that year Dr.

[12] Chapman Papers: Chapman to Pickett, 19 March 1904, MMS.
[13] See the diary of Joseph Doke, quoted in William H. Cursons, *Joseph Doke, The Missionary Hearted* (Johannesburg, 1929), 187ff.; Arthur J. Cross, *Twenty Years in Lambaland* (London, 1925), 24ff.

Walter Fisher, Northern Rhodesia's foremost medical evangelist, moved his family from a station on the low-lying Zambezi River to one in the high hills of the Mwinilunga District. He wrote enthusiastically to his brother-in-law: "We were pleased with the district, the hill we think most suitable [for a station] being 4,800 feet high, about 700 feet above the level of the country lying to the west and 200 to 300 feet higher than the country lying east. Within six miles are about twenty decent sized Lunda villages, and the people are friendly. . . ."[14] At a station known as Kaleñe Hill, Fisher established a sanatorium for missionaries that eventually became an outstanding rural hospital and an example of what medical science could do for Africans.[15] Other Brethren joined him at Kaleñe and, in time, they built a chain of stations throughout Lunda- and Luvaleland.

The missing link in the evangelical chain was supplied by the South Africa General Mission, a non-denominational sect formed in the Cape Colony in 1888 by a British evangelist and two operators of homes for invalided soldiers. (The original foundation, The Cape General Mission, in 1894 absorbed the South-East Africa Evangelistic Mission to become the South Africa General Mission.)[16] Like most of the Protestant missions in Northern Rhodesia, the Africa General offered a strict fundamentalist code to its African adherents. Its own

[14] Fisher Papers: Fisher to Darling, 8 February 1906, National Archives, Salisbury.

[15] For a further discussion of the missionary medical role, see Chapter Five.

[16] See John C. Procter, "The Cross in Southern Africa" (Johannesburg, 1943), an unpublished typescript; Scott Searle, "The South Africa General Mission" (Cape Town, n.d., but c. 1914), unpublished typescript; Mrs. George Osborn-Howe, *Through Fire and Cloud* (London, 1913).

creed typifies that of the Plymouth Brethren, the Primitive Methodists, the Brethren-in-Christ, the Nyasa Industrial, the South African Baptists, and the Church of Christ, and thus bears summation. Scripture was interpreted literally; the faith was propagated in a fervently evangelical fashion. In order to belong, its members were required to "give unmistakable evidence of conversion to God and the service of man." They were required to "live lives of danger and complete self-sacrifice and denial. They were to depend on freewill offerings for support—the bounty of God's promise." They abstained totally from alcohol and tobacco. They upheld the personal nature of the Holy Spirit, the fall of man, and the personality of Satan. They subscribed to a justification by faith in which good works were the proof and result of a saving faith; eternal salvation existed for the saved and eternal punishment for the lost. They understood the present and conscious assurance of salvation; absolution of sins was available only through the intercession of Christ and through the joyful anticipation of His return.

The Africa General Mission introduced its creed to the Kaonde in 1910. Arnot, then still intimately concerned with the propagation of the Gospel in Northern Rhodesia, had encouraged the mission to set its sights upon the Kaonde. Coryndon, then Governor of Swaziland, advised it to establish a station near the small Kansanshi copper mine, in Kaondeland, where it would also have a captive audience of mine laborers. Arnot guided Albert Bailey of the Africa General to the mine, helped him to build his first house, and then left him to learn the local lore and the local language by experience. Like the earlier pioneers, Bailey was optimistic: he wrote to his directors that, barring unforeseen misfortune, the South

Africa General Mission would soon occupy all of a "vast unevangelized tract westward to the Atlantic."[17]

By 1910 an outline of the Northern Rhodesian missionary map was almost complete. In the west the Paris Mission had opened up additional stations to serve the peoples of Barotseland. On its northern flank the Plymouth Brethren and the Africa General had begun to settle. To the east were the Primitive Methodists, the Brethren-in-Christ, the Jesuits, the Adventists, and the Nyasa Industrial Mission. The northern tier of Northeastern Rhodesia meanwhile contained the London missionaries and the White Fathers, both of whom had gradually expanded until their original foundations were no more than the nuclei of a system of flourishing stations among the Bemba and Mambwe-speaking peoples. There were also three stations of the Livingstonia mission, among the Namwanga, the Bemba, and the Lala, and three Brethren stations along the Luapula River. To the south, where in 1905 the White Fathers had unsuccessfully attempted to begin a station in the Luangwa Valley, the Dutch Reformed Church had asserted its paramountcy in the Cewa, Ngoni, and Nsenga strongholds. Already, wherever these various sects tended to overlap, there was a fierce competition for African converts. One last society soon added yet another glowing ember to the coals of religious confusion.

The Universities' Mission to Central Africa had been founded as a result of David Livingstone's direct appeal that his work in Africa should not be abandoned. It was essentially "high church" and somewhat "Anglo-Catholic" in ritual and appeal; the English Establishment, clerical

[17] South Africa General Mission archives, London (hereinafter, SAGM): Bailey to Middlemiss, 6 March 1910.

and lay, supported it. In its early years, the mission had been forced to withdraw from the Shire Highlands of Nyasaland to Zanzibar, which for several decades remained the center of its missionary sphere. Later it established a second diocese that catered to the African population of Likoma Island, Kota Kota, and Mponda in the basin of Lake Nyasa.[18] It soon became entangled, however, with the religious fortunes of the white community of Northern Rhodesia. In the early years of the twentieth century, when Fort Jameson was the capital of Northeastern Rhodesia, its small British official community naturally sought to acquire a chaplain. The Company built a substantial replica of an English village church and in 1905 persuaded the Anglican Society for the Propagation of the Gospel to supply a priest who was later supervised by the Bishop of Likoma.[19] The white officials and settlers who lived along the railway line in Northwestern Rhodesia likewise had their own Anglican chaplain, a priest of the Church Railway Mission who was responsible to the Archbishop of Cape Town. This was the state of affairs when the directors of the Universities' Mission began seriously to consider the creation of a third diocese to encompass Northern Rhodesia.

In 1907, at the jubilee celebrations of the mission in Cambridge, the Bishop of Southwark appealed for funds with which to establish a third diocese for the spiritual welfare of the Africans of Northern Rhodesia. He and other directors of the Universities' Mission had been

[18] For a general history, see George Herbert Wilson, *The History of the Universities' Mission to Central Africa* (London, 1936).

[19] A 3/11/3: Codrington to Trower, 14 November 1903, Lusaka archives. The British South Africa Company and the Society for the Propagation of the Gospel each provided £150 a year for the maintenance of the chaplain, W. J. Bell, of Kilmeaden, County Waterford, Ireland.

stimulated in their decision to propose a third diocese by the determined generosity of a single, then anonymous, benefactor.[20] As early as 1905, Thomas Edward Wilkinson, Bishop of East and Central Europe and sometime Bishop of Zululand, had offered £1,000 for the creation of a new missionary "kingdom" in Africa. He did so partially in order to spare the health of the then two bishops of the Universities' Mission. In his eyes, a third diocese would be a living memorial to those Bishops who had died while fulfilling the responsibilities of their office. He explained: "My offer is made because the lives of two very valuable Bishops of the Universities' Mission to Central Africa might, humanly speaking—have been prolonged had their area of work been divided and sub-divided. . . . It shall be my interest and my care as long as my life may be spared."[21] But as much as the Universities' Mission wanted to embark upon the creation of a third diocese, its directors were opposed by the Church of the Province of South Africa, by Bishop Gaul of Mashonaland, Southern Rhodesia, by Bishop Weston of Zanzibar, and, implicitly, by the Archbishop of Canterbury.

Each of the forces of opposition helped to shape the eventual character of the diocese. The South African clergy, Bishop Gaul and, in addition, Bishop Trower of Likoma, were concerned lest a Universities' Mission pay too little attention to the needs of Northern Rhodesia's European population.[22] Indeed, for a time it appeared as

[20] But see Lewis Gann, *The Birth of a Plural Society* (Manchester, 1958), 29; Wilson, *op.cit.*, 143.

[21] Universities' Mission archives, Central Africa House, London (hereinafter, "UMCA"): Wilkinson to the Society for the Propagation of the Gospel, 18 May 1906.

[22] At this time, British immigrants were erroneously expected to settle in large numbers in Northern Rhodesia.

5. Frank Elliot Lochner of the British South Africa Company attempting to persuade Paramount Chief Lewanika to sign a treaty with Queen Victoria and his Company, 1890

6. Francois Coillard being transported up the Zambezi River about 1900

7. Dorwald Jeanmairet's School at Leshoma, about 1890

8. The Paris Mission at Kazungula, about 1892

9. The White Fathers' church at Kayambi,
erected about 1905

10. London Missionary Society church at Mbereshi, about 1920

if the conflict over a third diocese would be confined to the advocates of a "colonial" as opposed to a "native" mission. But the Bishop of Zanzibar opposed the creation of another diocese simply because he assumed that it would detract from the funds available to finance the activities of his own missionaries. He was supported by the Mission's Oxford and Cambridge University Committees.[23] The way was clear only in 1908 when, after intensive lobbying, the South African clergy were persuaded to withdraw their objections after being assured by the Mission that it would always remember its duty towards the white population of Northern Rhodesia. The Bishops of Zanzibar and Likoma were likewise prevailed upon to agree. In 1909 the third diocese was officially sanctioned, and the Rt. Rev. John Edward Hine, a former Bishop of both the Zanzibar and Likoma dioceses, was consecrated the first Anglican Bishop of Northern Rhodesia. According to the general secretary of the Universities' Mission, within the new diocese "the white men of course will . . . need and will receive the ministrations of the Church, but the first concern of the missionaries . . . will always be . . . the spiritual welfare of the natives."[24]

The Universities' Mission claimed all of Northern Rhodesia as its sphere of evangelical work. Bishop Hine was faced with the difficult task of establishing new mission stations that would demonstrate this breadth of purpose without seeming to neglect the pastoral care of Europeans. Accustomed as he was to areas of Africa where

[23] UMCA: Donaldson to Travers, 27 November 1906; Ince to Travers, 29 November 1906; Cape Town to Montgomery, 2 January 1907; Gaul to Montgomery, 8 July 1905; Weston to Travers, 16 September 1910.
[24] *Central Africa* (1909), 309-313.

responsibility for whites was a secondary consideration, Bishop Hine early erred on the side of his African charge. In 1910, a few weeks after his arrival at the Victoria Falls, he set out on a 1,300 mile trek to acquaint himself with the terrain of Northern Rhodesia and to seek out likely sites for stations. In 1911 he walked another 1,400 miles. In the end he started stations among the Tonga— near the headquarters of the Brethren-in-Christ—near Fort Jameson, among the Nsenga, and suggested that other stations should eventually be started near the Luapula River, near Lake Bangweulu, and among the Lala. Thus, the Universities' Mission spread itself thinly across four different language groups, 1,000 or more miles apart.

Bishop Hine soon discovered that the whites were generally unhappy with his African policies. Symptomatic of this unhappiness was the mission's long conflict with the settler community of Livingstone, in 1910 the capital of Northwestern Rhodesia and, after 1911, the capital of Northeastern Rhodesia as well. In 1910 Livingstone also mirrored the racial attitudes of the other small white townships of southern Africa. No one had objected when the Paris Mission had begun to hold church services for Lozi who resided in the African sections of their town. But when Bishop Hine began to deny them their accustomed racial prerogatives and spiritual priority, the whites objected vociferously.

Should Africans be allowed to worship in the new "white" Church of St. Andrew in Livingstone? The Bishop said "yes, of course." The European community of Livingstone, the explorer's town near the Victoria Falls, said "no, never." Its members feared that a church "built by white people for white people" would, if "thrown open" to Africans, encourage them to think that they were equal to whites: "it would become the fashion for a native to attend the same place of worship as his master and mistress."[25] They viewed "with dismay the prospect of their children kneeling and sitting where all sorts and conditions of natives [had] knelt and sat. . . . [They] . . . objected most strongly on hygienic grounds. . . ."[26] The Bishop, astonished by such attitudes, refused to consecrate the church, or to release the funds that would remove its debt, until the principle of racial equality before God was generally recognized by the parishioners. "Access," he told them, "[may not be] barred on racial grounds to any member of Christ's Holy Church."[27] He also took issue with them in matters of hygiene:

"I think the Church Council forget—forgive me for reminding them—that I am myself a Doctor of Medicine of London University, and have had more experience (in the last twenty-two years) of native diseases than any of the medical residents here. I should not, therefore, be likely or so foolish as to admit anyone into the Church whose health was such that I felt any risk attached to his presence there. . . . [Furthermore], the people who will attend service in the Church need feel no anxiety about the native Christians to whom I refer defiling the seats by sitting on them. Our native Christians always are taught and required to sit on the floor. We don't have seats at all in our churches. I should [even] be quite

[25] Minutes of the Livingstone Church Council, 1 November 1910, statement by F. J. Clarke.

[26] UMCA (Northern Rhodesia): Baldock to Selborne, 1 September 1911.

[27] Minutes of the Church Council, 1 November 1910, statement by Bishop Hine.

83

willing to reserve a special chalice and paten for use at native celebrations."[28]

The Bishop merely wanted Africans to be able to worship in the church until such time as an African church could be built. He wanted to establish the right of Africans to the same limited use of St. Andrew's Church—for early Sunday morning services and occasional special services like confirmation—that they had in the cathedrals of Mombasa and Zanzibar, and the collegiate church of Dar-es-Salaam. "I wonder," he asked the settlers, "what Dr. Livingstone would think of his 'memorial' if he were acquainted with the restrictions that it is wished to place upon the use of it!"[29] In reply, the local church council, tacitly supported by the government, resolved that St. Andrew's Church was to be "exclusively for whites and that on no condition would natives be allowed inside."[30] In despair, the Bishop wrote to London: "I shall wash my hands of all responsibility, and retire into the country with my staff of men. I will do nothing to recognize the use of a church on racial lines. What the result will be I cannot say, but I have no alternative. I believe Mr. Selby is the great opponent, and he is mad on the subject of Niggers. . . . I am in hot water and the most unpopular person in Livingstone."[31]

Only the intervention of Lord Selborne, the British High Commissioner for South Africa, and the Archbishops of Cape Town and Canterbury, moved the local church council to compromise. Lord Selborne wrote

[28] UMCA (NR): Hine to Selby, 4 November 1910.
[29] *Ibid.*
[30] UMCA (NR): Baldock to Hine, 16 December 1910.
[31] UMCA (NR): Hine to Travers, 4 November 1910. Bishop Hine referred to Philip Hamilton Selby, an employee of the British South Africa Company.

strongly to the church council that he was "simply amazed that any of [his] friends in Northern Rhodesia should have suggested such [reservations]." He said: "I have never heard such a suggestion from any of my fellow members of the Church of England anywhere in South Africa, and to me—I say bluntly—it seems wholly incompatible with the holding of the Christian faith."[32] Randall Davidson, Archbishop of Canterbury, rendered a conclusive judgment: "I have considered carefully the statement of facts about the Church at Livingstone. I find it difficult to realize how men who hold the Christian faith can put the matter in the way in which some seem now to be putting it, i.e., that within the walls of this church no native of Rhodesia should ever under any circumstances join the worship of God and say his prayers! [To exclude Africans] is in my deliberate judgement, to set aside a fundamental principle of our Christian faith."[33]

In late 1911 the council agreed reluctantly to acknowledge the right of entry into the Church for Africans and to permit a small number of baptized Africans to take Holy Communion at a time separate from whites. But, for ordinary services, a special African church would be constructed. The Bishop's principles had been upheld. At the same time, the practical effect of his compromise with the council was the virtual segregation of the two congregations, each in their separate churches. In the towns, this segregation continued; in the rural areas, the mission became a true memorial to Livingstone.

Yet, in African eyes, the Anglicans were merely another

[32] UMCA (NR): Selborne to Baldock, 7 October 1911.
[33] UMCA (NR): Archbishop Randall of Canterbury to Hine, 29 July 1911.

of the many Christian bodies seeking to salvage their souls. Africans had already been more mystified than edified by subtle doctrinal differences. They had been amused and often surprised by the antagonism and rancor generated by denominational differences, by the lengths to which missionaries of one persuasion would go to seek advantage over another, and by the ways in which their villages were often used as pawns in the struggle for religious hegemony in rural Rhodesia. To a large extent, this rivalry was, in general, between the missions that refused to recognize secularly drawn spheres of influence —the White Fathers, the Jesuits, the Universities' Mission, and the Seventh-day Adventists—and the Protestant organizations that were willing, even anxious, to divide Northern Rhodesia into parishes wherein only one brand of Christianity would be available for African consumption. The evangelical division of Northeastern Rhodesia between the London, Livingstonia, and Dutch Reformed missionaries was indeed an early example of such successful cooperation. The London missionaries had also attempted to persuade the White Fathers to abide by similar *ad hoc* ecclesiatical boundaries. With reference to the Mambwe, the London Missionaries claimed priority. They "are our own, and as such we desire to retain our spiritual jurisdiction over them. . . . We appeal to your sense of honor and your sense of justice and ask you kindly that you desist. . . ."[34] But the White Fathers categorically refused to accept any restraints upon free competition.

The government of Northeastern Rhodesia attempted to impose a delimitation of spheres that would obviate

[34] LMS: Jones to White Fathers, 24 May 1892, in a volume of official letters.

such Christian squabbling. In 1905 Codrington issued regulations designed to limit the operations of the White Fathers, "whose avowed intention," he wrote, "is to occupy the whole country."[35] But the White Fathers, nonetheless, continued to compete aggressively with the London and Livingstonia missions and, latterly, with the Dutch Reformed Church east of the Luangwa River. With support from the government, the Dutch Reformed missionaries objected to this invasion of what they regarded as an exclusive religious domain. By threatening to ignore its existence and to "starve" it out, the Dutch missionaries also tried to prevent the Universities' Mission from opening a station near Fort Jameson; each battled for physical control of strategic villages until a compromise was at last reached in 1911. On its western flank the Dutch Reformed Church was also forced to compete with the expansive design of the Jesuits who, in turn, were anxious to exercise control over much of the country between the Victoria Falls and the Luangwa River at the expense of the Methodists and the Adventists. "The day may not be far," wrote a leading Jesuit priest, "when the country will be overrun by Methodists and other sects. . . ." He wrote: "There is still hope for us to make the Tonga nation a Catholic nation. [Moreover], I am now building our seventh outstation. It is a victory over the 'Adventists' who had tried hard to get it."[36] The Methodists likewise responded to the Jesuit threat by opening a number of schools in the villages claimed by their opponents. An English Methodist confided the dilemma to the pages of a diary that was dis-

[35] A 3/11/7: Codrington to Prentice, 2 September 1904, Lusaka archives.
[36] Campion Papers: Bick to Brown, 27 April 1924; Bick to Brown, 17 August 1924.

87

tributed among his British supporters: "We learned that the Jesuits are keen to start work in two places where we have existing work. . . . Their Father Superior in these climes is a Pole, or some such nationality. . . . Here we are in this district, doing the best we can. The Jesuits want to come in the same place, whilst to the North there is a huge area untouched. . . ."[37] The administration felt that it was "impossible to avoid the conclusion that the Jesuits are, with the relatively large funds at their disposal, endeavoring to establish schools . . . more for the sake of a footing than to provide education, for political rather than moral results."[38]

The records of missionary societies and the government of Northern Rhodesia contain references to an incredible number of similar controversies. The missionaries devoted considerable time and effort to the strategic needs of interdenominational war. When a society established a station, it did so in order to serve all the peoples of the surrounding area. A Methodist expressed this axiom simply: "We have planted this station to claim the whole neighboring country for our church . . . here was a whole country that can be ours just for the taking."[39] The more populous or healthy the region, the more it was coveted by others, and the more the resultant competition hindered the ability of Africans fully to appreciate the significance of the Christian message. No one gave this conclusion better expression than a Primitive Methodist schoolmaster: ". . . there is so much space and so much work needing to be done that it is more than a pity that

[37] The diary of Oliver Roebuck, 9 June 1923, in the author's possession.
[38] KDC 2/16/1: Williams to Melland, 30 October 1923, Lusaka archives.
[39] Roebuck, diary, 13 June 1922.

[many] missionary societies should be seeking to establish themselves in one village and that one society should want to establish within a stone's-throw of work already established by another mission. If this is to go on I am afraid that our Christianity will be wrecked. It is indeed a sorry spectacle which we show to the native people."[40]

[40] UMCA (NR): Fell to May, 16 November 1923.

Chapter V. The Growth of
a Secular Initiative

THE missionaries to Northern Rhodesia represented various denominations that differed doctrinally among themselves but that were nonetheless essentially evangelical, and united by a common response to the secular demands of their African environment. They had given priority to the propagation of the Christian faith. They soon found, however, that they were unable to devote their efforts exclusively to the spreading of the Gospel. Their scattered stations were isolated outposts of the West; Africans looked to them for protection, cloth, medicine, and education before they looked to them for new religious ideas. Where the missionaries were powerful, those who sought protection usually received it. Medical attention and, for a time, calico and other manufactured goods were also available only from the missionaries. Africans were thus attracted to their stations, and the missionaries, if only to enhance the appeal of their religion, became more and more the captives of a worldly web. In this way, they helped to introduce Africans to Western ideas and material possessions, thereby influencing significantly the subsequent modernization of Northern Rhodesia.

In the long run, the practice of curative medicine became one of the major secular contributions of the missions. It began, however, as a sideline; of the pioneer missionaries, only a few were trained doctors, and only one structure was ever called a hospital—the wattle and daub dispensary built in 1891 at Niamkolo by the London Missionary Society. The other missionaries possessed some rudimentary knowledge of medicine, acquired either by experience or as a result of a short course in a seminary. They knew how to bandage wounds, to drain sores, to set bones, and to nurse patients afflicted with fever. Indeed, to Africans, some of their cures appeared miraculous.[1] Gradually, these early missionaries and their wives developed an enviable reputation for being able both to alleviate pain and to heal the sick. They did not entirely supersede the popular traditional doctors, but by 1900 many were able to report that their clinics were full and that their limited knowledge of tropical medicine had generally proved inadequate to cope with the emergencies of rural life. They had also come to realize that it was not only right, but proper, that they should broaden the scope of their medical services. "The provision of these services had proved an avenue," as one missionary said, "for getting the Gospel into them [Africans]."[2]

On strategic grounds, the missionaries soon appealed to their societies for the assistance of ordained doctors. They indicated how beneficial doctors were in the struggle against "heathenism." They enumerated the missionary lives (wives and children included) that probably could have been saved by proper medical care. But their directors in England and France were only occasionally persuaded. Good doctors were difficult to find, expensive to

[1] One of the more famous early missionary "miracles" was performed on the Zulu chief Mpande. See Natal Missionary Conference, ed., *Uplifting the Zulus: Seventy-Five Years Mission Work in Natal and Zululand* (Durban, 1911), 14.

[2] Fisher papers: Fisher to Singleton Darling, 8 January 1907.

91

maintain, and, when available, usually sent instead to China and India.[3]

For many years the treatment of African ailments remained in the hands of gifted amateurs. Whenever they went on tour to the rural villages, missionaries carried a medicine chest and tended the infirm who gathered at each settlement through which they passed. At appointed hours on the stations their wives (or the Roman Catholic sisters) transformed a convenient verandah into a dispensary. Africans queued obediently for medicine, for ointment, or for bandages. They gradually gained sufficient confidence in the white man's medicine to bring their children; even the pregnant women came eventually. Of necessity, the missionaries also became dentists. Some, although their equipment might have consisted of only a single pair of forceps, gained experience and even achieved a widespread acknowledgment of their proficiency. They were amateurs nonetheless. Oliver Roebuck, an English Methodist, described his particular predicament:

"A dusky brother came in great pain pointing to an offending tooth, and intimated that he wanted it out. Well I have to start sometime [I thought] so here goes. . . . I proceeded to my medical box, and opened him to discover that I have an array of seven forceps for all sorts of purposes. Next I looked up my medical books and learned the name of the tooth to be extracted, and that done I chose my forceps. Then I examined the mouth [of the dusky brother] standing behind, looked wise, and felt as nervous as the shivering victim. . . . However I now took the forceps, flourished them twice over my own head and once over his. Then I called a halt . . .

[3] See Appendix II.

to roll up my sleeves. At last I made the plunge . . . Got him! A few twists, and a pull and the wretched tooth was out. . . . Dentistry I now regard as another of my accomplishments."[4]

Of the various missionary societies active in Northern Rhodesia before 1910, only the London, the Livingstonia, and the Brethren included qualified doctors on their rosters. By 1924 the Primitive Methodists and the Paris mission had also sent doctors to Rhodesia. These men were all extremely active; none, however, were as influential generally as Dr. Walter Fisher, a surgeon from Northern Ireland. He had joined the Brethren in 1889, and had spent the next seventeen years ministering to the sick of the Zambezi Valley in Angola. In 1906 he decided to establish a sanatorium.

During the search for a suitable site, he took careful note of the size of the spleens of children. An enlarged spleen meant malaria; only at Kaleñe Hill was there a low proportion of children with enlarged spleens, and Fisher chose, without any later regrets, to settle there, near the conjunction of the Angola-Congo-Rhodesia borders.[5]

Fisher held rather definite views on the way in which he could best be of service to the Africans of Northern Rhodesia. He desired both to cure their bodies and to save their souls. He thought that he could wean Africans from superstition and the worship of ancestors and eventually bring about lasting conversions by a demonstration of the power of the white man's medicine. By improving their lot physically, he assumed that he could

[4] The diary of Oliver Roebuck, 3 June 1922, in the author's possession.
[5] See above, 76.

increase African receptivity to the Christian message. At the very least, the successful treatment of their maladies would, he hoped, prevent Africans from using "fetish remedies" and other "sinful practices" that marred "their testimony for God."[6]

Their confidence was essential. Fisher gradually overcame their natural distrust and persuaded a few Africans to submit to simple, if effective, operations. Before the end of his first year in Northern Rhodesia he had successfully used the surgeon's knife on six occasions. "This assures us," he prophesied, "that we have already a wide open door ready for us to enter. . . ."[7] By 1909 a dispensary had been constructed. Soon thereafter he began to administer chloroform to his African patients without ill effect.[8] He pulled teeth, set bones, removed eye cataracts, excised tumorous growths, and tried, unsuccessfully, to cope with leprosy. Unlike most other missionary doctors—reluctantly, and for a stiff fee—he also treated Africans who had contracted venereal disease. In 1916 the operation of his dispensary—especially the provision of drugs and instruments—cost £700 a year, a large sum for the missionary exchequers of the day. Four years later Fisher at last believed that the power of the white man's medicine was beginning to destroy the influence of the local doctors. In 1920, 341 patients occupied beds in his hospital; 70 came daily to the outpatients' clinic. Africans had even allowed him to participate in the hitherto secret male initiation rites—the *makishi*—and to perform the actual circumcisions himself

[6] Fisher Papers: Fisher to Dorie, 21 March 1900.

[7] Fisher Papers: Fisher to Darling, 8 January 1907.

[8] Chloroform was first administered in Northern Rhodesia in 1894 by the London missionary Adam Purves.

in the mission hospital.[9] Furthermore, he had started to train a few local Lunda males to assist him in the hospital. Fisher was rightly satisfied. He had, within a relatively few years, transformed Kaleñe Hill from an isolated mission station into a major center of curative medicine. Other missionaries followed his initiative.

As Fisher healed the infirm, so his fellow missionaries contributed indirectly to the economic development of Northern Rhodesia. By them, Africans were introduced for the first time to the peculiar ways of Europe—to the sins of indolence and nakedness, and the virtues of chastity and obedience. They were told that the doors of heaven would open only to those who wore clothes, possessed property, and labored energetically in the Lord's earthly vineyard. They learned that they could be similarly rewarded, on earth, for copying the white man's speech, habits, and consciousness of time. Preferment and status had previously been obtained by exploit, by magic, or by ascribed rights of lineal succession; the missions instead recognized the prestige of achievement. And, in time, the missionary ethic became synonymous with a new, somewhat alien, notion of progress.

The economic pursuits of the missionaries were by-products of the missionary enterprise. On the one hand, financial support from home was often somewhat precarious and slow in arriving; missionaries were therefore

[9] The *makishi* ceremonies were more than circumcision rites. They constituted the main path for tribal acceptance and thereby served an important socialization function. Teen-age boys were generally isolated in a special enclosure for two or three weeks under the supervision of selected masters. There they were initiated into the secrets of their tribe, and into the demands of African manhood. For an early description of their costumes and dances, see Emil Holub, *Seven Years in South Africa* (London, 1881), II, 168-170.

thankful to learn that by trading they could easily lessen their dependence upon overseas support—most of which was derived from arm-chair enthusiasts anxious to know that the harvest of souls was commensurate with their individual investments. On the other hand, the missionaries were also conscious of the various ways in which they could improve their own material surroundings.[10] It was therefore natural that they should indulge in commerce, that they should try to live off the land as much as possible, and that they should make a profit of economic necessity. Moreover, before the widespread acceptance of coin, their only media of exchange were the truss of calico or the string of beads. Many of the original mission sites had been purchased for calico. The first houses had been constructed by Africans whose wages had been calculated in yards rather than in shillings or rupees. Porters had been paid from the contents of the loads that they had carried. New desires were thereby stimulated, and the missionaries, whether or not they supported Livingstone's theoretical coupling of commerce and Christianity, became intimately involved in the mercantile arrangements of a secular society.

Each mission had its store where Africans could buy calico, dresses, ornaments, shoes, soap, candy, religious translations, and, in time, almost any conceivable product of Western factories. In 1902, for example, one station imported fifteen tons of trade goods for resale—not an unexceptionable amount. The goods offered for sale included 1,600 fezzes, 4,300 fancy scarves, 1,850 pounds of soap, 5,400 yards of red calico, 39,000 yards of sheet-

[10] Arthur H. Cole, "The Relations of Missionary Activity to Economic Development," *Economic Development and Cultural Change*, IX (1961), 124.

ing and other calico, a ton of beads, and quantities of cheap jewelry, watches, umbrellas, and salt.[11] This particular mission regularly made a profit on its trading activities and, for a number of years, its treasurer devoted nearly all of his time to such entrepreneurial pursuits. He balanced the ledgers carefully, and forwarded elaborate profit and loss accounts to his directors. When they eventually complained of his excessive zeal, he could say that the store had justified itself not only economically but also as a magnet with which to draw people to church. As a canny French Jesuit told his Superior, "Take the store away and we shall very likely be left alone."[12]

Missionaries usually found some way to turn their talents to economic use. Gardens, for instance, when tilled by inexpensive labor, produced vegetables and grain for the European market. During one year a single mission station also sold more than 16,000 pounds of grain to Africans. Another exported beeswax and honey, and a third specialized in stock-raising. One Plymouth Brother supplied furniture from his small factory to a number of urban Rhodesian outlets, and other missionaries, of various societies, trained Africans to construct desks, chests, and tables for sale locally. And, if the entries in his diary accurately reflected his concerns, a Jesuit missionary worried more about pigs and potatoes than about his parish. Indeed, whenever their taste for the missionary life became jaded, all manner of men cheerfully preoccupied themselves with the affairs of trade or with the broader functions that may be called entrepreneurial.

[11] LMS: Wright to Thompson, 23 January 1903.
[12] The diary of Julius Torrend, S.J., 2 May 1919, available at Kasisi Mission, Northern Rhodesia.

The government of Northern Rhodesia ultimately complained that the missionaries were competing unfairly with the ordinary traders and the large commercial companies. In 1915 it insisted that missionaries should purchase trading licenses and that they should remove their stores from lands that had been acquired for religious use and for which the missionaries had originally paid very little money. A Jesuit was among those who purchased a trading license. His explanation was full:

"I have taken [out] a £5 trading license for half a year. Without it there is too much danger of going to gaol, because cash alone here will not do to pay servants, much less to buy grain for our own consumption. Yet, if I use goods for any of these purposes I am in constant danger of being sent to gaol, as happened two and a half years ago. . . . It was for paying three or four servants partly with such things as a singlet, an old worn coat, and I do not remember what else, that I was sent to gaol. Again with cash alone last year I was not able to buy as much as one-half the grain I needed for our own consumption. . . . [The] Judge . . . insisted that for a man in my position the only practical thing was to take a trading license and have done with all difficulties."[13]

These stores, and the other commercial activities associated with the missions, all helped to prepare the people of Northern Rhodesia for the part that they would later play in the modernization of their country. In their entrepreneurial roles, missionaries generated an African interest in economic betterment. They taught Africans new skills, inculcated new standards of dress and decoration and, with the help of the administration, encouraged Africans to regard regular work as a necessary, almost

[13] *Ibid.*, 29 August 1918.

98

inescapable duty. Africans had previously worked in order to live; instead, the missionaries preached that they should live in order to work. This accelerated the movement of Africans from rural villages to urban towns and, in its own particular way, assisted the development of the gold, diamond, and copper mines of southern Africa. The contribution of missionaries to the economic development of Northern Rhodesia was therefore subtle, frequently indirect, but nonetheless evident. It has often been underestimated.

In another sphere—national politics—their influence was more direct and usually overestimated. Like the missionaries who had gone to other parts of Africa, they tried to protect their early adherents from the raids of slavers. They sought to end the power of chiefs hostile to whites and to place Africans for whom they felt a sense of responsibility under the colonial umbrella of a European power. In Northern Rhodesia, the missionaries were to some extent responsible for Barotseland's first treaty with the British South Africa Company, for the Company's assumption of power in Bembaland, and for the peaceful extension of British rule to much of the remainder of the territory. But, in the early 1900's, after the Company's actual acceptance of administrative responsibility, the missionaries tended less and less to defend African interests. Indeed, their philosophy was similar to that of the Company: whatever the white man wanted was, in general, thought to be best for Northern Rhodesia and, therefore, for its African population. There were no early official attempts, as in Kenya, to dispossess Africans from large tracts of land. (When this threat arose, after 1920, some of the missionaries vigorously defended African rights.) Discrimination existed, but this practice was common to settlers, government officials, and missionaries alike; the status to which Africans were relegated thus was never an issue that claimed an inordinate amount of missionary thought. On the other hand, the missionaries protested sharply to the Company whenever European officials cohabited with African women, were cruel to their African subordinates, or attempted otherwise to take advantage of the indigenous population.

Missionaries welcomed the Company's administration. The relationship between church and state was, in fact, mutually beneficial. The Company supported evangelical efforts wholeheartedly, albeit with what cynical missionaries regarded as an ulterior motive: "The government agents," wrote one with experience, "personally may have very little sympathy with the faith and purposes of the missionaries, but they know quite well their value, and they know that the more work the missions can do the less it costs the government to keep the country in order."[14] Missionaries meanwhile counted upon the backing of the Company in matters large and small: the accessibility of its secular power enabled them individually to feel secure and their association with it gave the Gospel an added attraction. They were also satisfied with its overall approach toward the problems of Africa and were rarely reluctant to make use of its influence for their own ends. Like their colleagues in Nyasaland, they successfully urged the Company to introduce the taxation of huts in order that Africans might thereby be encouraged both to work for white employers and to reduce the number of polygynous marriages. A White Father later complimented the administration on its plan: "The benefit of taxation is very appreciated in all respects. . . . It will

[14] LMS: Thompson to Robertson, 22 February 1902, CA, 259.

100

have a good result against polygamy . . . as the wealth of a man is appreciated by the number of his wives. . . ."[15]

Missionaries helped the government to collect taxes, several made church membership conditional upon the payment of taxes, and nearly all failed to see the contradictory expectations that such actions would arouse among Africans. And although they and their message came, quite understandably, to be equated by most Africans simply as European in inspiration and application, the missionaries were untroubled. They were pleased to be instruments of benevolent colonial rule; they never ceased to believe that the Company, like other colonial governments, had as one of its chief aims the "uplift of the natives." This solidarity of purpose was natural: administrators and missionaries were both European, and were mutually occupied with the implementation of a kindred social system. In following their mutual callings, they were faced alike with conservative and often unwilling tribesmen. They were, in sum, united by the desire to transform indigenous authority wherever it interfered with their own.

Missionaries were generally content with the Company's method of governing Northern Rhodesia. They frequently said so, and defended the Company from overseas criticism. With regard to the derogation of African land rights, however, they fought the Company energetically in order to prevent the transfer of African lands to white settlers. This was a battle of the 1920's. Before then, there had been far less pressure upon the land than there had been in the Shire Highlands of Nyasaland, in South-

[15] A 3/11/2: Guilleme to Administrator, 3 April 1907, Lusaka archives. See also FO 2/614: "Report on the Hut Tax in Northeast Rhodesia" (1902), 274; below, 128-129.

ern Rhodesia, or in Kenya. During the early years of settlement, there had been ample land for both white and black farms. The indigenous population was, furthermore, less densely settled there than in any of the neighboring territories, partially because the soil was that much poorer than it was, for example, in the Shire Highlands. Thus, with the partial exception of the Fort Jameson District —the one important area of white interpenetration— African patterns of land use were little affected by the coming of Europeans to Northern Rhodesia, or by their subsequent alienation of much of the better and more accessible areas.

The British South Africa Company had acquired control of the land of Northern Rhodesia by virtue of the Lozi concessions and the treaties and certificates of claim that had been approved by Harry Johnston. After the Boer War, whites had begun to occupy homesteads on either side of what became the single railway line from Livingstone to Ndola, and in the isolated Fort Jameson district. They grew maize and grazed cattle and, at first, competed largely for local markets. Wherever African land holdings had interfered with the tracts that they had excised, the Africans had been removed. But, in the early years, settlers had been pleased to have had a ready source of labor resident upon their farms. Often, Africans who had refused to work had been evicted. But unalienated land had never been far distant, and Africans thus had not been loath to migrate. Instances of individual hardship should not be minimized but, in broad social terms, by 1920 the impact of white settlement had not been as severe as it had been elsewhere in colonial Africa.

Before this time, only Africans in the Fort Jameson

district had been threatened with a deprivation of their traditional rights to land. In that district the British had defeated the Ngoni in 1899. Their success had heralded a land rush; the North Charterland Exploration Company, which had taken over a concession wrung from Mpeseni, chief of the Ngoni, and had subsequently brought about the war that had resulted in his downfall, had thereafter alienated large blocks of land to European stockmen. On these lands frequently as many as 150 Ngoni lived on each square mile. This was the most densely populated area of Northern Rhodesia, and competition between white and black for available grazing land early threatened to become acute. In 1904 the first of many commissions investigated the situation and proposed that an Ngoni reserve be created. In 1907 a very small reserve was in fact gazetted, but no Africans were compelled to move into it.[16] Only with the arrival of European cotton and tobacco farmers, in the period from 1910 to 1913, did the settlers agitate to expel Africans from white-owned land. Administrative officials moved a number of villages during this period, despite African protests, but this compulsory transfer was found to be illegal, and reserves were not created.

At the conclusion of World War I, a new influx of settlers, and an attempt by the North Charterland Company to make its concession pay, combined to threaten African holdings afresh. The Company proposed to remove about 150,000 Ngoni, Nsenga, Cewa, and Kunda from their tribal lands in order to make way for an undetermined number of whites who might be induced to purchase Company property in the Fort Jameson

[16] ZP 1/1/1, Lusaka archives. But see Lewis H. Gann, *The Birth of a Plural Society* (Manchester, 1958), 146.

District at 1/- an acre.[17] But the Anglican missionaries resident within the controversial area at the Msoro station quickly protested against this proposal. They pointed out that Africans would be transferred from land that had been occupied for generations to a region quite incapable of sustaining them. To Alston Weller May, their Bishop, "it seem[ed] . . . a questionable proceeding to remove 2500 natives from a district which is admirably fitted for their requirements to another which is quite unfitted, in order that two or three Europeans may be settled."[18] He complained directly to the governor and also encouraged missionaries of other denominations to support the cause. John Fell, a leading Primitive Methodist schoolmaster, was in the vanguard of those who fought alongside the Bishop. Together they urged influential friends in London to see that the matter was raised in Parliament. "If you can interest some M.P. in the subject," Fell wrote, "and get him to have the thing worried into the officials responsible, then we may get fair treatment for the natives." He continued: "We do not want the whole thing settled behind closed doors without the native case being heard at all. Surely there is still a sense of British justice to which an appeal can be made? The native aborigine of the territory must have adequate provision made for him and his rights must be respected. I know that there are many . . . who believe that the native has no rights at all . . . [and that] he should be thankful that he is allowed to live at all and . . . remain in British territory . . . without any voice in Government."[19] Lord Cavendish-Bentinck asked

[17] May Papers: May to Spanton, 5 October 1925, privately held. See also UMCA (NR): Sandford to May, 22 July 1923.

[18] Bishop May in *Central Africa* (1922), 144.

[19] Fell Papers: Fell to Barkby, 16 February 1922, MMS.

the necessary questions in the House of Commons.[20] This unfavorable publicity, and the vigorous nature of missionary objection within the territory, finally persuaded the Company to forestall the delimitation of reserves within the North Charterland Concession.

Victory was, unfortunately, temporary. In 1924 the new colonial government re-opened the matter and appointed a local commission to investigate the Northern Charterland Concession. Its report recommended the very plan that had dismayed the missionaries in 1922.[21] For the sake of the three European homesteads then occupied, the commissioners proposed to alienate a large tract of African land and to compel Africans to move away from it into less productive districts. According to the Bishop, much of this land was devoid of water. He complained personally to the Governor, Sir Herbert Stanley, and once again mobilized the forces of Christian opinion. But his efforts proved unproductive. In 1926, despite the Bishop's prophecies of disaster, the Governor delimited reserves and forcibly removed Africans from the North Charterland Concession. The Bishop's vindication took twelve years. In 1938 a government agricultural specialist accompanied an administrative officer into the Fort Jameson reserves. Together they reported that the crowding of Africans into such agriculturally marginal areas had at times caused famine,

[20] *Parliamentary Debates*, fifth series (1922): Lord Frederick Cavendish-Bentinck to Winston Churchill, 155/1024; Cavendish-Bentinck, on the colonial vote, 156/269-270; Charles Roberts to W. G. A. Ormsby-Gore, 166/1642.

[21] The report of the North Charterland Concession Commission is contained in ZP 1/1, Lusaka archives. Its chairman was Judge Leicester Beaufort. He was critical of the way in which his two commissioners, Edward Humphrey Lane-Poole, a Native Commissioner, and J. R. Phipps, a settler, behaved during the inquiry.

periods of acute hunger, and a related, widespread feeling of discontent among the affected Africans.[22]

In Nyasaland, Tanganyika, Kenya, Uganda, and Southern Rhodesia there were missionaries who championed African rights. They spoke publicly, they wrote letters to newspapers, they addressed themselves privately to the leaders of their governments, they informed influential persons in Britain about colonial conditions, and they defended African interests during sessions of the various legislative councils. In Northern Rhodesia, however, Bishop May and John Fell, alone among the missionaries, championed African rights. Missionaries, in general, were therefore consulted less often by government officials; none were appointed to serve on the Advisory Council which existed from 1917 to 1924. Likewise, none were members of the Legislative Council until 1945, when the Anglican Bishop, Robert Selby Taylor, was asked to represent "native interests." In short, the missionary witness on behalf of Africans went largely by default.

[22] Sec/Nat/85: Report by R. H. Fraser and Kenneth Bradley, 21 July 1938, Lusaka archives. See also Sir Alan Pim and S. Milligan, *Report of the Commission Appointed to Enquire into the Financial and Economic Position of Northern Rhodesia*, col. no. 145 (1938), 60-62.

Chapter VI. The Beginnings of
an Educational System

AMONG their many secular preoccupations, the missionaries gave pride of place to the provision of educational instruction. By 1901—the end of the pioneer period—a scattered success had been achieved. The early missionaries had enticed some Africans to school and had at least introduced the notion of a type of Western education into the indigenous social fabric. But they could not always persuade Africans to indulge in the white man's mnemonic exercises.

In the period between 1901 and 1924 the missionaries usually complained about the difficulty either of attracting students to their schools or of sustaining their interest. For attention, the schools were forced to compete with a variety of other vocational demands. The pupils, often males aged between twenty and thirty, were required in the fields when grain was being planted, and later when it was ripening or being harvested. They were needed to carry salt, or to work the nets when fish were running well in the rivers. Even the adolescents, many of whom were eventually enrolled in the missionary classes, had tasks that frequently prevented their continuous attendance. The diversions were many. A Methodist's report was typical: "The attendance is very bad just now. The reason is the crops are ripening and at the present time the big birds find the mealies a feast easy to be got, and no end of children are away from school to scare away the birds."[1] The new education simply interfered with the old, predominantly agricultural and pastoral, way of life. For some years, the questionable attractions of the classroom therefore vied unsuccessfully with the distractions of the land.

Prospective pupils were usually offered a limited educational fare that included reading in the vernacular, simple arithmetic, geography, drawing, singing in the vernacular, physical drill, and memorization of the stories of the Bible. Some of the theologically more fundamentalist missions, however, provided a curriculum that contained considerably less stimulation. The South African Baptists, for example, wanted their students solely to commit to memory "selected portions" of Scripture and hymns.[2] In general, the missionaries wanted only to supply the educational tools that would help them to make Christians of the "heathen" population. The Lamba, for instance, were supposed to have "lived in the Devil's grip for centuries." The Baptists educated them because they believed that Africans could not "profit by the Word of God until they [could] read."[3] Like other missionaries, the Baptists furthermore "engaged in rudimentary education, and in training the mind so that [their] scholars might [become] teachers and evangelists to their own people."[4] In this way, the missionaries believed that they would be able to produce a loyal, indigenous cadre capable of rapidly introducing the new religion into untouched areas. "Our main object," a missionary later said, "was to get the Gospel into them; they learned one

---

[1] Oliver Roebuck, diary, 3 May 1922, in the author's possession.
[2] Llewellyn Phillips, in *Lambaland*, II (January 1917).
[3] *Ibid.*   [4] *Ibid.*

story and then preached it."[5] Or, as his contemporary
wrote: "The rising generation is growing up little better
than the former ones, and we desire to teach all we can
to read and write, so as to give them the Scriptures in
their own tongue."[6] But the pupils themselves instead
sought the specialized knowledge that would enable
them more readily to come to terms with the impact of
British government and the Western way of life. They
believed that the ability to read, write, and count would
open countless doors of opportunity and reward. One of
the Brethren presented the common missionary dilemma
to his supporters: "We fully realize that the increasing
desire for education is not at all generally prompted by
a desire for Spiritual things. But when these people ask
to be taught to read, what a wonderful opportunity we
have of teaching them and placing the word of God in
their hands."[7]

Africans begged to be taught English. "Their one idea,"
an Anglican priest reported, "[was] to learn English and
[to] go and earn money as house boys [servants]. . . ."[8]
Unfortunately, this aim was one with which the missionaries were unsympathetic. Most feared, understandably,
that training in the English language would immediately
divert Africans from the paths of religion. The missionaries assumed, perhaps correctly, that knowledge of English would unsettle Africans, that in the process the
student horizons would become less limited, and that it

[5] Herbert Pirouet, interview with the author (London, 24 October 1958).

[6] George Sims, letter of 15 March 1920, in *Echoes of Service*
(June 1920), 133.

[7] Stanley R. Coad, letter dated 1 November 1924, in *Echoes*
(March 1925), 60-61.

[8] Ronald Moffatt, in *Central Africa* (1916), 106.

would ultimately produce "half educated" Africans with an unfortunate awareness of their own independence. A missionary of experience was moderate in his expression of regret: "English is certainly in great demand, simply from its monetary value, but I doubt if we should at Mission expense provide it extensively. It is sought, not as a means of further study, but as opening up higher paid employment with others, and its study leads to the neglect of Native language, needs, and conditions, both by Teacher and the Pupil."[9] Administrators disagreed strongly with this type of reasoning. With missionaries, they often argued in favor of the teaching of English. "If [Africans] do come, even for . . . material ends, you get a chance of teaching them; and if you fail to get the message of Christianity into their hearts when you have them near you for a long spell, it will not be the fault of the message but of the teachers."[10] Nevertheless, missionaries usually remained unconvinced. By and large, they preferred their pupils to remain ignorant of English and of what one missionary was wont to call "high-class education."[11]

Without succumbing to the demand for English, the missionaries used a variety of blandishments to increase the appeal of their educational establishments. They gave presents to chiefs and headmen and, in return, expected them to send their young men to school. Invariably the missionaries clothed and fed pupils; they also offered them the opportunity of earning money. They drew a necessarily fine line, in fact, between bribery and

[9] Abel Papers: Robertson to Hawkins, 17 September 1912, privately held.
[10] SAGM: Melland to Foster, 11 September 1920.
[11] LMS: Draper to Thompson, 23 January 1902.

suitable inducement: "I certainly do not believe in bribing people," a director wrote to one of his first representatives, "but I cannot forget that the only side of Christianity which the natives around you can at present appreciate is its practical value in bringing some new temporal advantages to them. I should strongly discourage tempting either men or children by presents, but if you can open up work which will be for the good of the mission in the way of building, fencing, and planting, and can by this means employ labor, I am sure you will find the results satisfactory in many ways."[12]

The Africans attracted to school were usually boarded there by the missionaries. In this way a maximum of continuous supervision and a degree of physical coercion could be exerted. Their attendance could thereby be ensured, and they could help the missionaries to keep the stations and the schools in good repair. Edwin Williams Smith put his decision before the General Missionary Council of the Primitive Methodist Connexion: "On coming to Kasenga [station] I deliberately decided to board students . . . their attendance would be regular and they would constantly be under our supervision."[13] Missionaries expected the boarders to participate fully in all of the activities of a given station. They compelled them to attend morning services and Sunday meetings; they enjoined them to pray regularly and to live upright Christian lives.[14] In general, the missionaries severely circumscribed their lives. In 1914 one missionary expelled

[12] LMS: Thompson to Jones, 24 April 1890, LMCXXIII, 111. Cf. Roland Oliver, *The Missionary Factor in East Africa* (London, 1952), 214-215.
[13] Smith Papers: Smith to Guttery, 26 August 1910, MMS.
[14] See also Oliver, *op.cit.*, 52.

a group of students for leaving its compound without permission: "I dismissed a whole crew who, when in a batch of boys, deliberately disobeyed my command and went to the surrounding villages on a Sabbath afternoon. . . . I told them I could not have them in the school . . . if they liked the Villages better."[15]

Throughout Northern Rhodesia, the missionaries imposed severe restrictions upon the manifestation of improper sexual thought by their boarders; but it was often difficult, if not impossible, to do so successfully. The earlier students were certainly past the age of puberty. Some of the missionaries nonetheless attempted to restrain their movements by the erection of high fences or barricades. An Anglican Bishop even wanted boarders to live only in adequately lighted dormitories. He advised his fellow missionaries: "We should not forget that a mission school could be the seed ground of many sins, and great care should be given in surroundings so far as possible exposing younger boys to temptation of a special kind. . . . Dormitories . . . should have lights in them burning all night."[16] And to make its hold particularly secure, one missionary society directed its students to sign a formidable contract. It read: "I hereby make agreement with European missionaries to the effect that I will stay with them for two years to learn things of civilization and be instructed in the faith. They on their part agree to teach, feed, and clothe me. I will try to aspire to knowledge. I will obey them without fail. I promise never to criticize them. I will work as directed

[15] SAGM: Raymond Vernon, monthly report from Musonweji, October 1916.
[16] Bishop Hine, 20 June 1914, in the Livingstone station diary.

by them. I will live in peace and friendship with my friends, all students, loving them."[17]

At these boarding schools, missionaries trained the future leaders of Northern Rhodesia. The European teachers provided the elements of a primary education and introduced their students generally to the somewhat mystifying mores and folkways of the Western world. When school was in session, the classroom occupied them for only a few hours each day. During the remaining hours of daylight, the missionaries put the pupils to work on the station grounds and in the houses of Europeans. In exchange for clothes, soap, and rations, the pupils fetched wood, carried water, and kept the station tidy. They waited on the missionaries' table, and when the missionaries went on tour, the schoolboys accompanied them as guides and servants. The students did "a lot of necessary work which would otherwise have [had] to be done by hired labour"; and, in addition, the missionaries felt that only thus were they able to exert an "incalculable influence on African life."[18]

If the station boarding schools were, collectively, the heart of the Christian educational system, the many village schools were, in aggregate, its arteries. In these far-flung bush schools the students spent an hour or two a day—perhaps only for two or three months—memorizing one or two stories from the Bible, the letters of the Roman alphabet, and a few simple sums. After a year or two, the best pupils were usually promoted—if their parents approved—to the boarding schools. The others carried on as before, dismally reciting what they had

[17] From the Kafulafuta station notebook, 1912. The author is indebted for the translation from Cilamba to Mr. Rex. C. Mulenga.
[18] SAGM: Harris to The General Conference, 20 May 1913.

so often learned, and just as frequently forgotten. One missionary found the village schoolboys a challenge: "They seem to learn and recite easily, not many can read; they forget very quickly; however . . . a few . . . can read."[19] One aspect of the problem was that the missionaries tended to visit the village schools only occasionally.[20] Another aspect was that most of the first African teachers were of poor quality.

For the most part, these teachers had been trained hastily, after completing no more than a year or two at a boarding school. Their own knowledge had been obtained by rote; they naturally drilled the village pupils in the manner in which they themselves had been taught. Each simply repeated as much as he could remember. Occasionally, even men who had not themselves ever received any schooling were allowed to teach in the bush schools.[21] One missionary society insisted upon changing teachers every three weeks from one school to another.[22] Some teachers were simply incapable of teaching: after an inspection tour, for example, an Anglican priest reported that he had found "the alphabet being taught upside down."[23] In general, the teachers had been ill-prepared. The missionaries had wanted to disseminate the "glad tidings" as extensively as possible. They had therefore entrusted the most callow convert with the dual responsibility of teaching and preaching in the villages;

[19] William White, letter of 17 July 1903, in *Echoes* (October 1903), 394.

[20] LMS: Laws to Thompson, 3 August 1905, CA xiii. See also Robert Laws and James Chisholm, *Central Africa Mission: Report of Commissioners* (London, 1905).

[21] Gerrard Papers: Gerrard to The General Missionary Council, 15 December 1916, MMS.

[22] *Lambaland*, III (April 1917).

[23] The Chipili station diary, I, entry for 9 September 1915.

moreover, the missionaries themselves possessed little pedagogical experience that could be passed on to students. Some had not even completed their own primary education in Britain. As a result, "the teachers were like officers promoted from the ranks in the middle of an action to hold a post already occupied. There was little time and indeed inclination to train them, except in so far as the responsibility itself was training."[24]

Individual missionaries occasionally organized vacation courses in order to re-train their academic armies. They gathered the village teachers at a station, and tried to cram fundamental knowledge into their minds. "I was up early," a missionary wrote, "giving [the teachers] their drill." He continued: "Also took lessons in writing, Bible Characters, Hygiene, Geography, and letter writing. Geography was of great interest to them. I am giving them casual geography, and of course commenced with the shape of the earth. It is hard to convince [them] that the world is a globe. Many of them think that at a far distant place the earth and the sky meet and that that is the way that people go to Heaven. Others think that if they could walk far enough they would fall off the end of the earth. Others wanted to know what the earth rested on. . . . I cannot help but feel what a privilege it is to be able to give these leaders of their people a lift up."[25]

At another station, the teachers were brought in from the outschools in 1917 in order that the missionaries might make one last, desperate attempt to undo the unfortunate mistakes of their predecessors. "The 21 teachers . . . assembled each day from 9 to 12:15, and from 1 to

[24] A. Victor Murray, *The School in the Bush* (London, 1929), 91-92.
[25] Oliver Roebuck, diary, 7 March 1922.

3:15 for instruction in very elementary arithmetic, sing-ing and a little English. On the Thursday they were unable to make anything of three plus eight, minus seven, after several days of explanation. I lectured them for 15 mins., reported the state of things . . . to the Bishop . . . and sent them . . . to their teaching villages. Little wonder," this sad report concluded, "that . . . people never come near our schools: the so-called teachers have nothing to teach them." Furthermore, "to retain such [teachers] appears not only to be throwing our supporters' money into the bush, but also to endanger the thorough-ness of our work for all time."[26]

Some of the missions imported African teachers from outside Northern Rhodesia. On the one hand, both the Paris Mission and the Primitive Methodists hired mem-bers of their churches who had been trained in Basuto-land but, in the majority of instances, the missionaries reported that these men were no better prepared and no more efficient than local Africans. They further tended too frequently to compromise themselves morally; many were accused of such offences as adultery, illegal divorce, polygynous marriage, wife-beating, and drunkenness. On the other hand, the Livingstonia mission was staffed largely by Nyasas; few caused complaint and one, David Kaunda, father of the latter-day nationalist leader, Ken-neth Kaunda, founded and was in charge of the Lubwa mission station from 1908 to 1915.

In an attempt to improve the quality of their teachers, a few missions imposed their own standards and ex-aminations in lieu of a proper territorial educational code. In 1918 the sub-primary classes were therefore taught

[26] Sydney Ranger, 17 September 1917 in Msoro station logbook, I.

by men who were required to know how to do addition, subtraction, and single-figure multiplication and division. They knew how to "write clearly between lines in an exercise book" and to "teach intelligently the pronunciation and formation of all letters and figures." Teachers of the middle grade could do three-figure multiplication and long-division. They were able "to repeat the Ten Commandments" without error. Senior teachers could also figure sums of money and read the Gospel according to Luke. One missionary organization, in 1918, employed another seven teachers with superior qualifications: they all satisfied the examiners that they understood the multiplication and division of pounds, shillings, and pence, and that they could "read intelligently any portion of the four Gospels [in their own language], and that they had memorized the Apostles' Creed, the Lord's Prayer, and the Beatitudes."[27]

These reforms were unfortunately belated. By 1920 the missionaries had begun to compete unsuccessfully with the government, the traders, and mining companies for the services of the educated Africans. The missionaries paid Africans as little as they could. Like other European employers, they were content to hire Africans cheaply and to peg their remunerations at a level barely more than that which would permit a teacher to meet his tax obligations. (Whenever taxes were increased, missionaries throughout the country generally raised their scales of pay by identical amounts.) Some of the fundamentalist missionaries even thought that African Christians should teach without expecting financial reward. An influential Plymouth Brother wrote: "My aim has been that Christian boys who have a real desire to

[27] Chipili station diary, II, 20 March 1918.

117

serve the Lord should be enabled to settle down to an industrious life to secure their own support, and to teach children to read and write, not because they are paid to do so by us, but from a real anxiety to reach them with the Gospel. Their preaching and evangelistic efforts generally would then be spontaneous, and more effective because freed from the suspicion of being mercenary. . . ."[28] Many of the better teachers accordingly went to the towns in order to earn appreciably more money than they had been accustomed to receiving from the missions. By working in Bulawayo or in Elisabethville, they were able, for example, to double their real incomes. In 1912 one mission paid its teachers 9d. a month. Another's rate varied between 1/8 and 8/- a month, depending upon the level of competence attained by the teacher concerned. At the same time, government clerks with similar qualifications were receiving between £1 and £5 a month.[29] During the period between 1917 and 1922, the wages of "superior" teachers rose from 10/- to £1, although most teachers were receiving between 6/- and 10/- a month. Their expenses included three loincloths a year (@ 3/6), three shirts a year (@ 4/6), seven "sheeties" yearly for their wives (@ 5/-), and 5/- a year with which they paid their tax assessments. From a total yearly income (including that imputed) of £4-2-6 (i.e., 7/6 x 11 months), the teachers thus had a disposable income of 18/6 with which to clothe their children and feed their family for a year.[30] Is it any wonder that the

[28] George Suckling, letter of 19 July 1919, *Echoes* (August 1919), 183-184.
[29] J. M. Cronjé, *En Daar was Lig* (Bloemfontein, 1948), 84; LMS: Robertson to Hawkins, 17 September 1912; LMS: Nutter to Cousins, 12 April 1912. Rations were included.
[30] Chipili station diary, ii, 4 November 1917, 29 June 1918.

better teachers grew dissatisfied, and the missionaries distraught?

Only by training would-be teachers professionally could the missions ever hope to reform their inadequate methods of primary instruction. Clearly a college and an experienced staff were needed, but most missionaries for long thought that any white man could, if patient enough, teach Africans to teach. There were a few London missionaries, however, who realized that this was an inaccurate assumption. In 1905, therefore, they began to send prospective teachers to the Overtoun Training Institute at Livingstonia, Nyasaland. Dr. Robert Laws, its principal, welcomed them, but in 1908 the London missionaries refused to renew their contracts with Livingstonia. They claimed that Livingstonia had corrupted their innocent students, that its sophisticated atmosphere had turned their heads, and that they had in general returned more "cheeky" than they had gone.[31] Meanwhile, the Primitive Methodists had begun to think about the establishment of a teacher training college of their own. From 1910 to 1916 they tried continually to persuade their hesitant General Missionary Council to provide the funds with which to build such an institution. In 1916 a large donation from an anonymous businessman finally forced the Council's hand, and the Primitive Methodists began to develop Northern Rhodesia's first higher school.

In 1918, with the support of Northern Rhodesia's other Protestant missionary societies, the Primitive Methodists opened the Kafue Training Institute. John Fell, an aggressive English schoolmaster who came to have an important influence upon the education of the indigenous population of Central Africa, became its first principal. Before

[31] LMS: Freshwater to Martin, 1 September 1909.

his appointment, he had spent ten years at Primitive Methodist missions in the evangelically unprofitable Gwembe valley. There the teachers had generally been of the poorest quality, and he had frequently, if vainly, tried to introduce a number of pedagogical reforms. At the Institute, he was at last able to put many of his educational ideas into practice. He "set out primarily to train native Christian teachers and evangelists," but he also accepted other students (who paid £4 a year) for purely scholastic or vocational training. "In all departments," he explained, "our foremost aim is character. We do not desire to develop intelligence at the expense of spiritual facilities, nor train the hands without growth in Grace."[32] Fell insisted that the students should master the fine points of their own languages and the intricacies of higher arithmetic. He compelled them to memorize the Scriptures. He taught public speaking and the art of vernacular composition. Of greater importance, perhaps, he also wanted his pupils to learn how to read, write, and speak English.

The Institute was an educational innovation. But Fell continued to cling to the usual missionary practice of clothing and feeding his students in order to have "a hold over them." He disciplined them rigidly. "Unseemly conversation" resulted in "instant dismissal."[33] He carefully indoctrinated them so that they might later persuade their village pupils that the social changes demanded by the church were beneficial. Controlled debates among the pupils were also organized as part of the indoctrination process. Students asked: "Is it good to pay dowry?" "Should we drink intoxicating beer?" "Are schools good

[32] Fell Papers: Fell to Hirst, 9 February 1918, MMS.
[33] Fell Papers: Fell to Barkby, 22 February 1919, MMS.

for Black People?" "Who should inherit a dead man's goods?"[34]

Most of the Protestant missionaries sent their better pupils to be trained at the Kafue Institute. The White Fathers and the Plymouth Brethren held aloof, however; the Jesuits and the Adventists sent their better students to Southern Rhodesia; and the Universities' Mission elected to train its own at the stations. Missionaries of the Africa General mission were also reluctant to permit their pupils to go to Kafue. They thought that its theological presuppositions were too liberal, and they therefore tried to urge their students to stay at home. Two diary entries for 1921 illustrate this point of view:

"Maruva [a teacher] left to [go] to Kafue. Only reason given was to learn, although he admitted he was learning here [at the Musonweji station]. Evidently his heart was set only on English. Responsibility to God and to his tribe was clearly set before him. Determined to go."[35]

"Solomon [a student] went to his village. Said he wished to think things over as his 'heart was not sitting well.' At last . . . he said that there were three things on his heart, viz., 'To stay here and learn,' 'to go out to the village to preach,' [or] 'to go elsewhere to learn.' The last was the temptation and this he had evidently given way to as we have now heard that he has [gone] to Kafue. Much prayer has been offered in his behalf and we are still hoping that he may return. He realized, as do the other boys, that it was not God's will for him to go. Why he was dissatisfied we do not know. . . ."[36]

The Kafue Institute became the leading educational

---

[34] *The Star* (March 1922), a duplicated monthly newspaper of the Kafue Institute.
[35] Musonweji station diary, 30 September 1921.
[36] Musonweji diary, 12 October 1921.

foundation in Northern Rhodesia. Arts subjects were the core of its curriculum, but it was also the first school to offer technical instruction on a large scale. As early as 1904, the British South Africa Company had unsuccessfully tried to persuade missionaries to train Africans in proper agricultural methods and in useful trades. The Administrator of Northwestern Rhodesia wrote at length to a number of the more important missionary societies: "I am convinced from my experience that technical work is the only way to labour among the natives if one wants that real success which it is the endeavor of my administration to encourage. . . . The Board of the Company would be much more inclined to assist a society which approached matters in such ways rather than purely theoretical and dogmatic religious teaching. . . ."[37] But most missionaries were unwilling to see their African students become accomplished farmers, carpenters, joiners, or blacksmiths. Instead, they generally saw this question in the same light as had Frederick Stanley Arnot: "How to teach the native to profess honest trades . . . is . . . a difficult problem. Sometimes a promising lad is spoiled and lost to the work by being taught the elements of trade, enabling him to earn at some neighbouring mining camp better wages than his teacher ever saw. Missionaries, I hold, have nothing to do with training boys in order to bring them into competition with white men, in white men's towns. We are bound to help them to be good keepers at home, and to be content with humble Christian living and seeing to the upbringing of their sons and daughters."[38]

[37] A 2/3/3: Coryndon to Pickett, 22 February 1904, Lusaka archives.

[38] Frederick Stanley Arnot, *Missionary Travels in Central Africa* (Bath, 1914), 128.

Before the Kafue Institute was established, only two London missionaries—one of whom tried to start a cotton plantation near Lake Tanganyika[39]—and an irrepressible Jesuit attempted to introduce serious agricultural or technical training. In 1905, the Company gave the Society of Jesus 10,000 acres at Chikuni, among the Plateau Tonga, with the understanding that the priests would teach Africans how to use a modern plough and to make their herds of indigenous cattle more productive.[40] Joseph Moreau, a Breton and the first priest to make Chikuni his home, readily accepted the "apostolate of the plough." "I am quite willing, and even anxious," he explained, "to try to teach the native to get more good and better food and live a life a little more human."[41] He personally demonstrated the effectiveness of the iron plough to Africans who had rarely used any implement more sophisticated than a digging stick. Later he helped many to obtain plough and oxen: when an African Christian married, Moreau taught him how to till the soil and lent him a plough and a team of oxen until the young farmer was able to purchase his own. There was, however, one provision—that the plough and oxen could be used only under Moreau's supervision. This plan worked rather well, and the Company came to appreciate all that Moreau had done. But, for him, there had also been a spiritual satisfaction that moved him to deny the accusations of his critics. "Yes," he wrote, "I am only a farmer. I have done a deal of farm work, but if I had not done

[39] B 1/1/a36: "Industrial Development of South Tanganyika," Lusaka archives.
[40] See M. A. Prokoph, "Chikuni, 1905-55," *The Catholic Teacher*, IV (September 1955), 9.
[41] Campion Papers: Moreau to Brown, 11 December 1924.

that, it is not sure [that] I should have done more good to the people even [from] a spiritual point of view."[42]

At the Kafue Training Institute, Fell likewise chose to emphasize the importance of agricultural instruction. In this regard, his beliefs were reinforced by what he observed during a visit to the Hampton Institute (Virginia) and the Tuskegee Normal and Industrial Institute (Alabama) in the United States. His students were taught to manage a dairy herd, a pig farm, a chicken run, and to "handle every kind of implement except the very large three-furrow disc plough."[43] By 1924 methods of carpentry, brickmaking, and building were also included in the syllabus. Fell's idea was, however, not to train men in these various fields, but to "give all prospective teachers some instruction in these things so that, when they started their work in the village schools, they could teach them and demonstrate them to the people there."[44]

These efforts were all aimed at the education of men. Young women were rarely encouraged to attend school. There were a number of traditional obligations which tended to occupy their time, and most missionaries, being men, were wary of instructing African women, lest they be compromised thereby. They were also loath to permit male African teachers to do so. The sex shibboleth proved all-powerful. Yet the missionaries were aware that women were the key to the successful conversion of Northern Rhodesia's African population. "We must put the girls under our care," they said, "if we are to break [Africans] of the bad habits of village life."[45] They agreed that they "must grow good wives for [their] Christian boys," other-

[42] Campion Papers: Moreau to Parry, 8 December 1919.
[43] John T. Lyon, *in litt.* (23 November 1958).
[44] Fell Papers: Fell to Hirst, 4 September 1926, MMS.
[45] Barlow Papers: Barlow to Horton, 29 September 1926, MMS.

wise converts would be compelled to marry "heathen girls who wear only a thin loincloth." They would be "tempted to sin" by "heathen women" and the labor of years thus "would be wasted."[46] Wives of Protestant missionaries occasionally tried to teach African women in village schools, but encumbered as they were with family responsibilities, these women rarely had the time to sustain an initial enthusiasm. Only after various societies had begun to employ unmarried female missionaries especially to cope with this problem were schools for women established. The first of these dedicated women was Mabel Shaw, a schoolmistress from Wolverhampton, England, who was sent in 1915 to the people of the Luapula Valley by the London Missionary Society. She later established an outstanding training center for women at the Mbereshi station and was largely responsible for encouraging other missions to imitate her example. Two other ladies, the Dutch Reformed missionaries Issie Hofmeyr and Ella Botes, established a school for the blind at Magwero, in Ngoni country, and set an enviable standard of education for the sightless. Miss Hofmeyr started the school in 1905 and, in 1910, after her death, Miss Botes produced the first primers in Cinyanja Braille. She was still actively helping the blind at Magwero in 1959.

In all these schools the increase in the number of students was impressive. In 1924 about 80,000 Africans were on the rolls of 1,200 schools run by fifteen societies. Of the total number, 14,000 were students in 300 schools of the London Missionary Society, an increase of 4,000 students since 1910. By contrast, in 1919 the Primitive Methodists reported an enrollment of 250; ten years later

[46] Mapanza station diary, 26 May 1917, 187.

1,808 pupils were in its schools.[47] And for the first time, a full primary education was possible. Inspired by the Kafue Institute, some schools took students beyond Standard III (the fifth year in a system that began with Sub-A and Sub-B) to Standards IV and V. The government had, moreover, begun, albeit meagerly, to subsidize missionary schools (there was then only one official school),[48] and Fell and Bishop May had persuaded the colonial authorities to appoint the Protectorate's first director of education. They and their fellow missionaries had, in sum, constructed the foundations of an educational system that was, in the future, to become increasingly more elaborate.

[47] See *Proceedings of the General Missionary Conference of Northern Rhodesia* (1924), 86. The totals are estimated because both the White Fathers and the Plymouth Brethren refused to supply the conference with complete statistics.

[48] For a history of this school, see M. A. Mortimer, "History of The Barotse National School" *Northern Rhodesia Journal*, III (1957), 303-310.

Chapter VII. Social Change and the
Encouragement of an Indigenous Church

THE many secular pursuits of the missionaries were but aspects of a larger enterprise. Their main concern was "to get the Gospel into them"—to introduce the African population of Northern Rhodesia to the joyful message of Christ. To the missionaries, and even the Roman Catholics were surprisingly evangelical, this was a straightforward message of sin, redemption, and salvation. Indeed, to the more fundamentalist of them, the fierce fires of Hell were a burning image. Their sermons neatly contrasted heathen damnation with the eternal blessedness of the Elect before God. If only Africans would confess their sins, preached the missionaries, they would "be born again," and "be truly saved." This was a doctrine of professed faith that could be demonstrated by a willingness to exchange pagan practices for Christian precepts. It presupposed the wholesale transformation of African life.

Of the many indigenous customs abhorrent in missionary eyes, polygyny was considered the most important bar to the salvation of the peoples of Northern Rhodesia. In their tribal society, polygyny was the ideal state of marriage. It contributed significantly to a man's status and economic well-being, for women alone could produce the staple food and the grain for the all-important beer. Clearly, "the labour of a single wife [could not] suffice for the requirements of a great man."[1] Nor could it for an ordinary tribesman. A missionary explained: "The ordinary native will tell you that the system of monogamy may be alright for missionaries and white men, but for him one wife is no good, he would never be able to get enough to eat."[2] Wives also played a religious role, especially in connection with the worship of ancestors. In its many particulars, polygyny gave evidence of being a complex institution. But most missionaries nonetheless assumed that the practice was merely a sinful manifestation of heathen life and that it could be destroyed without causing serious disturbance to the traditional social fabric.

They urged Africans to forswear polygyny. They denied church membership and baptism to polygynists and their wives, and eventually persuaded some men to cast aside all of their wives but one. In this regard, the missionaries were acting in accordance with a decision of the Council of Trent: "whoever shall say it is lawful for a Christian to have more wives than one . . . let him be anathema."[3] But there were occasionally men among the missionaries to Northern Rhodesia who tended to question the applicability of such assumptions to Africa.

[1] Emil Torday, "Principles of Bantu Marriage," *Africa*, II (1929), 260. There is an extensive anthropological literature relevant to this discussion of marriage customs in pre-missionary Northern Rhodesia. See, for example, Elizabeth Colson, *Marriage and Family among the Plateau Tonga of Northern Rhodesia* (Manchester, 1959); Max Gluckman, "Kinship and Marriage among the Lozi of Northern Rhodesia and the Zulu of Natal," in A. R. Radcliffe-Brown and Daryll Forde, eds., *African Systems of Kinship and Marriage* (London, 1950), 166-206.

[2] Chapman Papers: Chapman to Slater, 27 November 1903, MMS. See also William Shaw, *The Story of My Mission in Southeastern Africa* (London, 1860), 419.

[3] *Canones de Sacramento Matrimoni*, 7.

They drew support from St. Augustine of Hippo, himself an African: "When polygamy was a common custom," he wrote, "it was no crime; it ranks as a crime now because it is no longer customary."[4] These later missionaries could likewise understand the anguish of Africans who wanted to join the church without forsaking their wives. Like John William Colenso, the nineteenth-century Bishop of Natal, they wondered if it would not be as great a sin to make an African cast off his wives as it would be to make him marry more. Colenso defended his belief eloquently: ". . . to force an honest polygamist to divorce his wives is to attack his feelings of justice and duty with reference to his wives. The question as to which wife is to be kept offers endless difficulties. What is to become of the dismissed women and their children?"[5]

In Northern Rhodesia, the medical evangelist Walter Fisher could similarly find nothing in the New Testament that would move him to deny the sacraments to an African solely because he had married several women. "Are we ever justified," he asked, "in laying down laws which are not in the Word of God? Should we not rather give the people the Word of God, and by example and precept and prayer, expect God to constrain them to love Him and His words, and so restrain them from following their sinful inclinations?"[6] Several of the London missionaries took a similar stand, but their colleagues, and their directors in England, were unwilling to compromise. The pronouncement of the secretary of the London Missionary

[4] St. Augustine, *Contra Faustium Manichean*, XXII, 47, in Philip Schaff, ed., *A Select Library of Nicene and Post-Nicene Fathers* (New York, 1887), v, 267-268.

[5] Quoted in C. W. Cox, *Life of Bishop Colenso* (London, 1888), I, 63-68.

[6] Fisher Papers: Fisher to Darling, 19 March 1907, Salisbury archives.

Society was unequivocal; it expressed the prevalent opinion of Edwardian Christians:

"Polygamy is a form of license which is not allowed in the Christian church. A man who is a polygamist must make up his mind which wife is his true wife and there is not much difference as a rule in this by native custom, because throughout Africa I imagine this custom has been fully recognized that where a man has more than one wife one of them is the chief wife by virtue of birth or some other tribal understanding, the others being really secondary wives. Having decided upon his legal wife, the man should make proper provision such as he would make if he were under native custom divorcing any of his wives, and should set the others free to return to their homes."[7]

Nonetheless, Africans were not easily persuaded, or always able to understand why polygynous marriages were evil. A Lunda evangelist, in all seriousness, could even tell a chief that he must divorce his wives because "the bread and the wine at the Lord's table is very little, and if you and one wife come you will get a little, but if you bring a lot of wives there will not be enough."[8]

A number of other marital customs were condemned by the missionaries to Northern Rhodesia. In the first place, they compelled Christians to marry only other Christians —if there were any. The Universities' Mission had a typical regulation: ". . . a Christian ought to marry a Christian—but seeing that there are no unmarried Christian women apparent—a Christian may marry a catechumen if the Padre agrees and then reports the case to

[7] LMS: Thompson to Robertson, 8 April 1905, CA xxxiii.
[8] Fisher Papers: Quoted in Eileen Darling to Singleton Darling, 29 January 1909.

the Bishop afterwards. . . . Again, if a Christian cannot find either a Christian or a catechumen partner, he may marry a heathen. But first the case must be reported to the Padres, and the Padres must receive the Bishop's consent before marriage may be transacted."[9] Traditional marriage ceremonies were firmly eschewed because of the "disgustingly sinful" arrangements associated with them. The missionaries also prohibited divorce and wife-beating. They opposed the passage of marriage earnests, misconstruing the concepts expressed by *ciko, nthengo, mpango*, and *lubono* as simple bride-purchase.[10] Like the earlier missionaries to South Africa, they failed to understand that *ciko* (etc.) was the transfer of cattle or other items of value (iron hoes or cowrie shells) in order to solemnize or formalize a forthcoming marriage between members of two lineages. They likewise misunderstood the importance of widow inheritance as a basis for contracting a second union or as a means of preserving kinship ties. It often resulted in a stable marriage, since the widow was inherited, along with her fields, into the deceased's kinship group. But to the missionaries this practice appeared to defile the sanctity of marriage. A cognate custom—sexual intercourse with a widow by a dead man's kinsman in order to remove the contamination of the latter's death—was also condemned by missionaries.[11]

[9] Chipili station diary, I, 19 June 1917.
[10] See A. R. Radcliffe-Brown, "Bride Price, Earnest or Indemnity," *Man*, XXIX (1929), 131; Colson, *op.cit.*, 102-103; Audrey Richards, "Some Types of Family Structure Amongst the Central Bantu," in *African Systems*, 225-233; John Fell, "Report of the Commission on Objectionable Native Marriage Customs," *Proceedings of the General Missionary Conference of Northern Rhodesia, 1922* (Lovedale, 1923), 64.
[11] See Audrey Richards, "The Bemba of North-Eastern Rhode-

Then there were the habitual evils. Adultery and pre-
marital intercourse were prohibited, and offenders were
frequently excommunicated or flogged, even if the offence
were adultery in intent rather than in fact. Drunkenness
was likewise a punishable offence; most missionaries
(the Roman Catholic priests excepted) even attempted
to eliminate the brewing and drinking of beer. Tribal
dancing, drumming, and singing similarly offended missionaries and their wives. A Plymouth Brother responded:
"A man came and asked if he might have a dance to
propitiate the ancestor of a woman who was sick. We
said we did not object to the dancing on our own account,
but because we knew that in so doing they were not
putting their trust in one who could help them, and
spurning the real Lord and Giver of Life."[12] Smoking,
particularly the smoking of Indian hemp, known locally
as *bhang* and *dagga*, was banned. The list of evils included the practice of all forms of gambling, necromancy,
trials by ordeal, and belief in divination. The Brethren-
in-Christ prohibited the wearing of gold ornaments and
bright clothes and the eating of freshly killed meat.[13]
And to end the catalogue, they and the Primitive Methodists tried vainly to prevent the Ila from practicing their

---

sia," in Elizabeth Colson and Max Gluckman, *Seven Tribes of
British Central Africa* (London, 1951), 181-182: "The surviving
partner of a marriage must perform an act of ritual intercourse
with a man or woman, respectively, who is the potential successor
to the dead husband or wife. Unless this custom, known as . . .
'to take back the death,' is carried out, it is believed that the
mupashi of the dead man or woman cannot return to its own
family, and that it will avenge itself on the surviving partner if he
or she subsequently marries someone else."

[12] George Suckling, *Echoes of Service* (September 1923), 205-
206.

[13] Minutes of the Brethren-in-Christ African Conference, 4
November 1907.

timeless, "disgusting" habit of knocking out the four upper center front teeth of infants.

Within the various Christian communities—the many mission stations and their satellite villages—the missionaries were, to some extent, able to enforce these prohibitions. Punishments varied, but the missionaries almost always denied communion or other sacraments to offenders, and suspended from church membership those Africans whose behavior was thought to be incorrigible. Some simply prescribed "customary discipline for ordinary offences" and removed adulterers, for example, from the church rolls for three months. A few either sent converts guilty of adultery "back to the enquirers' class until such time as [the offenders] proved themselves worthy," or excommunicated them "on the spot."[14] Others whipped adulterers, beat "prostitutes and pimps," and generally reserved the *cikoti* for all cases of "unseemly" behavior. (An Nsenga was once given ten lashes by an Anglican missionary for disturbing a Sunday service.)[15] Indeed, church discipline was often meted out to offenders guilty merely of disobedience: at one station, Christians unwilling to gather thatching grass for the missionaries were refused the Eucharist. In general, these punishments were accepted by the many Africans who were almost wholly dependent upon the missionaries. Remunerative employment was reserved for faithful Christians.

In the rural hinterland Africans were less beholden to the missionaries, who were therefore unable to transform indigenous behavior by the threat of physical or economic reprisal. They instead relied primarily upon

[14] Minutes of the Brethren-in-Christ Native Conferences, 1914 and 1919.
[15] Fort Jameson station diary, 5 December 1910.

verbal persuasion—upon the evangelical propagation of the faith. At one time or another, every missionary participated in this crusade against indigenous evil by taking the Gospel to those isolated villages that were still "in darkness." These tours were known as "itinerations," and it is impossible fully to appreciate the Christian assault upon Northern Rhodesia without some understanding of the nature of these extended journeys. While it is difficult to find out precisely how village Africans reacted to these visits, they played a major role in the lives of missionaries, no individual's correspondence being complete without a thoughtful reference to his most recent itineration. Of these many accounts, the most graphic and detailed descriptions are contained in the diaries of William Freshwater, a member of the London Missionary Society from Market Harborough, England. The following extracts are from his diary entries for 1903 and 1905. They convey, better than any summary can, the nature, the purposes, and the problems of rural evangelism:

"Crossing the ferry in a native dugout [one Sunday] we held the third service [of the day] at Mwamakupa's village. . . . There was a good attendance altogether. Over 20 of the sages of the village [came]. . . . I was also enabled here to speak a few words in addition to our native teacher, and at the close of the service I asked them, as we had given them the school, to each give a mat to cover the floor and thus add to their comfort. They smiled. I wonder how many I shall see next Sunday! If this is successful, it will be a good plan to ask them to give white-wash for the inside.

"I am just beginning to feel the great difficulty in making known to these dark minds the meaning of the

134

atoning work of the Lord Jesus Christ, to explain what connection that death has with sin and with forgiveness, and that by salvation, a new life is received by faith alone in this one great fact; to explain God the Father and God the Son and God the Holy Ghost not as three Gods, but one triune God, to show that Jesus Christ is ever present in the person of the Holy Spirit and yet that Jesus Christ is *not* one of their *mupasi*, a departed spirit which returns at death and enters again the house of the deceased, or enters some tree, stone, water or garden, to wait for the mother to pray this *mupasi* to enter into her son. One needs to live very long with the people, it seems to me, to get such a grip on their own language, so as to be able to minister adequately to their needs. A few years is not sufficient; many years are needed. . . . I returned home with great joy, as the sun was setting, in being privileged to take some little part in this glorious service.

"A quiet, yet busy uneventful week has passed and now it is again the day . . . I welcome it. . . . I held morning and afternoon . . . open air meetings at Mpoja's little village. . . . He . . . deemed it quite an honour to have me in his hut. It was soon crowded, and here was another fine opportunity of presenting the Gospel. I therefore seized this opportunity and as far as I was allowed by my vocabulary, I told them what was on my heart. They listened with great attention, and to show that he had understood, Mpoja repeated, as far as he remembered, what I had said. . . . I suppose it was etiquette on my part to let him have this say. . . . We held our third service in the school at Mwamakupa's.

"The days have been going by without anything of great moment to record. One needs here to plod on day after day and not be weary in well doing. I believe it is only by such plodding that any impression will be made upon the native. Today I made another attempt at speaking at our week-night service. I spoke of John baptising Jesus with water, but God baptising Him with the Holy Ghost. Some of my enquirers here have asked for baptism, and I wished to tell them that it would be very sinful for a person who knew he had a sinful heart to be baptised. Though the missionary might not know it, God would know and we could not tell Him a lie. I also tried to show them that only Christ could take away sin, that the baptism of water would leave a man's heart the same. . . . I think most if not all understood my meaning. [But] How I did long to speak from the inside as it were of their language.

"[Later] a messenger came to me from Chief Mwabu-mukupa . . . asking me not to be angry if I heard the drum beating for dancing as the people wanted to pray to Mwamba, their great chief who died about seven or eight years ago. This praying festivity is only another name and an excuse for a drunken orgy. . . . This was anything but good news to receive just after Christmas, and I according[ly] sent back a message to the chief that I should be angry if he allowed this performance. In a little while, however, the drums began and I knew that the praying had started. . . . Only two days before I had been there and preached the Christmas message of 'peace to men of goodwill.' . . . It is these public beer drinks that form one of the evil customs of these people. They drink and dance until beside themselves with excitement and intoxication, while all restraint is lost and unnameable wickedness is the result. . . ."[16]

[16] The diaries of William Freshwater, entries of 9 March 1903,

Despite the similar effort of other itinerant preachers, missionaries were for the most part discouraged by their lack of evangelical success. Although Africans occasionally came to Sunday services, they usually refused to acknowledge the relevance of the Christian message, or to forsake their "heathen" customs. A Primitive Methodist was candid: "Some [people] walk eight or ten miles for services. But this does not mean there has been a spiritual awakening or an earnest desire to hear the Word. With many it is a kind of holiday and affords them an opportunity of meeting friends from other villages and of having a smoke and chat with them. Then it pleases the missionary."[17] Apparently the missionaries had mistaken the initial burst of indigenous curiosity for a lasting enthusiasm. "Alas," one missionary lamented, "the good will shewn towards us at the beginning does not exist any longer. The services were received with considerable enthusiasm at first. . . . There is a novelty and charm about having a white man speaking to them in their . . . language. When this is worn off the reaction takes place in spite of one's earnestness and determination. . . . By now they have found out that their material welfare has not improved by these visits."[18] The missionaries, in fact, were welcomed as neighbors and "as means for the exchange of goods, and also by many for . . . medicines; but as the prophet of the Lord, no!"[19]

---

16 March 1903, 3 April 1903, 26 December 1905. The author is indebted to the late Mrs. Nancy Freshwater and Dr. B. B. Freshwater, of Darlington, England, for permission to quote from the diaries.

[17] Baldwin Papers: Baldwin to Burnett, 5 August 1899, MMS.

[18] LMS: Nutt to Thompson, 25 July 1895, CA ix/3/c.

[19] W. R. Phillips, letter of 24 July 1918, in *Lambaland*, IX (October 1918).

The missionaries were likewise discouraged by the performance of their African converts, each of whom had passed through several stages of Christian indoctrination. They had been put "on trial" as "hearers" or as "catechumens," and had usually spent two or more years "under instruction." In preparatory classes they learned to recite the Lord's Prayer, the Ten Commandments, and the Beatitudes. They were warned against sin, and were urged to demonstrate their willingness to follow the ways of God. Bishop May provided a lucid answer to the frequent question: Why must a catechumen wait two years to be baptised?

"He waits for two years so that he may hear the words of God and understand them. And again, he waits, so that he may learn to give up bad heathen customs, and that all men may see that he has given them up, and is trying to refuse Satan and walk in the way of God. And again, he waits so that he may learn to pray to God and to worship him. If a man has done these things for two years and has tried to live well, then it is right that he should be baptised. But perhaps one man does not come well to learn; perhaps he has not understood the words of God. Then it is not right that he should be baptised. He must wait. Perhaps he has not given up bad heathen customs and is not trying to refuse Satan. Then it is not right that he should be baptised, he must wait. Perhaps he has not prayed; perhaps he has often sat in the village at the time of the Eucharist on Sunday. Then, again, it is not right that he should be baptised. He must wait till the Padre sees that he is trying seriously to do well. Perhaps he must wait three years, perhaps four, perhaps longer."[20]

[20] Chipili diary, II, 16 May 1921.

Of the comparatively few catechumens who were ever baptised, most were partial to acts of apostasy—to what the missionaries preferred to call "backsliding." By taking an extra wife, committing adultery, drinking beer, or merely absenting themselves from church, innumerable African Christians thus slid backwards into "the abyss of utter heathendom." As a result, purges of whole congregations were not uncommon. In 1905, for example, the London mission suspended nearly its entire membership: "We feel that a drastic treatment is essential, for although there are many truly Christian people in our churches, there is a lot of rubbish, ignorance, and carelessness."[21] In 1918, at a station of the Universities' Mission, 104 catechumens were eliminated from the church rolls in three days, the first baptisms among this group taking place four years later, after the former members had begun to repent. This was also the experience of other missions. Each had its own tale of apostasy and in 1924 each was still hoping to create a strong indigenous church.

Of the approximately 1,500,000 Africans in Northern Rhodesia in 1924, no more than 18,000 had been baptised. This total included nearly 8,000 Roman Catholics, 2,000 Presbyterians, 1,000 London adherents, 300 Methodists, 200 followers of the Paris Mission, 200 African Anglicans, 48 Baptists, and 23 converts of the South African General Mission.[22] No indigenous ministers had been ordained,

[21] Abel Papers: Robertson to Thompson, 14 August 1904, privately held.

[22] These figures are derived from the *Proceedings of the General Missionary Conference of Northern Rhodesia, 1924* (Lovedale, 1925), 86; *Lambaland*, xxi (April 1924), "The History of the Nanzela Mission" (unpub. typescript, 1920); and from estimates based upon the various diaries and private papers noted in the bibliographical appendix.

and none of the missions had tried seriously to encourage the participation of African congregations in the government of the local churches.[23] There existed, in fact, only the bare bones of an indigenous church, and a widely held, keenly experienced feeling of failure.

From the wave of self-criticism that swept over the missions two major points emerged: First, it was felt that missionaries had wrongly sought the wholesale eradication of "heathen" customs because, by doing so, they had simply accelerated the decay of traditional institutions and had condoned the destruction of the cohesion of indigenous society. This point of view was expressed best by Bishop May: ". . . it is the greatest possible mistake for missionaries to encourage the abandonment of native custom (especially marriage custom, which is the keystone to the whole social fabric amongst Natives as amongst more civilized people) unless it is absolutely necessary. There are plenty of influences at work to bring about the break-up of tribal life, and probably it is bound to come sooner or later, but it is not the [task of the] missionary of all people to make confusion worse confounded by precipitating it."[24]

In the second place, there were missionaries who were disturbed by the extent to which the Church had countenanced, even furthered, racial discrimination. African and European congregations were affected by different sets of rules and regulations. The missionaries chastised Africans, for example, who drank or brewed beer, while

[23] In 1932 Leonard Shapela became the first ordained Northern Rhodesian. He was a coloured member of the Primitive Methodist Church. By 1940 the London Mission, the Livingstonia Mission, the Africa General, the Universities' Mission, and the Society of Jesus had ordained local Africans.

[24] May Papers: May to Laura, 31 August 1922, privately held.

ignoring the similar habits of their white parishioners on
the Copperbelt. The Wesleyan Methodist leader, John
White, tried to persuade his colleagues against making
temperance mandatory for African Christians: "I have
urged against this because there is no New Testament
authority for such a rule; it is racial legislation as we
would not think of making such a rule for Europeans.
. . ."[25] A number of missionaries also refused to extend
to Africans the ritual kisses with which they customarily
celebrated the sacraments. "Africans have horrible
diseases," they wrote, "and we have therefore decided
to discontinue the custom of greeting with a kiss at the
time of baptism and communion."[26]

Of greater importance, a few missionaries condemned
the racial light in which African Christians were characteristically regarded by their European padres and
priests. They questioned the way in which the churches
were segregated—European families sat on chairs or pews
while Africans squatted in the dust—and they called
attention to the innumerable other ways in which Africans were made to feel inferior. They were unable, however, completely to understand the extent to which
this practice of discrimination vitiated the appeal of
the young church. Africans, however, many of whom
were later to renounce the Church and, in time, to become nationalist politicians, were intimately aware of
this conflict between the ideals of the Bible and the practices of those who were its paternal advocates in Northern Rhodesia.

This disillusionment with the Church was later expressed simply by Kenneth Kaunda, the son of an early

[25] White Papers: White to Burnett, 6 October 1923, MMS.
[26] Minutes of the Brethren-in-Christ African Conference, 26
September 1914.

African minister: "In my days at Lubwa [mission], I had begun to question certain things in the life of the mission which seemed incompatible with the teaching of Christ in the Bible. I could not see why the European missionaries should have special seats in church and why the Rev. Paul Mushindo [an African] went about on foot or on a cycle while the missionaries rode around in cars."[27]

Despite these criticisms, most missionaries continued to preach and to act, after 1924, in their accustomed pattern. At the same time they grew more professional; some were even able to draw upon new sources of financial support in order to improve their physical facilities and to expand the services offered to the peoples of Northern Rhodesia. Africans, who had come to participate more fully in Western life, gladly took advantage of these new services—of the new hospitals, new schools, and the instruction by a new corps of qualified teachers. They overflowed the available accommodation and at last demonstrated the enthusiasm for which the missionaries had waited so patiently. The number of Christians likewise increased out of all proportion to the total for the period from 1882 to 1924. As a result, the old centers grew in size, and new ones were established regularly until there were more than 300 stations staffed by representatives of 19 different missionary societies.

It is difficult to say whether the influence of the Church in Northern Rhodesia increased with this rise in its apparent affluence. In the period before 1924 it provided almost the only schooling and medical care available to Africans. It was the foremost purveyor of Western goods and Western ideas; it was an important source of

[27] Kenneth Kaunda, *Zambia Shall Be Free* (New York, 1963), 146.

employment. The main roads to material and intellectual enrichment all passed through the mission gates. But, after 1924, with the rapid industrialization and urbanization of Northern Rhodesia, and with the increased attention paid to the rural areas by colonial administrators, more direct paths were provided, and the missions, most of which were located at places distant from the main centers of European life, lost their singular attraction. They were no longer the primary embodiment of the West; they accordingly competed with less and less success for the undivided attention of Africans.

Chapter VIII: Epilogue

N 1964, Northern Rhodesia approached independence. The frontier atmosphere of the pioneering days prevailed no longer, and the missionaries—like white farmers, traders, and miners—had long since settled into an evangelical and educational routine. They could look back to the nineteenth century, however, with some satisfaction. In the once virgin bush, churches and cathedrals stood; Africans crowded mission-run schools and hospitals. Missionaries of many denominations in innumerable ways continued to enrich the life of their adopted country. Like the earliest of their predecessors, they gave much, and asked little of material importance in return. At the same time, their own roles had altered significantly. They had for some years devoted most of their energy to educational and administrative tasks. Latterly, they had also turned their attentions to the urban areas, where the needs of parishioners differed strikingly from those who resided in rural areas. Moreover, they no longer labored alone; almost everywhere, Africans worked beside the white missionaries. Transformed, the Church continued to make its presence felt in Northern Rhodesia. But a central question remained: to what extent had the Church harvested the fruit that had been nurtured by its first, doughty, pioneers?

The missionaries had entered trans-Zambezia during the historical period of the European partition. They had actively abetted the advance of the secular partitioners and, as representatives of the West, individually contributed to the inclusion of trans-Zambezia within the British sphere of influence. The missionaries thereafter introduced a novel system of values that enshrined individualism and provided a number of new ethical hurdles for the would-be participants. To often mystified Africans, they preached of sin and redemption, of industry and thrift, and of abstinence and continence. They ministered to the sick. They built schools and attempted to educate Africans along Christian and European lines. By the employment of a variety of other secular means, they sought to gather Africans within their different religious communities. They struggled, in sum, for the souls of the indigenous inhabitants of Northern Rhodesia.

Occasional successes there were, but total victory eluded and has continued to elude the missionaries. From the start, the missionaries compromised their message. As absolute power supposedly corrupts absolutely, so the isolation of their stations and their own heightened sense of moral and racial superiority tended to corrupt the attitudes of the missionaries and to perpetuate the apparent tension between sermon and action, Biblical pronouncement and observed deed. Although the indigenous inhabitants of Northern Rhodesia appreciated the sacrifices that the missionaries claimed to have made in order to "save" African souls, they nonetheless responded to the missionaries ambivalently and, in many cases, with real animosity. They often resented what appeared to be pretense and hypocrisy; they noted the apparent lack of congruence between utterance and action, envied the comparative wealth of the missionaries, and disliked the ways in which the missionaries abused them physically and mentally. To African dismay, the missionaries preached brotherhood and treated Africans as inferiors. They thus resembled white settlers, traders, and officials in their inability to come to terms with the aspirations of Africans and the African mental environment. In this respect, the experience of most of the missionaries in Northern Rhodesia differed decisively from that of their colleagues in neighboring Nyasaland, where the Scottish churches seem successfully to have recruited a cadre of exceptionally well-qualified representatives. (Appendix II contains a further discussion of the sociocultural background of the missionaries who served in Northern Rhodesia.)

Africans might well have expected missionaries to have interceded with the Administration on their behalf, and to have fought valiantly against the forms of segregation and discrimination that began to impinge upon African rights after the end of World War I. But Africans waited in vain; by and large, missionaries sided politically with their fellow whites. Few championed African interests and, during the long eventually unsuccessful African battle against the amalgamation or association of Northern Rhodesia with Southern Rhodesia, the voice of the Church was rarely heard in support of Africans. Thus, as the organization of voluntary associations and political parties heralded the rise of nationalism in Northern Rhodesia, so Africans came to see with increasing clarity that their missionary teachers had unwittingly encouraged aspirations that could not be fulfilled within the essentially static colonial milieu. They felt cheated, spoke at length of their disillusionment, and joined new political organizations or the popular, African-run, separatist churches.

Of the men who brought about the end of colonial rule and created the new Republic of Zambia, nearly all had been trained by missionaries, and many had once been members of the elite of the Church. But most had broken with the missionaries and the Church. Some had denounced missionaries; most, however, had simply refused any longer to countenance what they called the hypocrisies of their youth. In relation to its original role, the Church no longer occupied a position of real prominence. In that sense, and in terms of their early aspirations, the missionaries had sown the wind and, apparently, reaped the whirlwind.

APPENDICES

Appendix I: A Chronological Account

1878. François Coillard visits the Victoria Falls.
1880. London missionaries explore the Lofu estuary.
      Father Anthony Teroerde of the Society of Jesus dies at Mweemba's in the Zambezi valley.
1881. Jesuits visit Lealui.
1882. Frederick Stanley Arnot settles in Lealui.
      Jesuits re-visit Mweemba's.
1883. The London Missionary Society establishes a station at the mouth of the Lofu River.
      Jesuits return briefly to Lealui.
1884. Arnot leaves Lealui with Silva Porto.
      Coillard arrives in Sesheke.
1885. The Paris Missionary Society opens a station at Sesheke.
      The London Missionary Society establishes a mission center at Niamkolo but later abandons its stations at Lofu and Niamkolo.
1886. The Paris Missionary Society opens Sefula mission.
1887. The London Missionary Society establishes Fwambo mission.
1889. The London Missionary Society re-opens a station at Niamkolo.
      The Paris Missionary Society begins work at Kazungula.
1890. The London Missionary Society moves from Fwambo to Kawimbe.
      The Primitive Methodists arrive at Kazungula.
1891. The White Fathers establish the Mambwe mission.
1892. The Paris Missionary Society closes Sefula and Coillard opens a station at Lealui called Lwatili.
1893. The Primitive Methodists finally reach Nkala.
1894. The London Missionary Society opens Kambole mission.
      The Paris Missionary Society begins work at Nalolo (Nangoma).
1895. The White Fathers establish Kayambi mission.
      The Primitive Methodists open Nanzela mission.

The United Free Church of Scotland begins work at Mwenzo.

1896. The White Fathers close the Mambwe station.

1897. The Plymouth Brethren contemplate starting a station at the Johnston Falls.

1898. The Paris Missionary Society establishes a station at Senanga.

1899. The White Fathers open missions at Chilubula and Chilonga.

The Dutch Reformed Church Mission of the Orange Free State establishes a station at Magwero.

The Paris Missionary Society rebuilds Sefula mission.

1900. The London Missionary Society opens stations at Mbereshi and Mporokoso.

The Paris Missionary Society establishes Mabumbu station.

1901. The Primitive Methodists establish a station at Sijoba in the Zambezi valley.

The Plymouth Brethren return to Johnston Falls.

1902. The Paris Missionary Society establishes a station at Seoma.

A party of Jesuits looks for possible mission sites in Northwestern Rhodesia.

1903. The Dutch Reformed Church Mission opens a station at Madzimoyo.

The White Fathers start a station on Chilubi island.

1904. The White Fathers open a mission at Kambwiri, in the Luangwa valley.

The Primitive Methodists close Nkala station.

The Paris Missionary Society begins work in Livingstone.

1905. The White Fathers abandon Kambwiri.

The Nyasa Industrial Mission establishes a station at Kafulafuta.

The Dutch Reformed Church Mission opens stations at Nayanje and Fort Jameson.

The Society of Jesus establishes Chikuni mission.

The Society for the Propagation of the Gospel supports a chaplain in Fort Jameson.

The Seventh-day Adventists open a station at Rusangu, near Chikuni.

The Primitive Methodists begin work at Nambala and close Sijoba.

The White Fathers open missions at Kapatu and Lubwe.

David Kaunda establishes Lubwa Mission for the United Free Church of Scotland.

1906. The Society of Jesus opens Kasisi Mission.

The Plymouth Brethren establish themselves at Kaleñe Hill.

The Brethren-in-Christ start a station at Macha.

1907. The Primitive Methodists open Mudodoli mission.

The United Free Church of Scotland starts a station called Serenji.

The Paris Missionary Society closes its Seoma mission.

1908. The Dutch Reformed Church establishes Nsadzu mission.

The Paris Missionary Society opens a station at Lukona.

1909. The Primitive Methodists open a station at Kasenga.

The Plymouth Brethren close Johnston Falls mission and open a station at Kaleba.

The United Free Church of Scotland moves from Serenji to Chitambo.

The Wesleyan Methodists look for mission sites in Northern Rhodesia.

The Universities' Mission to Central Africa establishes its third diocese, in Northern Rhodesia.

1910. The South Africa General Mission opens a station at Chisalala.

The Universities' Mission establishes stations at Livingstone and Fort Jameson.

The Primitive Methodists move from Mudodoli to Kanchindu and open a new mission at Kampilu.

The White Fathers open Chibote mission.

The Society of Jesus transfers its work from Miruru in Moçambique to Kapoche and Katondwe in Northern Rhodesia.

153

1911. The Universities' Mission opens stations at Msoro and Mapanza.

The Plymouth Brethren establish a mission at Bwingi.

1912. The Wesleyan Methodists open Chipembi mission.

The Primitive Methodists close Kampilu station.

The South Africa General Mission opens a mission at Lalafuta.

The Plymouth Brethren close Bwingi mission and open a station at Lufimba.

The Universities' Mission begins work at Ng'omba and Shakashina.

1913. The Universities' Mission closes Msoro mission.

1914. The South African Baptist Missionary Society becomes responsible for the Kafulafuta mission.

The Dutch Reformed Church Mission opens Hofmeyr mission.

The Society of Jesus opens a station at Chingombe.

The Plymouth Brethren begin work at Chitokoloki on the Upper Zambezi River.

The White Fathers open and close Mpongwe mission and establish Ipusukilo station.

The Paris Missionary Society closes its Senanga station.

Because of hostilities on the East African front, the London Missionary Society vacates Kawimbe mission.

1915. The South Africa General Mission moves from Lalafuta to Musonweji.

The Primitive Methodists move from Nambala to Namantombwa.

The Plymouth Brethren close Lufimba mission and open a station at Chilubula.

The Universities' Mission reopens its Msoro station, closes Shakashina and Ng'omba, and opens Chilikwa (later Chipili) mission.

1916. The Primitive Methodists begin a mission station at Kafue.

The London missionaries return to Kawimbe.

1917. The Seventh-day Adventists establish a station at Musofu.

154

1918. The Plymouth Brethren open a station at Mwenso wa Nsoka and close the Chilubula mission.

The South Africa General Mission move the Musonweji station to a new site farther up the Musonweji River.

The Universities' Mission opens a station at Old Mkushi.

1919. The Plymouth Brethren close Mwenso wa Nsoka and open a station at Mansa (later Fort Rosebery).

The Universities' Mission closes its station at Old Mkushi.

1920. The Plymouth Brethren establish a station at Chunwe.

1921. The Plymouth Brethren close Chunwe and open a mission at Mubende.

The Seventh-day Adventists open a mission at Chimpempe.

The Dutch Reformed Church Mission establishes a church in Broken Hill.

1922. The United Free Church of Scotland opens a mission at Chasefu.

The Society of Jesus begins work at Lusaka.

The White Fathers open stations at Malole and Rosa.

The Dutch Reformed Church Mission opens Merwe station.

The Plymouth Brethren return to Johnston Falls and establish a new station at Chavuma, on the Upper Zambezi.

1923. The London Missionary Society establishes stations at Senga Hill and Kafulwe.

The Society of Jesus begins work in Broken Hill.

The Brethren-in-Christ open a station at Sikalongo.

The Church of Christ establishes Sinde Mission.

The Plymouth Brethren begin stations at Kamapanda and Kanganga.

1924. The Dutch Reformed Church Mission opens a station at Tamanda.

The Universities' Mission establishes Fiŵila.

Appendix II: The Missionaries as Missionaries

THE MISSIONARIES to Northern Rhodesia came from diverse backgrounds and brought to Africans the experience of a variety of occupations. They were fiercely independent men and they fought bitterly with one another and with their overseas directors, usually to the detriment of their evangelical objectives. In their individual journals and correspondence, expressions of fractiousness, spitefulness, and jealousy compete with one another for space in numerous letters supposedly written more in sorrow than in anger. Indeed, missionaries seemed to spend as much time and energy committing these quarrels to paper as they did in seeking to accomplish conversions. Their actions reflected both their training and the ways in which collectively they were organized.

The Northern Rhodesian missionary societies that concentrated decision-making powers in a few episcopal hands were able to limit dissension and to ensure a useful continuity of policy. The authority of Roman Catholic Bishops and their delegates may have been questioned by junior priests, but only the markedly individualist Father Julius Torrend ever openly disobeyed this authority. Similarly, the Bishops of the Universities' Mission to Central Africa administered their Northern Rhodesian diocese autocratically. Despite its sprawling nature, and the necessarily difficult problems of communication, all actions—even the meting out of church discipline—were invariably referred to Livingstone for the Bishop's approval.[1] Questions of theological interpretation arose, and occasionally there were expressions of priestly discontent, but such disagreements were rarely allowed to disturb the precise distribution of ecclesiastical authority. Furthermore, unlike the members of non-conformist sects, priests were forbidden

[1] Father Bernard Icely kindly allowed me to read the extensive correspondence of Bishop May.

to publicize disputes or to communicate with the directors of their society in London.

The Brethren-in-Christ, an American fundamentalist sect with strong Middle European associations, retained an episcopal structure while permitting its representatives more individual initiative than any of the Catholic societies. The local bishop often deferred to the decisions of other missionaries meeting in periodical conferences, and each of the missionaries, within his own parish, exercised a degree of independence greater than any priest. Indeed, the freedom of action allowed to Brethren-in-Christ missionaries approached that given to their representatives by the more democratic societies; personal idiosyncrasies therefore appreciably influenced overall policy.

In practice, this was the administrative pattern of the Paris Missionary Society, the Wesleyan Methodist Missionary Society, the Livingstonia Mission of the United Free Church of Scotland, and the Seventh-day Adventists. Each delegated financial and political responsibility to one locally resident representative. If he were a dominant personality, like François Coillard or Robert Laws, the representative settled disputes between colleagues, safeguarded the mission purse, decided where missionaries should be based, and served as the main, if not the only, direct channel of communication with directors overseas. Whenever this system functioned properly, it avoided the strife that was endemic within the more democratic societies. It also allowed the missions to expand rapidly, and along ordered paths. Sometimes, however —usually during a period of weak leadership—this system broke down, and the chaos of the more democratic societies captured those that compromised between episcopal and presbyterian control.

The London Missionary Society, the Primitive Methodist Missionary Society, the South Africa General Mission, the South African Baptist Missionary Society, and the Dutch Reformed Church Mission of the Orange Free State permitted local synods to determine day-to-day policies. But their boards in London, Cape Town, and Bloemfontein retained ultimate authority and were not infrequently unwilling to approve radical changes proposed by the synods. The inevitable lengthy delay before Rhodesian synodal decisions could be ratified or rejected by the boards also meant that missionaries often put innovations into practice only to find subsequently that they had failed to receive the sanction of the appropriate directors. The synods therefore became centers of revolt.

Most disagreements between missionaries and directors concerned money. Although directors regularly denied funds to their missionaries for various new projects, the missionaries themselves often went ahead regardless, or juggled their station accounts in order to provide what they themselves assumed to be essential. Sometimes in exasperated tones, directors explained that funds were short. They counselled the missionaries to be patient and long-suffering. "You scarcely seem to realize our position," his director wrote to Edwin Williams Smith, "we simply cannot go beyond what we have allowed."[2] Moreover, directors were understandably reluctant to supply large sums of money and numerous reinforcements to missions that had failed to produce results comparable to those in other parts of Africa or in Asia. One secretary wrote to a Rhodesian synod: "It does not seem as if we are getting at the teeming multitudes of Central Africa, and in comparison with the vast multitudes clamoring for help in other parts of the world, it is difficult to make out a case for maintaining a strong staff in Central Africa."[3]

Often only the barest minimum of confidence and trust existed between missionary boards and their many agents. Edwin Williams Smith, for example, complained bitterly that the Primitive Methodist Missionary Society had "less confidence in me after ten year's service than the youngest in the field. They have never restricted a man as they have . . . me. Others are given a . . . free hand. I am bound down hand and foot. . . ."[4] But, in turn, the society's secretary accused Smith of widening the breach: "I have grown uneasy as to your long silence. You are the only brother on the field from whom I do not hear frequently, not merely on matters of

[2] Smith Papers: Guttery to Smith, 10 October 1910, MMS.
[3] LMS: Thompson to Swann, 10 March 1893, CA xxv, 121-122.
[4] Smith Papers: Smith to Guttery, 2 June 1910, MMS.

business, but in that friendly correspondence that is precious and helpful. . . ."[5]

Private correspondence from the field is eloquent testimony to the missionaries' feeling of estrangement. They regularly persuaded themselves that their directors possessed "absolutely no understanding" of affairs in Northern Rhodesia. The missionaries thus took matters into their own hands with alacrity and, as Laws reported in 1923, "it was a case of democracy run mad."[6] The congregational policy had resulted in "each man or groups of men . . . doing what seemed right in their own eyes . . . and successors . . . overturning the plans and work of their predecessors before they even knew what was happening. . . ."[7]

In one case, color discrimination was the cause of damaging dissension within a synod. The London Missionary Society sent James Hemans, an outspoken West Indian, to its Lake Tanganyika stations with an early group of pioneers. He was a trained teacher and agriculturalist but, from the beginning, he was ostracized by his fellow missionaries and deprived of ordinary spiritual fellowship. The Society also denied him privileges that would otherwise have accrued to him because of his age, seniority, and experience. His salary was always less than that of his colleagues. Once, when the Bemba paramount chief wanted specifically to ask Hemans about Christianity, the synod forbade him to visit the chief. They thought that a white missionary should be the first to explain the Society's principles, and to discuss the possible expansion of the London mission into Bembaland. For the chief, however, only Hemans would do. He said: "I do not want to see the white man just now. I want the one who is of my colour and who can speak so that I might understand him, to come and see me. I will hear whatever he has to say and I will go by his words. He will be my friend."[8]

[5] *Ibid.*, Guttery to Smith, 12 February 1912, MMS.

[6] Edinburgh Papers: Laws to Ashcroft, 18 October 1923, National Library of Scotland.

[7] LMS: Laws to Thompson, 3 August 1905.

[8] LMS: Hemans to Thompson, 3 July 1894, CA 1x/2/c. The paramount chief sent a small elephant tusk to Hemans as an indication of his good will.

But the synod was obstinate. It sent a white missionary, who was refused an audience with the chief, and the White Fathers instead occupied most of the Bemba country. Increasingly, Hemans was ignored by his colleagues and criticized behind his back in their letters to the directors. Finally, after a deputation had investigated the causes of such evident disharmony, Hemans was retired "for the good of the mission." The secretary of the society agreed with the deputation that dark-skinned missionaries could never be accepted on equal terms by their colleagues, and that their presence was therefore harmful to good relations between missionaries. "I [originally] opposed . . . the appointment of any . . . West Indian or American coloured," he wrote, "because I saw only too clearly from what I already knew of the relation of such native workers to European colleagues in other missions and other parts of the world, that there were bound to be difficulties which would probably be of a serious kind. They do not understand us and we, I suppose, do not understand them. . . ."[9]

Two groups had few of these problems. The Plymouth Brethren and the Church of Christ refused, in fact, to be considered societies at all. Their members controlled sites individually and eschewed any centralized direction. Friction between individuals was therefore rectified fissiparously by the establishment of new bases, and many of the Brethren stations were started precisely in order to avoid internal quarrels at the existing centers. Moreover, although funds for the Brethren were cleared through a secretariat in England, there were no superiors with whom missionaries could disagree. The government of Northern Rhodesia, however, found the lack of any central authority to be a source of continuous administrative frustration. Brethren of all kinds and persuasions were free to embark upon missionary adventures, to occupy new areas, or to join existing teams. Neither quality nor quantity of personnel were controlled. There was no selection process. The use of available resources was unplanned and, for example, three trained teachers could settle at a sta-

[9] LMS: Thompson to Robertson, 16 June 1906, CA xxxiv, 55.

tion where there was only one school, while another station with ten schools might be unable to obtain any teachers at all.

The majority of the two hundred missionaries who went to Northern Rhodesia before 1924 possessed a minimum of formal education and were of predominantly working-class backgrounds. Fewer than thirty-five had received a university education. The others had usually left school at an early age, worked at a trade, and perhaps studied in a Roman Catholic seminary or a Protestant Bible-training institute. Before entering the ministry, their occupations ranged from rate-collecting to cabinet-making, and one Methodist had, successively, been a stationmaster, grocer's assistant, lawyer's copyist, manufacturer's chemist apprentice, boiler worker, and cost clerk. One Plymouth Brother made cycles, three representatives of the South Africa General Mission were respectively a bank clerk, a printer, and a factory laborer. Only four women and one man had been teachers.[10] As a group they were descended from craftsmen or tradesmen, and occasionally from fishermen, farmers, or graziers. The fundamentalist Protestants had characteristically been converted during adolescence and had worked long hours during their early manhood in order to obtain the religious training that would qualify them for a missionary career. They were men of upright character who guided their own and African lives according to inflexible conceptions of right and wrong.

They were representative of their age, and of a section of a highly stratified European society. Yet, unlike others, they had escaped the dreary destiny of their class and, to their delight, in Africa they found themselves in positions of greater authority and responsibility, and surrounded by far more material comfort, than they could ever have achieved in Europe. The comments of James Stephen on the representatives of the Church Missionary Society in New Zealand could well have been applied to those men sent to Northern Rhodesia by Roman Catholic and Protestant societies—with the exception of the Universities' Mission. "One and all," Stephen

[10] Detailed biographical sketches at the end of this section give a more complete picture of the missionary background.

wrote to Macvey Napier, "they seem to me too solicitous to produce a striking effect, and to have too large an infusion of dramatic nature for persons of their high calling. The fact is they have been, almost all, low men at first, and are embarrassed on appearing in the conspicuous stations assigned to them."[11]

Northern Rhodesia usually received the least qualified of the many British men and women who offered themselves for missionary service overseas. Society directors believed that mission fields in Asia were more deserving than those in Africa, and they wanted the better educated candidates to be sent to China and India, where more sophisticated heathen and "superior" cultures would, they believed, be encountered. Since Africa was widely thought to be devoid of history and civilization, its conversion could safely, so they thought, be entrusted to missionaries of the "second rank." Eventually the experience of a few discerning missionaries demonstrated that such common suppositions were fallacious but, by then, the damage had been done. To some extent, the rapid development of a strong indigenous church had been forfeited and, to compound the problems of the missionaries already in the field, the meager returns in the form of souls saved had made societies reluctant to provide more than token human and material support. As a result, poorly trained and generally underprivileged missionaries continued to influence the course of the evangelical endeavor in Northern Rhodesia.

[11] Quoted in E. T. Williams, "The Colonial Office in the Thirties," *Historical Studies: Australia and New Zealand II* (1943), 160.

Appendix III: Some Missionary Biographical Sketches[1]

ADAMSON, David (UFCS): 1875-1932. A carpenter and builder by trade. In 1909 married Annie Rodger Chalmers, a teacher. In Northern Rhodesia, at Lubwa and Mwenzo, 1914, 1921-1927.

ALEXANDER, Thomas Thomson (UFCS): b. 1881, Penicuik, Scotland. Attended Penicuik Public School and Edinburgh University, M.A. 1903. Studied at New College, Edinburgh, 1903-1906. Asst. Minister, Lady Glenoschy's United Free Church, Edinburgh; Missionary in Canada, 1907; ordained there; Minister in Whalley Range Presbyterian Church, Lancashire; Minister, Orkney, 1911. Went to open the new Senga station, 1914. Invalided and sailed to United Kingdom, 1915. Inducted Holm Congregation, Orkney, 1915.

ALLISON, Grace R. (UFCS): Received Diploma of School for Christian Workers. Member of Bon Accord Church, Aberdeen. Worked as a nurse for three years. Served at Tamanda and Chitambo, 1922-1925. Resigned because of ill-health.

[1] ABBREVIATIONS USED IN THE APPENDIX

BC	— Brethren-in-Christ
CC	— Church of Christ
DRC	— Dutch Reformed Church (OFS)
LMS	— London Missionary Society
NIM	— Nyasa Industrial Mission
PB	— Plymouth Brethren
PMS	— Paris Missionary Society
PMMS	— Primitive Methodist Missionary Society
SAB	— South African Baptist Missionary Society
SAGM	— South Africa General Mission
SDA	— Seventh-day Adventists
SJ	— Society of Jesus
UFCS	— United Free Church of Scotland
UMCA	— Universities' Mission to Central Africa
WF	— White Fathers (now four vicariates)
WMMS	— Wesleyan Methodist Missionary Society

ANDERSON, William Harrison (SDA): 1870-1950; b. Mexico, Ind. Brought up in an Adventist family on a farm near New Waverly, Cass Co., Ind. Attended local schools for eleven years, American Normal and Commercial College (Logansport, Ind.) for three years, and Battle Creek (Mich.) College for six years. He received a B.Sc. degree from Battle Creek College in 1905 and an M.A. degree in 1918 from Emmanuel Mission College. Ordained in 1905; at Rusangu mission, 1905-1907, thereafter active in Southern Rhodesia, Bechuanaland, Angola, and South Africa.

ARNOT, Frederick Stanley (PB): 1858-1914, b. Glasgow. Son of a shipper. Resided Hamilton and Tayport, Scotland. Left school at fifteen. Laborer and draper's assistant. Arrived at Sesheke, 1882, lived at Lealui, 1882-1884. Founded missions in Angola and Katanga and was the moving force behind Brethren foundations in Northwestern Rhodesia.

BAECHER, Aloysius (SJ): 1869-1952, b. Wecsan, Germany. At Katondwe mission, 1912-1915.

BAILEY, Albert William (SAGM): 1873-1955, American. Minister in New York and Maine with the Christian and Missionary Alliance. Served in the SAGM mission at Durban, 1909, established Chisalala in 1910 with Arnot, opened Lalafuta station in 1912, and transferred his activities permanently to Angola in 1913. He resigned from the mission in 1948.

BALDWIN, Arthur (PMMS): 1864-1937, b. Otley, England. Educated at Otley Collegiate School. Joined the PMMS in 1887 and went to Northern Rhodesia with the pioneer party of 1889. He returned to Great Britain in 1903 and later became financial secretary for the society.

BARNES, Herbert (UMCA): 1866-1937. Educated at Wells (England) Cathedral Grammar School, 1876-1883, B.A. London 1889. Ordained priest at Llandaff, Wales, 1896. Missionary, diocese of Nyasaland, 1899-1904; principal, St. Michael's College, Likoma, 1902-1904; parishes in South Africa and, after 1911, with Community of Resurrection in Rosettenville, and Penhalonga, Southern Rhodesia, 1914-1920. In Northern Rhodesia, with UMCA, 1920-1928.

BARTLING, Irene Anna (SAGM): b. 1892, American. At Musonweji and Mukinge Hill, 1922-1930.

BERT, Charles (SJ): 1869-1952, b. Bruges, Belgium. At Chikuni from 1923.

BICK, Charles (SJ): 1861-1939, b. Strasbourg, Alsace. At Chikuni, 1908-1914.

BILLES, Leslie Seymour (SDA): b. 1902. In Northern Rhodesia, 1922-1926.

BIRCH, Arthur Clarkson (UMCA): b. 1889. King's College, Cambridge, and Cuddesdon Theological College. Assistant curate of Cottingham, Yorks, 1912-1915. At Msoro, 1915-1917, resigned and returned to England. Curate of Hessle, 1918-1922, and Vicar of Cloughton, 1932-1957.

BOISSELIER, Joseph (WF): 1858-1940, b. Blouère, France. Studied at the minor seminary at Beaupréau before completing his education at the White Fathers' seminary in Carthage, Tunisia, where he was ordained in 1894. He taught briefly in the White Fathers' school for former slaves on Malta. In 1897 he began a long period of service in Northern Rhodesia. He resided at Kayambi (1897-1898, 1900, 1915-1919), Chilubula (1899, 1901-1903), Chilonga (1904-1906, 1911), Lubwe (1907-1910), and Kapatu (1912-1914, 1920-1940), where he died.

BOTES, Ella M. (DRC): b. 1890, Transvaal. In Northern Rhodesia, principally Magwero, 1912-1960. Teacher, instructor of the blind, and trained nurse.

BREDENKAMP, Ovid Ogden (SDA): b. 1895. In Northern Rhodesia, 1921-1923.

BROWN, Alexander (UFCS): b. 1872. M.B.,Ch.B., Aberdeen; D.T.M. & H., Liverpool. In Bandawe, 1906. Went to Chitambo with Mr. and Mrs. Moffat, 1907. Transferred to Kalma, India, 1913.

BROWN, Annie Howie (UFCS): b. 1877. Parents belonged to Renfield United Free Church, Glasgow. Received Diploma for Housewifery, Cookery, and Laundry, and Certificate for First Aid. Worked as a teacher for four years under London County Council. Member of Ilford Presbyterian Church. In Loudon, 1907-1911, 1913. At Mwenzo, 1916, until her marriage.

BROWN, David McCulloch (UFCS): 1880-1947, b. Falkirk, Scotland. Educated at Motherwell; McGill University, M.D., 1910; studied theology in Glasgow, 1910-1913; F.R.G.S., 1924. Ordained and inducted as Minister, United Free Church, Saline, Fife, in 1914. Captain in R.A.M.C. during First World War. Ministerial and medical work after World War I in Orkney. Married Elizabeth Yuille Caldwell, 1917. She died in Annan, Scotland, 1957. In Itete, Tanganyika, 1921. In Lubwa, 1927. Returned to Scotland, 1946, but retired to Africa later, and died in Lubwa, Northern Rhodesia.

BUCKENHAM, Henry (PMMS): 1844-1896, b. Fakenham, England. He had churches in Burton-on-Trent and Dereham, England, and founded the Primitive Methodist Mission at Aliwal North, Cape Colony. He served there from 1870-1875. He took churches at Rugby and Torquay, England, and then served at another new mission on Fernando Po from 1882-1885. He had churches again at Worthing and at Burton-on-Trent, before going to Northern Rhodesia as the leader of the first Methodist mission. He founded Nkala mission with Baldwin, and died while returning to Europe.

BUCKLEY, Stanley Edwin (PMMS): 1888-1946, b. Scarborough, England. A carpenter. Courses at Hartley College. In Northern Rhodesia, 1913-1930, at Kanchindu and Nambala.

BULSIEWICZ, Ladislaus (SJ): 1879-1919, b. Jaslo, Galicia. At Katondwe, 1913-1919.

CAMPBELL, Dugald (PB): 1870(?)-1955. Lived in Glasgow. His father was a baker. Campbell worked in a carriage factory. He went to the Katanga, 1893-1900; opened Johnston Falls mission in 1901, and a succession of Northern Rhodesian stations from 1910-1919, when he became an inspector at the Étoile du Congo mine near Elisabethville. He later went to Kano, Nigeria.

CARSON, Alexander (LMS): 1850-1896, b. Stirling, Scotland. B.Sc. Glasgow. Engineer with the Lake Tanganyika and Central Africa mission. At Kavala Island, 1885-1891, and Fwambo, 1892-1896.

CARTER, Herbert (WMMS): b. 1887, Warminster, England. Resided in Wiltshire and Derbyshire. A bookkeeper for eleven years. Attended Headingly Theological College (Leeds, England) and was ordained there. In Northern Rhodesia for varying periods, 1915-1923, being stationed more regularly in Southern Rhodesia. Sometime Secretary and Chairman of the Christian Council of Southern Rhodesia.

CASSET, Ambrose (SJ): 1863-1928, b. Myans, France. At Chikuni, 1909-1920.

CHAPMAN, William (PMMS): 1869-1947, b. Strubly, England. Founded Nanzela mission, 1895, with Frederick Pickering, and opened work at Nambala in 1905. Left Northern Rhodesia in 1914.

CHISHOLM, James A. (UFCS): 1872-1936. L.R.C.L. & S., F.R.G.S. Ordained in 1905, in Inverness. Married Miss MacGilvray in 1900, a trained nurse. She died at St. Leonard's-on-Sea, Sussex, 1947. In Mwenzo, 1900-1914. Left owing to German raid on the border. War service with Rhodesian forces in East Africa in 1916. Returned to Mwenzo, 1933, and died there.

CLARK, Ernest Howard (LMS) b. 1878, Walthamstow, England. Diploma in teaching at Cheshunt College, 1901, and one year at Livingstone College (1902-1903) for medical training. In Northern Rhodesia, 1903-1936, at Niamkolo, Mporokoso, and Kawimbe. Married Harriet Emily Thorn, a nurse, in 1904.

COBBE, Benjamin (PB): Originally from Belfast. A missionary in Katanga and at Luanza from 1894-1896, when he died.

167

APPENDIX III: BIOGRAPHIES

COLE, Elizabeth B. (UFCS): 1865-1938, b. Co. Monaghan, Ireland. Received a nursing certificate from the Western General Hospital, Glasgow, a Fevers Certificate at Tooting Fever Hospital, London, and took a Maternity Course in Belfast. She worked as a sister at Kroonstad, the Orange Free State, during the Boer War and later became assistant matron, Western Infirmary, Glasgow. At Livingstonia, 1910; Tamanda, 1923. Retired, 1927. Became Matron, Gordon Memorial Hospital, Sibasa, South Africa. Died in Auckland, New Zealand.

COLIBAULT, Jean-Marie (WF): 1880-1954, b. Orouges, France, into a farming family. Attended local schools, a minor seminary, and the major seminary of Rennes (1900-1902), before entering the White Fathers' seminaries of Binson, France, and Carthage, Tunisia, where he was ordained in 1907. Thereafter he served in Northern Rhodesia at Chilubula (1907), Kapatu (1908-1909, 1915-1919), Chibote (1910-1912), Chilubi (1913-1914, 1920-1923), Lubwe (1924-1931, 1939-1941, 1946-1954), Kabunda (1932-1938), Lufubu (1942-1944), and Kasala (1945).

COOKE, Christopher Crosbie (UMCA): d. 1951. M.A. Keble College, Oxford. Vicar of St. Thomas', Acton Vale, London. In Northern Rhodesia, principally at Livingstone, 1920-1932. Later vicar of Ashton Hayes and Freeland, England.

COWL, Fanny Priscilla (SAGM): b. 1886. At Luampa, 1923-1926. Later joined the YWCA, Durban, Natal.

CRAWFORD, Daniel (PB): 1870-1926, b. Gourock, Scotland. The son of a shipmaster who left school early. Became a clerk and a bookkeeper in Greenock, Scotland. Converted in 1877. A missionary in the Congo and later in Northern Rhodesia, 1890-1926. Founded Luanza mission, and explored Northern Rhodesia, particularly the Luapula and Bangweulu regions.

CUNNINGHAM, Hugh (PB): 1869-1940, lived in Kirkcaldy, Scotland. At Kavungu and Kalunda, 1899-1922, at Kamapanda, 1923-1940.

CURRY, Wilfred Edwin (PMMS): 1896-1956, b. Thornley, England. Hartley College. Minister of a church in South Wales, then Northern Rhodesia, 1924-1937, primarily at the Kafue Institute. Later chaplain to the High Sheriff of Exeter, 1937-1939, and missionary in the Gold Coast, 1939-1945. Received the Military Medal for actions as a pilot in World War I.

CZARLINSKI, Felician (SJ): 1868-1921, b. Brachnowka, Prussia. At Chingombe, 1914-1921.

DAVIDSON, Hannah Frances (BC): 1860-1935, b. Smithville, Ohio. High school and college in Kalamazoo, Michigan. Took an M.A. degree there and later studied at the University of Chicago. She taught at McPherson College, Kansas, for seven years before answering an appeal by the BC for missionaries. Her family was deeply involved in BC activities. She helped to found Matopo mission in Southern Rhodesia, and single-handedly founded Macha mission in Northern Rhodesia in 1906. She retired from Northern Rhodesia in 1924 and taught for eight years at Messiah College in Harrisburg, Pennsylvania.

DAVOUST, Donatien (WF): 1874-1958, b. Hambers, France. His father was a railway station-master. Davoust became a priest in 1898 after attending French schools. From 1901 he devoted the rest of his life to Northern Rhodesia and, in particular, to the peoples who resided near Kayambi (1901, 1906, 1922-1929, 1932-1933), Chilubula (1902-1903, 1908-1913, 1957-1958), Kambwiri (1904), Chilonga (1905, 1915-1921), Chilubi (1907), Kapatu (1914), Lubushi (1930-1931), Ipusukilo (1935), Rosa (1936), Malole (1937-1939), Twingi (1940), Lwena (1941-1946), and Kalabwe (1947). He compiled a standard dictionary of Cibemba.

DAY, Gordon Philip Jodrell (UMCA): M.A. St. Catherine's College, Cambridge; Ely Theological College. Ordained a priest in 1912 and became curate of St. Thomas the Martyr, Oxford, 1912-1915. At Chilikwa, 1915-1917, and at Livingstone, 1919-1922. Later curate of St. Saviour's Cathedral,

Pietermaritzburg, 1922-1925, chaplain of St. Catherine's College, 1926-1929, Candidate's secretary, Society for the Propagation of the Gospel, 1929-1933, Vicar of St. Giles', Norwich, 1933-1935, when he returned to South Africa. Later Priest-in-Charge, Gordon's Bay, Cape Town.

DEERR, William Ernest (UMCA): 1873-1920. King Henry VIII School, Coventry; B.A. Emmanuel College, Cambridge, 1894; and Cuddeson Theological College. Joined UMCA diocese of Zanzibar, 1902, as a teacher and became principal of St. Andrew's teacher-training college, Kiungani, 1908-1911. Joined Northern Rhodesian diocese, 1911, and subsequently opened Ng'omba in 1912, Chilikwa 1915, and Old Mkushi, 1918. Ordained 1918. Died of cancer in Livingstone.

DELAMARCHE, Julien (WF): 1858-1898. Served three years at Kayambi before dying of blackwater fever.

DE LA PRYME, Alexander George (UMCA): 1870-1935. Educated at Haileybury School and M.A., Trinity College, Cambridge, 1896. Priest in Stepney and Whitechapel, England, 1895-1899. Diocese of Nyasaland, 1899-1909. In Northern Rhodesia, at Fort Jameson, 1910-1919.

DEWER, Alexander (UFCS): d. 1943, South Africa. At Mwenzo, 1893. In Karonga, 1899. Returned to Mwenzo, 1900-1904, to assist Dr. Chisholm. Resigned in 1905. He joined the Free Church and went to South Africa in 1908 in charge of the Free Church of Scotland mission. He became the Moderator of the Free Church of Scotland, 1927-1928.

DOKE, Olive C. (SAB): b. 1891. Daughter of Joseph Doke, a Baptist minister who lived successively in Bristol, England, in New Zealand, and in Johannesburg, and who was responsible for the South African Baptist Missionary Society's takeover of Kafulafuta mission in 1913. She has been at Kafulafuta since 1916. Awarded the O.B.E.

DRAPER, Walter (LMS): 1861-1927, b. Hoddesdon, England. Artisan missionary at Urambo, Tanganyika, 1888-1898. At Kawimbe, 1900-1915.

DRWIEGA, Martin (SJ): b. 1887, Posada Olchowska, Poland. At Kasisi from 1923.

DUPONT, Bishop Joseph (WF): 1850-1930, b. Gesté, France, the son of a farmer. Achieved the Baccalauréat ès Lettres in 1874 after studying at the major seminary in Angers, France. He saw action in the Franco-Prussian war. Afterwards he entered Holy Orders, and then took a scientific course for missionaries that was sponsored by the Société de Géographie of Paris. From 1881 to 1885 he taught science at the White Fathers' training college in Carthage, Tunisia, and in their seminary in Algiers. After leading the pioneer White Fathers' mission to the Lower Congo (1885-1886), he spent the next four years recovering his strength and teaching in French seminaries. From 1890 to 1895 he served the White Fathers in German East Africa, initially at Karema and then at Kirando in Ufipa. In 1895 he became the superior of the White Fathers' mission to Northern Rhodesia. He opened the Kayambi station, on the borders of Bembaland, to replace the first Rhodesian station of Old Mambwe, or Mambwe-Mwela. Two years later, he became Vicar Apostolic of the Vicariate of Nyassa-Bangweolo and titulary Bishop of Thibar, *in partibus infidelium*. In 1898 he took advantage of the instability that resulted from the death of Chief Mwamba, and established the Chilubula mission near modern Kasama. In 1899 he opened the Chilonga mission near modern Mpika. In the same year his health failed, and Bishop Dupont returned to Europe. From 1905 to 1911 he again directed the activities of the White Fathers in Northern Rhodesia and Nyasaland. He resigned in 1911, and retired to Tunisia, where he died.

EDWARDS, Henrietta (LMS): b. 1885, Rhyl, Wales. Trained at Carey Hall, Birmingham, England. At Mbereshi, 1915-1919. Married Capt. E. K. Jordan of Johannesburg in 1919.

ETIENNE, Louis (WF): 1886-1963, b. Ploézal, France. He became a priest in 1912 after completing his training in White Fathers' seminaries in France and in Carthage, Tunisia. Thereafter he lived continuously in Africa, and served the communities that surrounded twelve different Northern Rhodesian mission stations: Kayambi (1913), Chibote (1914, 1930-1931), Chilubula (1915-1916, 1919, 1939, 1947, 1955-1960, 1963), Lubwe (1920), Rosa (1921, 1928, 1933-1934, 1936), Kapatu (1923-1926, 1932, 1942-1944), Chilonga (1929), Ipusukilo (1935, 1937-1938, 1949-1951, 1961-1962), Chilubi (1940), Lubushi (1948), and Kasama (1952-1954). From 1916 to 1919 he was a chaplain with the Rhodesian troops in the East African campaign. He became an Officer of the British Empire and a Chevalier of the French Legion of Honour.

FAULKNER, Henry J. T. (PB): b. 1892, London. To Chitokoloki in 1921. Later to Mutshatsha, Belgian Congo. Now resides near Kolwezi.

FELL, John R. (PMMS): 1879-1947, b. Pontefract, England. A schoolteacher. Later attended Hartley College. He had churches in Belfast and in Abergavenny, Wales. Worked with his mission in Northern Rhodesia from 1907-1927, first in the Zambezi Valley, at Kanchindu, and after 1916 at Kafue Institute, which he founded. He became the first principal of the Northern Rhodesian Jeanes School in 1927.

FISHER, Walter (PB): 1867-1935, b. London. His father and grandfather were both fish traders. He was trained at Guy's Hospital, London, and went to Africa in 1889. He lived at Kavungu and Kazombo (Angola) before founding Kaleñe Hill in 1906, where he lived until his death. His wife, Anna Darling, was a trained nurse.

FOSTER, Charles S. (SAGM): b. 1892, St. Leonard's-on-Sea, England. His father was a builder. Young Foster became a bookkeeper. With his family he emigrated to Detroit in 1909, and became a laborer in an automobile factory. Later he studied briefly at Northwestern College and then at the Moody Bible Institute, Chicago. He was ordained a Baptist minister and had a church at Chattanooga, Tennessee. He has been in Northern Rhodesia, at Musonweji and Mukinge Hill, since 1917.

FRESHWATER, William (LMS): 1872-1936, b. Market Harborough, England. His father was a grazier. Freshwater went to a local state school until the age of fourteen, when he was apprenticed to a cabinet-maker in Birmingham. Later he studied at Harley House, London, and trained at Livingstone College. He was sent to Mbereshi in 1902, later serving at Mporokoso and Kafulwe. Married Nancy Swingler (1874-1959) of Market Harborough, a teacher, in 1908.

GERRARD, Herbert S. (PMMS): b. 1886, Swinton, England. Attended a Primitive Methodist school in York, England, until the age of sixteen. His father was a builder. Gerrard worked as a builder for four years, then went to do medical training at Victoria College, Manchester. He took three months of tropical medical training at Liverpool. In Northern Rhodesia, 1915-1934, primarily at Kasenga. In Kenya, 1934-1941.

GINTER, Lila Coon (BC): b. 1893, in Ohio. Taught at Macha mission, 1921-1925. Left BC to found Bible Class mission in Choma. Married Charles Ginter, 1938.

GOETSTOWERS, Corneille (WF): 1867-1897, b. Rucphen, Holland. Studied in secondary schools in Holland before entering the White Fathers' seminary in Carthage, Tunisia. He became a priest in 1893. He served at Old Mambwe and Kayambi before succumbing to fever.

GRANT, Margaret (UFCS): b. 1892, Coatbridge, Scotland. Trained in dressmaking. At Livingstonia, 1919. Later served at Mwenzo. Married in 1927.

GRAY, S. Douglas (WMMS): 1888-1963, b. Didsbury, England. At Chipembi, 1912-1941. Awarded the M.B.E.

GUILLÉ, Raoul (WF): 1866-1897, b. Sains, France. In 1894, after studying in a seminary in Rennes and the White Fathers' training college in Carthage, Tunisia, he was sent to Old Mambwe. He helped to establish Kayambi, where he died.

GUILLEMÉ, Mathurin (WF): 1859-1942, b. Ste. Marie, France. Studied locally and in a French White Fathers' seminary. He became a priest in 1883, and served at Zanzibar from 1884 to 1885. For the next twelve years he labored in German East Africa, before becoming pro-Vicar Apostolic of the Haut Congo vicariate of the White Fathers from 1895 to 1897. After a year in Marseille, he joined Bishop Dupont at Chilubula, in Northern Rhodesia, and helped to found Chilonga mission during the same year. From 1899 to 1905 he was the administrator of the Nyassa-Bangweolo vicariate. During this period he established a number of stations in Nyasaland before becoming the Visiteur Regional to the White Fathers' missions in Tanganyika and the Haut Congo. In 1911 he became Vicar Apostolic of the Nyassa vicariate, a position which he resigned in 1934. He died at Likuni mission.

GUILLERME, Louis (WF): 1874-1960, b. Bangor, France, of peasant stock. He proceeded from a minor seminary in France to the White Fathers' seminary in Carthage, Tunisia, where he was ordained in 1900. After establishing the first, abortive, station in the country of Kazembe's Lunda, he spent four years (1901-1904) at Chilubula, and then opened the Kapatu station, where he resided from 1905 to 1914. Thereafter he was stationed at Chilubi (1916-1919, 1923-1926), Lubwe (1921-1922, 1954-1960), Chilonga (1927-1933), Kayambi (1934-1936), Rosa (1937-1951), and Twingi (1952-1953). In 1921 he became the first organizer and director of schools for the White Fathers. He compiled a short dictionary and a grammar of Cibemba.

HALLIDAY, Alexander (UFCS): 1887-1946, b. Perceton, Ayrshire. Son of Thomas Halliday, a miner. Attended Dreghorn Public School and the Bible Training Institute, Glasgow. Ordained to the ministry in 1927. In the Army for four years in Egypt and Palestine. In Livingstonia, 1921, and served at Mwenzo and Karonga. Went to Chasefu in 1930 and returned to Scotland in 1946. Married Janet Simpson Fulton, 1921, daughter of James Fulton, a miner. Halliday was killed on a railway near Dreghorn.

HANKIEWICZ, Stanislaus (SJ): 1877-1928, b. Krysowice, Poland. At Chingombe and Kasisi from 1914.

174

HANSEN, Thomas (PB): b. 1883, of Danish parents. Resided in Sunderland, England. A joiner by trade. He emigrated to Johannesburg in 1908. At Kabompo, 1916-1920, at Kanganga, 1920-1942, and afterwards at Kabulamema. Now resides in Bulawayo.

HARRIS, Ernest Alfred Martin (SAGM): 1866-1933, English. Served at Chisalala, 1911-1918.

HEMANS, James Henry Emmanuel (LMS): 1856-1908, b. Manchester County, Jamaica. At Niamkolo, 1888-1906. Married Maria Cecilia Clementina Gale, 1884. Both were residents of LMS missions in Jamaica.

HENDERSON, John Mathieson (UFCS): 1863-1943, b. Ecclefechan, Scotland. Attended the Bible Training Institute, Glasgow, in 1893, and was ordained to the ministry in 1920 by the Livingstonia Presbytery. He worked as a teacher and missionary in the Wynd Free Church, Glasgow. In Karonga and Livingstonia after 1896. Invalided, 1906. Missionary to Tamanda, 1913. In Mwenzo, 1924. Invalided, 1926. Married Catherine Young Riddell, 1902.

HEWITT, George Herbert (UMCA): b. 1893, Ripon, England. Father was curate of Ripon. Hewitt attended Ripon School, Fitzwilliam Hall, Cambridge, and Westcott House, Cambridge. He was assistant priest in Rotherhithe before joining the Northern Rhodesia diocese in 1920.

HIGGINS, Bernard (UMCA): b. 1893, Hereford, England. His father was the rector of Stoke Hamond, Bletchley. Educated at Berkhamsted School, Keble College, Oxford, and at Cuddesdon Theological College. He became curate of St. Paul's, Foleshill, Coventry, England, 1921-1923. In Northern Rhodesia, 1924-1931. Later curate of Heene, England, and returned to Northern Rhodesia, 1933-1949.

HIGGINS, Thomas (PB): 1877-1945, b. Queenstown, Essequibo, Guiana. At Luanza, and Koni (Congo), 1898-1920. In Northern Rhodesia, at Chunwe and Mubende, 1920-1945.

HINE, John Edward (UMCA): 1857-1934, b. Mapperley Park, England. Son of a manufacturer. Educated at University College School, University College, London, M.B. 1879; M.D. London 1883; M.A. Oxford 1891; D.D. Oxford 1896; D.C.L. Durham, 1908. Surgeon at the Radcliffe Infirmary, Oxford, 1880-1882. Curate of Richmond, 1886-1888. Priest, diocese of Zanzibar, 1889-1893. Priest, diocese of Nyasaland, 1893-1896. Bishop of Likoma, 1896-1901. Bishop of Zanzibar, 1901-1908. Chaplain, Tangiers, 1908, and Constantinople, 1909. Bishop of Northern Rhodesia, 1910-1914. Later Bishop Suffragan of Grantham, England, 1920-1930.

HOGG, Walter (PMMS): a carpenter. In Northern Rhodesia, 1901-1905, when he died at Sijoba.

HORE, Edward Coode (LMS): 1848-1922, b. London. Sailor and master mariner for twelve years. To Zanzibar and Lake Tanganyika with the first LMS party in 1878. Explored the southern half of the lake in 1880-1881, returning home that year. Married Anne Boyle Gribbon of Leeds in 1881. Again on Lake Tanganyika, 1883-1888, at Kavala Island, Lofu, and Niamkolo. From 1894-1900 he was in charge of the mission steamer *John Williams*, which called at the islands of Oceania. He settled in Tasmania and died in Hobart. Mrs. Hore died in 1922 in Sydney.

HOWIE, John Struthers (UFCS): 1882-1961. He worked five years as a joiner and five years on a farm (three of which were spent at an agricultural college gaining appropriate certificates). A member of the Reformed Presbyterian Church, Greenock. Arrived at Livingstonia, 1906. At Chitambo for building work, 1910. In 1914 he became a dispatch rider for the government of Nyasaland. Then he went to the United Kingdom, where he gained a commission in the R.A.F. Awarded the Military Cross. He became a major in the Serbian Relief Commission in 1919. Re-appointed, and sailed for Chitambo, 1929. Ordained by Presbytery of Livingstonia at Chitambo, 1933. Married Mary Gilmour, M.A., in 1915. She died in 1960. Howie died at Myrtle Cottage, Dollar, Scotland, and is buried there.

HUME, Douglas T. (PB): b. 1894, Toronto. A market gardener. Arrived Kazombo (Angola) in 1917. Commenced

176

at Kanganga in 1923, and joined the Sudan Interior Mission in 1928.

HURLOW, Herbert John (SDA): b. 1886, Cardiff, Wales. Attended local schools in Watford, England, 1890-1900. Obtained a male nurse's diploma at Caterham Sanatorium, 1906-1909. In Nyasaland and Northern Rhodesia after 1915.

INNES, Francis Alexander (UFCS): 1875-1944. His father was the minister of the Skene Free Church. He received the M.A. and M.B.,Ch.B. at Aberdeen. Ordained to the ministry in Rutherford Church, Aberdeen, 1903. Arrived Bandawe, 1899, and served at Ekwendeni, Karonga, and Livingstonia. On war service at Mwenzo, 1917. Left Livingstonia, 1919, and resigned from the mission, 1921. He became a government medical officer in West Africa, 1927-1932. Married Mary A. Innes, 1903. He died at Alloa, Scotland.

JAKEMAN, J. W. Victor (SAGM): 1883-1942, English. A bank clerk. A missionary in the Transkei, Swaziland, and Angola before founding Luampa in 1923. He remained in Northern Rhodesia until his death. He married Eva Milton of White Springs, Florida, in 1922. She was educated at Belmont College, Nashville. A Baptist, she attended the Moody Bible Institute.

JEDRZEJCZYK, Andrew (SJ): 1858-1921. b. Maluszyn, Poland. At Chingombe from 1921.

JEWELL, F. Burton (SDA): b. 1875, Ithaca, New York, of English parents. Attended public schools in Rochester, New York, from 1890-1892, Battle Creek College from 1898-1900, and the Battle Creek Sanatorium, 1903-1906, from which institution he received a male nurse's diploma.

JOHNSON, Harry (LMS): 1868-1964, b. Market Harborough, England. Attended Cheshunt Theological College. Ordained 1896. In Northern Rhodesia, 1896-1905, primarily at Kambole. Later pastor of the Congregational Church of Wilsden, Bradford, England. He subsequently retired to New Zealand.

177

JONES, David Picton (LMS): 1860-1936, b. New Quay, Wales. Attended Carmarthen College. Ordained in 1882. At Uguha (Congo), 1883-1886, founded Fwambo, 1887, Kawimbe, 1890, and Kambole, 1894. To Southern Rhodesia, 1897-1903. He later became a minister of churches in Glamorganshire, Wales.

JONES, Percy William (LMS): 1871-?, b. Malvern, England. Studied at Nottingham Institute. Ordained in 1896. In Northern Rhodesia, 1898-1899. Asked to resign.

KERSWELL, John Ambrose (PMMS): 1877-1944, b. Teignmouth, England. Attended Hartley College. Minister of a church in Aldershot, England. In Northern Rhodesia, 1908-1937, primarily at Nambala and Namantombwa.

KODRZYNSIK, Leo (SJ): 1881-1951, b. Lesna, Czechoslovakia. At Katondwe, 1913-1951.

KONIGMACHER, Samuel Martin (SDA): 1877-1950. In Northern Rhodesia, 1917-1934.

KOPEC, Maxim (SJ): b. 1878, Karwina, Silesia. At Katondwe and Kasisi from 1919.

KRAUPA, Apolonius (SJ): 1871-1919, b. Kozlow, Galicia. At Katondwe, 1913-1919.

KUPFERER, Alice A. L. (SAGM): b. 1894, St. Louis, Mo. Registered Nurse. In Northern Rhodesia, 1924-1933, primarily at Musonweji and Mukinge Hill.

LAMMOND, William (PB): b. 1876, Glasgow. Of a Free Church family. A fitter for nine years before arriving at Luanza, in 1901. In Northern Rhodesia, 1905-1963, primarily at Johnston Falls and Kaleba. Compiled a Cibemba vocabulary. He has received the Pioneer Medal of the Belgian Congo, the Bronze Medal of the Royal African Society, and the M.B.E.

LARUE, Bishop Etienne (WF): 1865-1935, b. St. Christophe-en-Brionnais, France. Studied at seminaries in Semur and Autun before completing his formal education in the

White Fathers' seminary in Carthage, Tunisia, between 1888 and 1891, when he was ordained into the priesthood. He later taught in seminaries in Jerusalem and France. In 1899 he became Bishop Dupont's secretary. Three years later he became Vicar General of the Vicariate of Nyassa-Bangweolo. He served at Chilubula from 1902 to 1905, and again from 1908 to 1909. During the intervening years he represented Bishop Dupont in Nyasaland, where he served as the regional superior from 1909 to 1912. In 1913 he became Vicar Apostolic of the newly separated Vicariate of Bangweolo, a post he filled until his retirement and death in France.

LAWSON, Agnes T. (UFCS): She was an Anglican who became a Presbyterian. In Livingstonia, 1906, Mwenzo, 1907. Resigned and married Charles MacKinnon, the Magistrate at Fife, Northern Rhodesia, in 1907.

LAWSON, James (LMS): 1874-1903, b. Blackburn, England. Studied at Nottingham Institute. Ordained in 1902. At Niamkolo, 1902-1903. Died at Mbereshi of blackwater fever.

LAZAREWICZ, John (SJ): 1865-1930, b. Lancut, Poland. At Katondwe and Chingombe from 1912.

LEEKE, Charles Harold (UMCA): 1887-1958, b. Lincoln, England. His father was sub-deacon of Lincoln Cathedral. All four of his brothers were priests. Educated at Marlborough College and M.A., Trinity College, Cambridge, 1914; Ely Theological College. Ordained in 1912. Curate of Boston, 1912-1914. At Chilikwa (Chipili), 1915-1929, Broken Hill, 1930-1933. Later vicar of Newport, England, 1933-1939, and vicar of Grantham and Canon and Prebendary of Lincoln Cathedral, 1939-1958.

LETORT, François (WF): 1859-1908, b. Theil. He became a priest in 1884 and joined the White Fathers in 1890. He served in North Africa from 1891 to 1896, and reached Kayambi toward the end of that year. Later he was associated with the Chilubula station before being transferred, in 1901, to German East Africa, where he died.

179

LEWIS, Ernest Winbolt (LMS): 1876-?, b. Madras, South India. M.B., Ch.B., Edinburgh. In Northern Rhodesia, 1902-1905, 1906-1910.

LONGA, James (SJ): 1857-1937, b. Kisszalok, Hungary. At Kapoche and Kasisi, 1931-1937.

LOVELESS, James H. (WMMS): 1884-1924, b. North Walsham, England. Headingly College. In Northern Rhodesia, intermittently, 1912-1924.

LYON, John T. (PMMS): b. 1890, Huggate Wold, England. Father a farmer. Educated at Cottingham Council School and Hartley College. Decided to be a missionary after reading a copy of "Livingstone's Life." A sergeant during World War I in the Royal Army Medical Corps. In Northern Rhodesia, 1919-1934, primarily in charge of farming at Kafue Institute.

MABEN, Pearl Ross (SAGM): b. 1887, American. In Northern Rhodesia, at Chisalala and Musonweji, 1922-1925.

MC CALLUM, Peter (UFCS): d. 1931, Hampshire, England. Artisan-Evangelist. In Livingstonia, 1881, and later Ekwendeni. In Mwenzo, 1896. Left Africa 1899, and resigned, 1900.

MAC DONALD, Alexander (UFCS): 1879-1941, b. Swordale, Stornoway, Scotland. Attended Knock School, Nicholson Institute, Stornoway, and Aberdeen Grammar School. Studied at Aberdeen University, 1900-1904, and the United Free Church Divinity College, Glasgow, 1908-1910, 1911-1912. Assistant Minister in Inveravon United Free Church and Greenock Gaelic Church. In Lovedale, South Africa, for one year. Ordained by the United Free Presbytery of Kirkcaldy, 1913. In Chitambo and Bandawe, 1913. In Nyasaland and German East Africa during World War I. In Chitambo, 1920, 1930-1932. In Chasefu, 1922. Resigned in 1933. Married Ruth Mary Livingstone Wilson, 1920. Died in Edinburgh.

MC FARLANE, Wilfrid (LMS): b. 1878, Edinburgh. One of fourteen children of a wealthy wire-cloth manufacturer and the publisher of *The Scottish Leader*. Member of the Congregational Church, Edinburgh. Left George Watson's School at sixteen to work in an insurance office. Later M.B., Ch.B., Edinburgh. He was fascinated as a boy by missionary life, and as a young man he conducted missions in a suburb of Edinburgh. In Northern Rhodesia, 1904-1913. Resigned over a disagreement with LMS policy. Awarded the Military Cross in World War I. With the Church of Scotland, Blantyre, 1920-1936.

MC GILL, Andrew Haugh (SAGM): b. 1885, Dumfries, Scotland. Emigrated to Canada in 1906. In Northern Rhodesia, 1917-1918, later with the SAGM in Angola and Southern Rhodesia. A Presbyterian.

MACKAY, James George (LMS): 1860-1924, b. Inverness, Scotland. Studied theology at East London Institute and medicine at London Hospital. L.R.C.S., Missionary in Madagascar, 1886-1895. Transferred to Northern Rhodesia (Kambole), 1897-1901. Resigned because of a disagreement with LMS policies.

MAC KENDRICK, George (LMS): 1869-1901, b. Wishaw, Scotland. Pastor of an Evangelical Union church at Langholme, Scotland. In Northern Rhodesia, 1900-1901; died at Niamkolo.

MAC LENNAN, John Edward (UMCA): 1870?-1916. Accountant, from Liverpool. Joined the Zanzibar diocese, 1904-1908. Attached to the diocese of Bloemfontein, 1908-1911. In Northern Rhodesia, 1911-1916, first as a teacher, later as a priest (ordained in 1914). Died of pneumonia and complications, in London.

MC MINN, Robert Donald (UFCS): 1870-1956, b. Dalquharren, Dailly, Ayrshire. Attended Kilgrammie School, Dailly, 1876-1882; Brown's Institute, Galston, Scotland, 1883-1889; Cliff College, Derbyshire, 1891-1893; and Harley College London. Member of Galston Free Church. Ordained at Livingstonia, 1906. In Bandawe, 1893, Mwenzo, 1911, Lubwa, 1913-1933. Resided at Lubwa and Shiwa Ngandu in retirement, 1939-1946. Died in South Africa in 1956.

MALIN, Christian (SJ): 1877-1942. b. Satteins, Austria. At Chikuni from 1920.

APPENDIX III: BIOGRAPHIES

MANN, Roy Hess (BC): b. 1898, Washington Borough, Pa. Converted at sixteen. Attended missionary courses at Messiah College. In Northern Rhodesia, 1922-1924. Mrs. Grace Miller Mann, b. 1900, Morrison, Ill., died at Macha in 1924.

MARKIEWICZ, Vincent (SJ): 1888-1924, b. Dyon, Poland. At Chingombe, 1921-1924.

MARTIN, Jessie (UFCS): Her father was the Free Church Minister of Ballgate, Scotland. Niece of Edward Irving. Worked as a teacher and nurse. Nurse at Belleville mission, Paris. In Livingstonia and Karonga, 1900, Mwenzo, 1905. Retired, 1909.

MASTERSON, Christina (UFCS): In Lubwa, 1922. Resigned in 1927 on marriage to the Rev. Mr. H. S. Kelp, of the Church of Brethren mission, Nigeria.

MASTERSON, John (SJ): 1878-1959, b. Edinburgh, Scotland. At Chikuni, 1912-1915.

MATHER, Charles Benjamin (LMS): 1858-1898, b. Tunbridge Wells, England. Son of the Rev. Mr. Robert Cotton Mather, A.M., LL.D., missionary to Benares, India. Charles Mather became M.B., Ch.B., Edinburgh. L.R.C.S., L.R.C.P. In Northern Rhodesia, 1888-1898, when he died at Fwambo.

MAY, Alston James Weller (UMCA): 1869-1940, b. Stoke-on-Trent, England. Seventh of eleven children of a retired naval officer and a sometime government factory inspector. He grew up in Congleton and Leeds, England, and attended Macclesfield and Leeds Grammar Schools. He was a scholar of Oriel College, Oxford, where he took first-class honors in classical moderations and a second class honors in Lit. Hum. He also rowed in the college boat. He taught at Rugby and then attended Cuddesdon Theological College, where he was ordained. He served in parishes at Richmond, Leeds, and at Portsmouth, and was Curate of Chertsey, England, 1911-1913. Bishop of Northern Rhodesia, 1914-1940.

MAY, John (LMS): 1866-1901, b. Saltcoats, Scotland. Studied at Cheshunt Theological College. Assistant Minister of Caterham Church. Ordained in 1897. At Kawimbe, 1897-1901, where he died.

MAZUREK, Stephen (SJ): 1891-1959, b. Polubicze, Poland. At Chingombe and Kasisi, 1923-1959.

MEIER, Francis Xavier (SJ): b. 1883, Switzerland. At Chikuni from 1915.

MELDRUM, James D. (UFCS): d. 1928. In 1906, relieved Mr. and Mrs. Moffat at Mwenzo until the return of Dr. Chisholm in that year. He arrived in the United Kingdom in 1907 and resigned because the Mission Committee had no funds with which to send him back to Africa. He later accepted a non-mission post in Nyasaland.

MOFFAT, Malcolm (UFCS): 1870-1939, b. Kuruman, Bechuanaland. A civil servant in the Cape Colony. Ordained to the ministry, 1907. In Nyasaland in 1894 as an agriculturist and evangelist. In Mwenzo, 1905-1906, during the leave of Dr. James Chisholm. In Serenje district, 1907, to establish Chitambo. Left Chitambo in 1930. Married Maria Martin Jackson (1868, Scotland—1958?, Mkushi, Northern Rhodesia) in 1900, a trained nurse of the Royal Infirmary, Glasgow, who came to Bandawe as a missionary in 1897. Their three sons are prominent in the affairs of Northern Rhodesia. Moffat died at Kalwa, Northern Rhodesia.

MOFFATT, James Ronald (UMCA): b. 1878. Attended Kelham Theological College. In Northern Rhodesia, primarily at Mapanza, 1912-1918. He later held a succession of South African parishes and became priest-in-charge, Sekukuniland, 1925-1929, returning again to Northern Rhodesia, at Broken Hill and Fort Jameson, 1938-1947.

MOLINIER, Louis (WF): 1872-1910, b. St. Amans-Soult, France, of a working-class family. Studied in French secondary schools and at a Roman Catholic school in Algeria before matriculating at the White Fathers' seminary in Carthage, Tunisia. He was ordained in 1896. In Northern Rhodesia, he served at Kayambi in 1898, founded the Chilonga mission in

1899, and then established the Lubwe station in 1906. He wrote a Cibemba version of the life of Christ and died at Lubwe.

MOREAU, Joseph (SJ): 1864-1949, b. La Bruffiere, France. At Chikuni, 1905-1949.

MORRIS, Sidney Herbert (LMS): 1875-1918, b. Market Harborough, England. Son of a missionary to Madras, India, and a sometime pastor of Market Harborough church. He became M.B., Ch.B., Edinburgh. In Northern Rhodesia, 1901-1902, when he resigned and entered government service. He subsequently returned to England.

MOSKOPP, Gaspar (SJ): 1869-1923, b. Koblenz, Germany. At Kapoche, 1913-1923.

MOWAT, Gavin Henry (PB): 1882-1950, b. Leith, Scotland. Emigrated to Buffalo, where he was a bank clerk. His father was a clerk in a wholesale provision store. In Angola, 1911-1923, Chavuma, 1923-1927.

MURRAY, William M. (UFCS): ?-1923, b. Sutherlandshire, Scotland. A carpenter by trade. At Mwenzo, 1907. Returned to Scotland in 1910. Ordained by the Free Church of Scotland and appointed to South Africa in 1911. Married Miss Sutherland in 1905 and had two children. Died in Scotland.

MYERS, J. Lester (BC): b. 1892, Franklin County, Pa. Converted at sixteen. Attended Elizabethtown College and Messiah College. Taught public school in Franklin County. In Northern Rhodesia, 1920-1924. Later Bishop of Montgomery County (Pa.) district of the Brethren.

NAVE, J. Ward (WMMS): 1885-1935, b. Willington Quay, Wales. Trained at Didsbury College. At Chipembi, 1924-1929.

NEILSEN, Christine L. (SAGM): b. 1895?, American. Attended Moody Bible Institute. In Angola, 1920-1924, in Northern Rhodesia, 1924-1925.

NICOT, Victor (SJ): 1858-1935, b. Champagne, France. At Chikuni, 1920-1921.

NUTT, William Harwood (LMS): 1869-1942, b. Beeston, near Nottingham, England. Artisan missionary in Northern Rhodesia, 1892-1896.

NUTTER, Henry Cecil (LMS): 1873-1942, b. Thwaites Brow, England. Studied at Harley House. Ordained in 1901. In Northern Rhodesia, primarily Mbereshi, 1901-1930.

O'FERRALL, Ronald Stanhope More (UMCA): b. 1890. M.A. Trinity College, Cambridge, 1916; Ely Theological College. Curate of Chesterfield, England, 1914-1918; house master, St. George's School, Jerusalem, 1919-1923; in Northern Rhodesia, 1924-1926. Bishop of Madagascar, 1926-1940. Assistant Bishop of Derby, 1941-1953.

OOST, Achille van (WF): 1859-1895, b. Hontkerque, France. Ordained a priest in 1883, he thereafter labored at Tabora (1890), Karema, Mpala, and Kibanga in Tanganyika (1891), before establishing Mambwe-Mwela, or Old Mambwe, in late 1891. During 1894 and 1895 he prepared the way for the thrust by Bishop Dupont into Bembaland. On a journey into the heart of Bembaland, however, he succumbed to an attack of blackwater fever.

PACEK, Francis (SJ): 1868-1945, b. Brangkowka, Poland. At Chingombe and Broken Hill, 1914-1945.

PACZKA, Adalbert (SJ): 1875-1955, b. Siedleoska, Poland. At Katondwe, Chingombe, Kasisi, 1913-1955.

PICKERING, Frederick (PMMS): 1863-1935, b. Bridlington, England. A member of the Church of England until age sixteen. Attended Hartley College. Missionary at Fernando Po, 1892-1895. In Northern Rhodesia, primarily at Nanzela, 1895-1901. Later at Aliwal North, Cape Colony.

PIROUET, Herbert Geffrand (SAGM): b. 1877, London. His step-father was a vicar of the Church of England. Attended Malvern College. Later worked in a stock-broker's office. In Northern Rhodesia, at Chisalala and Mutanda Bridge, 1919-1933.

POMEROY, Henry James (PB): 1871-1924. At Luanza, 1896-1899. Later active as a missionary in Algeria and Nigeria.

POTTIE, Michael (PMMS): A Transvaal farmer, originally from Scotland. At Kasenga, 1916.

PRESCOTT, William John (PB): b. 1897, Devon, England. A carpenter and joiner. His father was a builder. Prescott left school after obtaining an elementary education. In Northern Rhodesia, 1923-1963.

PRICE, John W. (PMMS): b. 1878, Norwich, England. Attended Hartley College. Minister of a church in Norwich, 1903-1906. In Northern Rhodesia, primarily Nanzela, 1919-1934. Later churches in Manchester, Dunstable, and Watton, England.

PUETH, Eugène (WF): 1874-1954, b. Sablieres, France, into a farming family. Studied in local schools, a Roman Catholic school in Algeria, and at the White Fathers' seminary in Carthage, Tunisia, where he was ordained in 1901. Thereafter, devoted himself to Northern Rhodesia, where he wrote a number of booklets in and on Cibemba, until his death. He resided at Kayambi (1901-1904, 1909-1922), Chilubula (1905, 1939-1944, 1951-1954), Chilonga (1906-1908), Chilubi (1923-1927, 1935-1938), Malole (1928-1933), Ilondola (1934), Lubwe (1945), Twingi (1946-1948), and Lwena (1949-1950).

PULLEY, Gerrard Todd (UMCA): b. 1888, Forest Hill, England. Son of a Church of England vicar. Marlborough College and M.A. Trinity College, Cambridge, 1914. Ely Theological College. Curate of Camberwell, 1912-1914, and of Westminster, 1914-1915. At Chilikwa, 1915-1923. Resigned because he was not entirely in sympathy with Africans. Originally joined the UMCA because of his long friendship with Leeke. Joined the Society of St. John the Evangelist in 1926.

PURVES, Adam Darling (LMS): 1865-1901, b. Dunse, Scotland. Artisan missionary in Northern Rhodesia, 1892-1901. He died at Mbereshi.

RAND, Frederick Bacon (UMCA): b. 1882. Member of Society of Sacred Mission from 1898. Curate of Sneinton, England, 1906-1907. Missionary in South Africa and Basutoland, 1908-1913. In Northern Rhodesia, 1914-1919. S. Rhodesia diocese, 1926-1929. Priest in Truro, England, 1937-1941.

RANGER, Apsley Sidney Burdett (UMCA): b. 1879, Hertingfordbury, England. Son of a priest of the Church of England. Marlborough College and Pembroke College, Cambridge, Cambridge Clergy Training School and Leeds Clergy School. A hockey blue, and a hockey international for England. Curate of St. Peter's, Leicester, England, for ten years. At Msoro, 1913-1926. Rector of Islip, England, 1927-1949.

RHINEHART, Jesse Abraham (SAGM): 1888-1944, American. At Chisalala, 1922-1924. Later in Angola, 1924-1932.

ROBERTSON, William Govan (LMS): 1869-1928, b. Whithorn, England. With the United Free Church of Scotland in Nyasaland, 1891-1896. Ordained in 1897 in Glasgow. In Northern Rhodesia, primarily at Kawimbe, Mporokoso, and Senga Hill, 1897-1928.

ROBINSON, Christopher (SDA): b. 1880, in England. In Northern Rhodesia, 1909-1911.

RODENBÜHER, Stephen (SJ): 1872-1948, b. Nemetker, Hungary. At Kapoche, 1913-1915.

ROEBUCK, Oliver (WMMS): b. 1896, Sheffield, England. Left school at thirteen. His father was a stationmaster. He became a grocer's office boy, a lawyer's copyist, an apprentice to a manufacturer's chemist, an apprentice in a boiler works, and an apprentice in an electrical engineering factory. Later he became a cost clerk. He became a lay preacher in Oldham. He served in World War I with the 17th Manchester Regiment, and was taken prisoner in 1917, remaining in German hands until 1919. He spent two years in Handsworth College, and was in Northern Rhodesia (Chipembi and Broken Hill), 1921-1924.

ROGERS, Thomas Lambert (PB): d. 1916 at Chitokoloki of blackwater fever. A student of civil engineering. In Northern Rhodesia, 1913-1916, at Kabompo and Chitokoloki.

ROSS, James Arthur (LMS): 1877-1958, b. Skipton, England. Resided in Nelson, England. Studied at Nottingham Institute. A skilled carpenter. At Kambole, 1904-1929.

RUCK, Cecil George (UMCA): 1890-1958. B.A. London University; Cuddeson Theological College. Priest in the parish of Rosbarton, 1913-1916, and chaplain to the forces, 1916-1919, during which time he was awarded the Military Cross. In Northern Rhodesia at Mapanza, 1921-1942, Ndola, 1942-1943, 1948-1952, Chingola, 1943-1948, Chipili, 1952-1953. Vicar of Tunstall, Blackburn, England, 1954-1958.

SCHOEFFER, Georges (WF): 1868-1942, b. Nozay, France. His father taught in a local school. He himself studied in local secondary schools and at the White Fathers' seminary in Carthage, Tunisia, where he was ordained in 1896. After ordination the young Schoeffer obtained a doctoral degree in theology in Rome. He served briefly in Uganda. He is reputed to be the first priest to evangelize in the surrounding villages while his colleagues devoted their attention to the station, where an orphanage occupied much of their time. He trained the first Roman Catholic catechists. He also wrote the first book sponsored by the Rhodesian White Fathers. It was a summary of the Old Testament in a mixture of Swahili, Cibemba, and Cimambwe. He also composed an early Cibemba grammar. In Northern Rhodesia, he served at Kayambi (1899-1909, 1929-1930), Chilubi (1910-1918, 1937-1942), Kapatu (1922-1923, 1936), Chilubula (1924-1925), Chibote (1926), Ipusukilo (1927-1928), and Chilonga (1931-1935). He died at Chilubi.

SCOTT, John Cameron (LMS): 1878-?, b. Manchester. In Northern Rhodesia (Mbereshi), 1908-1911. Resigned to join government service.

SCOTT, Robert (UFCS): M.B.,Ch.B., Glasgow. House Surgeon of the Perth Infirmary. In Bandawe, 1898. In Mwenzo, 1899-1900.

SEIDEL, Waldemar (SJ): 1882-1957, b. Rosdin, Czechoslovakia. At Kapoche and Katondwe from 1921.

SERVICE, Ruth (UFCS): 1894-?, b. Paisley, Scotland. Trained in Deaconess Hospital School of Edinburgh, and Royal Infirmary, Edinburgh. She held a certificate of the School for Christian Workers. Awarded the M.B.E., 1955. In Lubwa, 1922-1955. Resides in Coldingham, Berwickshire, Scotland.

SHAW, John (PMMS): b. 1889, Thackley, England. Left school at fourteen. His father was a Primitive Methodist lay preacher. He worked in a textile factory and studied at night in Keighly. He desired to be a successful businessman, but instead entered Hartley College in 1912. He contemplated taking a church in Canada or becoming a missionary in China. Instead he took a mission circuit in the Orange Free State. Transferred to Northern Rhodesia in 1916. At Nanzela, 1916-1925, Kafue, 1926-1932, and Lusaka, 1932-1960. During World War II he was chaplain to the Northern Rhodesia Regiment and was awarded the M.B.E.

SHAW, Mabel (LMS): b. 1888, Bilston, England. Resided in Wolverhampton, England. Studied at the Ryde Boarding School and at the Women's Missionary College, Edinburgh. She taught in elementary schools in Wolverhampton for four years and held teaching diplomas and a pianoforte certificate. At Mbereshi, 1915-1941, where she was in charge of women's education. She was awarded the O.B.E. in 1931. During 1942-1952, she was a missionary with the Church Missionary Society in Kenya and India.

SHOOSMITH, Edith May (SAGM): b. 1891. Resided Brighton, England. Elementary education at St. Nicholas' Church School, Brighton. A short-hand typist. In Northern Rhodesia, 1920-1952.

SHORT, William N. (CC): b. 1895, American. A stone mason. Educated at Cornell Christian College, Iowa. In Bulawayo and then opened CC stations in Northern Rhodesia, 1923-1960. Began Sinde in 1923, Kabanga in 1926, and Namwianga in 1932.

APPENDIX III: BIOGRAPHIES

SIMS, Ernest Herbert (PB): b. 1884, London. Left school at age fifteen, worked as an overseer and a rate-collector for the Tottenham (London) Borough Council. To Angola in 1913, to Northern Rhodesia, 1922-1960. He helped to establish Chavuma and Lukolwe missions.

SIMS, George (PB): b. 1881, Swindon, England. Completed form II in Swindon. Was a cyclemaker. At Luanza, 1907-1910, in Northern Rhodesia, primarily at Kaleba and Mansa, 1910-1960.

SMITH, Arthur Harry (UMCA): b. 1886. Attended Dorchester (England) Missionary College. In Zanzibar diocese, 1911-1919, in Northern Rhodesia, 1920-1960. At Msoro, 1920-1935, at Fort Jameson, 1936-1943, at Luanshya, 1943-1952, at Lusaka, 1953-.

SMITH, Edwin Williams (PMMS): 1876-1957, b. Aliwal North, Cape Colony. Son of a Primitive Methodist missionary. He was educated at Enfield College, England. He entered the Primitive Methodist ministry in 1897, and became a missionary in 1898. Served first in Basutoland and then at Aliwal, at Nanzela, and at Kasenga. In 1916 he joined the British and Foreign Bible Society, first as secretary for Italy, then as secretary for Western Europe. He became its literary superintendent in 1922 and its editorial superintendent in 1932. He retired from the Society in 1939. From 1939-1943 he lectured at the Hartford (Connecticut) Seminary Foundation and at Fisk (Tennessee) University. President of the Royal Anthropological Institute, 1934-1935. Founding member of the International African Institute. Editor of *Africa* and the *Journal of the Royal African Society*. Received the D.D. from the University of Toronto in 1942. Received the Rivers Memorial Medal of the Royal Anthropological Institute, 1931. Silver medalist, Royal Anthropological Society, 1939. Wrote or edited twenty books. Married Julia Fitch, who died in 1953.

SMITH, James (UFCS): b. 1898. Attended the Bible Training Institute, Glasgow. At Tamanda, 1923, Chasefu, 1925-1927. He later became connected with the Zambesi Industrial Mission, Nyasaland.

SPENDEL, John (SJ): 1880-1945, b. Stein, Czechoslovakia. At Katondwe, Kasisi, and Broken Hill, 1921-1945.

STECKLEY, Elizabeth Engle (BC): 1876-?, b. Lancaster County, Pennsylvania. Resided in Kansas. Converted in 1892. A practical nurse. In Northern Rhodesia, irregularly, 1907-1941. Married Lewis Steckley in 1916.

STOFNER, Joseph (SJ): 1865-1936, b. Sarntheim, S. Tyrol. At Katondwe, 1913-1936.

SUCKLING, George R. (PB): 1883-1952, resided London. In Northern Rhodesia from 1911. Founded Chitokoloki in 1915 and lived there until his death. He was awarded the O.B.E. in 1943.

SWANN, Alfred James (LMS): 1855-1928, b. Shoreham, England. Mate in the LMS marine department, 1882-1887, and 1888-1894. He later joined the administrative service of the British Central Africa Protectorate.

TANGUY, François (WF): 1886-1961, b. Bannalec, France. He was ordained in 1912 after completing his studies in White Fathers' seminaries in France and in Carthage, Tunisia. After service at Chilonga (1913-1914, 1920-1924), Chilubi (1915), Chilubula (1916-1918, 1925-1926), Lubwe (1919), and Rosa (1927-1932), he succeeded Father Guillerme as the foremost White Father educationist, headed his mission's teacher-training college at Malole from 1933 to 1949, and for many years filled the position of mission education secretary. He was awarded the honor of Officer of the British Empire, and died at Kasama.

TAYLOR, Myron (BC): 1873-1931, b. Lapeer County, Michigan. At Macha, 1907-1931, when he was killed by a lion. He married Adda Engle in 1909. She, b. 1869, Bainbridge, Pennsylvania, had been a church worker in Lancaster and had aided Frances Davidson at Macha in 1906. She helped her husband open Sikalongo mission in 1923. She lived there until 1932.

THOMAS, William (LMS): 1859-?, b. St. Clears, Wales. Studied at Carmarthenshire and Lancashire Colleges. For eight years, he was pastor of the Waterhead Congregational Church, Oldham, England. In Northern Rhodesia, 1893-1896.

THOMPSON, Frank Elwell (SDA): b. 1890, Northfield, Indiana, into an Adventist family. Son of a farmer. Attended local schools, 1897-1905, high school during 1907-1908, Beechwood Academy (Fairland, Indiana), 1909-1910, and later studied by correspondence. A carpenter by profession.

TORREND, Julius (SJ): 1861-1936, b. Privat d'allier, Haute-Loire, France. At Chikuni, Kasisi, and Broken Hill, 1905-1936.

TURNER, Bernard Raleigh (LMS): 1878-1943, b. Hackney. Studied at the Haberdasher's Guild School, London. In Northern Rhodesia, 1903-1940, principally at Mbereshi.

UHLIK, Francis (SJ): b. 1877, Poland. At Katondwe, 1912-1921.

VERNON, W. Roy (SAGM): 1887-?, American. In Northern Rhodesia (Musonweji) 1913-1919.

WALKER, Walter W. (SDA): b. 1887, Sopchoppy, Florida. Attended public schools in various Florida cities from 1892-1903, the Winyah Lake School in 1917-1918, and the Southern Junior College from 1919-1920. Worked as a farmer, in packing houses, as a carpenter, as a chauffeur, as a male nurse, and, from 1916-1917, as the manager and secretary of the Ogden, Florida, Citrus Growers' Association.

WAREHAM, Harold Edgar (LMS): 1873-1955, b. Guildford, England. Son of a LMS missionary to India. M.B., Ch.B. Edinburgh. In Northern Rhodesia, 1902-1931, primarily at Kawimbe, Mbereshi, and Kafulwe.

WATNEY, Martyn Herbert (SAGM): b. 1887, Pangbourne, England. Eton College, M.A. Trinity College, Cambridge, M.B. St. Thomas' Hospital, London. A member of the Church of England. At Kaba Hill, 1923-1930.

WEBSTER, William George (UMCA): d. 1954. A compositor. Trained for the priesthood at St. Augustine's College,

Canterbury, England. Ordained in 1901. In Zanzibar diocese, 1900-1906. M.A. Durham, 1910. At Livingstone, 1910-1912. In the Southern Rhodesia diocese from 1912. Canon of Salisbury Cathedral, 1923-1925; Canon of Cape Town, 1934-1950.

WELFELÉ, Eugène (WF): 1877-1956, b. Chatenois, France. After completing his studies at the major seminary of Besançon, he matriculated at the White Fathers' seminary in Carthage, Tunisia. He became a priest in 1903, and served in Northern Rhodesia from 1914 until his death. Together with Father Schoeffer, he helped to transform the methods of the White Fathers in Northern Rhodesia by preferring village proselytism to the reliance upon the gathering of Africans into orphanages on the stations. He is said to have introduced the cultivation of cassava to the Bemba. From 1926 to 1947 he acted as the Supérieur Régional, or religious superior of the White Fathers, in the vicariates of Northern Rhodesia and Nyasaland. He wrote a number of short books in simple Cibemba, including summaries of the Old Testament and the Gospels. He was attached to a number of stations: Kayambi (1904-1914), Chibote (1917-1919), Chilubula (1920-1925, 1953-1956), Mulobola (1948-1950), Malole (1951), and Kapatu (1952).

WENGER, Jesse (BC): b. 1876, Englewood, Ohio. Active in street evangelism in Dayton, Ohio. At Macha, 1907-1909, 1912-1914.

WHEELER, Clarence Edward (SDA): b. 1890, Tyro, Kansas, into an Adventist family. Attended local schools from 1896-1905, Kansas State Agricultural College, 1905-1911, Union College, 1913-1915, and Washington Missionary College, 1916-1917. From the last named he received a B.A. in 1917. At Rusangu, Musofu, and Liumba Hill from 1920-1943. A farmer by occupation.

WILHELM, Augustinus (SJ): 1866-1952, b. Wroclaw, Poland. At Kapoche and Katondwe from 1919.

WILSON, Augustus Albert (SAGM): b. 1887, Canada. A printer and a Baptist. Studied at Toronto Bible College. At

193

Musonweji, 1914-1921, Angola, 1923-1945. Returned to Canada in 1951.

WILSON, Hubert Francis (UFCS): b. 1884, Kendal, Westmorland. Son of Frank L. Wilson of Kendal and Sierra Leone, and grandson of David Livingstone. Educated at Kendal and Carlisle Grammar Schools. Received B.A. (Cambridge), M.B., Ch.B. (Glasgow). Member of the Wellington United Free Church, Glasgow. In Chitambo in 1914 and again in 1919 to relieve Malcolm Moffat. At Livingstonia, 1920. Left Chitambo and resigned from the mission in 1928. In 1953, assisted at Mwenzo Hospital for six months. Gained Military Cross in 1916-1918. Married Mary Rhoda Mackie (b. 1895) in 1923. They have three children, one of whom was a missionary doctor at Lubwa, and reside in St. Fillans, Perthshire, Scotland.

WILSON, John Victor (SDA): 1889-1955, b. Port Elizabeth, Cape Colony. Attended local schools for ten years, and Union College (Kenilworth, Cape Colony) from 1902-1907. At Rusangu 1915-1922.

WILSON, Ruth Mary Livingstone (UFCS): b. 1882, Kendal, Westmorland. Daughter of Frank L. Wilson, grand-daughter of David Livingstone, and sister of Hubert Wilson. Educated at Kendal Friends School and Miss King's Private School, Herne Bay, Kent, England. She trained as a nurse for four years, taking a course in midwifery. A member of the New North Free Church, Edinburgh. In Livingstonia and Chitambo in 1914. Left Africa in 1919 and married the Rev. Mr. Alexander Macdonald in 1920.

WRIGHT, Robert Stewart (LMS): 1858-1926, b. Edinburgh. His father was a master boot-maker. The family lived in Newcastle-upon-Tyne. Wright left school at age fourteen. He became an office boy with the local railway, and thereafter worked as a draper's assistant in Newcastle and in Edinburgh. He spent two years at Rotherham College, and was ordained in 1887. He served the London Missionary Society at Fwambo during the balance of that year, and was stationed during

194

1888/1889 at Kavala and Niamkolo. He returned to England, where he ministered to a congregation in Haydon Bridge, Northumberland. From 1896 to 1899 he worked for the African Lakes Company in Nyasaland. During the next year he was in the employ of the British Central Africa Protectorate in Blantyre. He rejoined the London Society, and resided at its Niamkolo and Kambole stations from 1902 to 1916, when he took a second English pastorate. In 1920 he went to Australia on behalf of the London Society, and thereafter settled in New Zealand, where he died.

ZUREK, Augustinus (SJ): 1846-1917, b. Lubliniec, Silesia. At Katondwe, 1913-1917.

Appendix IV: An Essay on the Sources

MUCH of the unpublished material on which this book is based was found in musty missionary society boardrooms, in little-used sheds and attics, under piles of more immediately important papers at innumerable remote mission stations, or in the old tin trunks and battered cardboard boxes of retired missionaries and their families. In bulk, it contains fascinating documentation for a variety of books and for further studies of other aspects of the history of Northern Rhodesia and Nyasaland. The following is a brief guide to the unpublished sources from which this book was written.

The archives of the various missionary societies differed considerably in the quantity and quality of the documentation available. The incoming and outgoing correspondence files of the London Missionary Society's Central Africa Mission, carefully preserved in London, is the most extensive and the best catalogued of the missionary materials relevant for a history of Northern Rhodesia. The archives of the Primitive Methodist Missionary Society, also in London, contain letters to and from its missionaries in Northern Rhodesia, the papers of Edwin Williams Smith, and the diary and journals of Arthur Baldwin. The files of the Wesleyan Methodist Missionary Society, housed together with those of the Primitive Methodists, are important largely for letters to and from John White, the Wesleyan superintendent in Central Africa.

The numerous file-boxes of the Paris Missionary Society are housed in Paris. The local archives of the Society, at Sefula, Barotseland, contain important correspondence, baptismal registers, and several volumes of unsorted letters. The Society's Archives de Morija, Basutoland, are well-organized and of great value for Northern Rhodesia. Particularly important are the Procès Verbaux, 1877-1889, and the annual reports of the Assemblée Générale. The National Archives of Rhodesia hold the collected papers of François and Christina Coillard.

196

The English headquarters of the Society of Jesus contained almost no unpublished material pertaining to Northern Rhodesia. In Rome, at the Curia Praepositi Generalis Societatis Iesu, there are eight volumes of incoming letters relating to Jesuit missions in Northern Rhodesia. There are also volumes of outgoing letters, including all of the letters from superiors of the Society of Jesus to missions belonging to the English assistency. Unfortunately, however, these archives are closed until 2022. But in Salisbury, Southern Rhodesia, the Society's office was found to house various boxes containing correspondence to and from the Chikuni, Kasisi, Katondwe, Kapoche, Miruru, and Chingombe missions, the journals and letters of Fathers Weld, Depelchin, and Teroerde, and several unpublished manuscripts. At Chikuni, there were letters and papers written by Father Moreau. The diary of the Broken Hill mission dates from 1923 and the diaries of the Miruru and Katondwe missions, while they date from 1885, are written in Latin, German, Polish, English, and Serbo-Croatian. Father Torrend's diary for 1914-1921 is available in Lusaka.

The activity of the White Fathers in Northern Rhodesia is reflected in the diaries and logbooks kept by their various mission stations. Each had its official journal, but not all were compiled either regularly, or legibly. For the period before 1924, the diaries of Kayambi (and Old Mambwe), Chilonga, Chilubi, Kapatu, Malole, Lubwe (St. Joseph de Ngumbu), Chibote, Ipusikilo (Chibofwe), and Rosa are valuable. Most are in various stages of deterioration. A few valuable letters have been preserved at Mulilansolo mission. In Rome, the Generalate, Padria Bianchi, holds the Lavigerie letters (to 1892), the Livanhac letters (1895-1922), and the Voillard correspondence (1922-1936). Each contains about 1,500 folios. The Generalate also contains seven volumes of annual reports from 1889 to 1939.

The files of the Universities' Mission to Central Africa were scattered after a bomb shattered the windows of its London headquarters in 1944. The correspondence of the Mission, then carefully catalogued, was undamaged, but in the consequent confusion much material of value was lost.

197

Only a volume of official papers, two volumes of applications from prospective missionaries, and four small collections of assorted correspondence now remain for the historian of Northern Rhodesia. Fortunately, the loss of this official correspondence is balanced by the existence of the diaries kept at each of the Mission's stations.

Overzealous "spring cleaning" in 1939 destined all of the then available correspondence of the Plymouth Brethren clearing house at Bath, England, to the incinerator. Many of these letters were, however, printed without alteration in numbers of *The Missionary Echo* or the *Echoes of Service*. Many of the diaries and papers of Frederick Stanley Arnot and Walter Fisher were also found in Northern Rhodesia—in an old wicker basket; they are now housed in the National Archives of Rhodesia.

The correspondence of the South Africa General Mission, contained in fifteen loose-leaf volumes, was rescued from an attic in London. It consists primarily of letters and enclosures from missionaries in Northern Rhodesia, transmitted to and from London via the Mission's office in Cape Town. Further records of interest were found in Cape Town and Johannesburg. At Mukinge Hill mission, in Northern Rhodesia, there are diaries, minute books, baptismal records, and loose papers. Nearby, at Mutanda Bridge mission, are other documents of importance.

The records of the United Free Church of Scotland were, to a large extent, destroyed during World War II. What remains—of limited value for the study of the history of Northern Rhodesia—may be consulted in the National Library of Scotland. At Livingstonia, Nyasaland, there are minute books, ledgers, and correspondence files of supplementary importance, and at the Church's Mwenzo, Chitambo, and Lubwa missions there are a few letters and papers, the most useful of which is the Native Conference Minute Book (in Cilala) at Chitambo. At Mwenzo, there is a large collection of sermons, ethnological notes, statistics, and correspondence in Cinamwanga.

Documentation of the activities of the South African Baptist Missionary Society and the Nyasa Industrial Mission is limited to logbooks and letters at Kafulafuta, and to letters published in *Lambaland*. Minutes of the local conferences of the Brethren-in-Christ are found in Bulawayo. The records of the Seventh-day Adventists in Northern Rhodesia appear to have been destroyed at the stations, at the mission's Bulawayo, Salisbury, and Johannesburg headquarters, and at its international offices in Washington. The records of the Dutch Reformed Church Mission of the Orange Free State are located in Bloemfontein, but I was refused access to them. The stations of this mission house almost no unpublished materials; in the absence of original correspondence the *Notule Van Die Uitvoerende-Raad Van Die N.G. Kerk Sending Van Die O.V.S.N.O. Rhodesia (1909-1926)*, I (Mkhoma, 1926) is useful.

Private papers are also invaluable. The letters and diaries of the missionaries William Freshwater, Charles Leeke, W. Govan Robertson, and Harold Wareham are held in England. The vast collection of letters to and from Bishop Alston James Weller May (1914-1940) are likewise in England. The papers and journals of the missionaries Herbert Carter, Douglas Gray, Oliver Rocbuck, E. Herbert Sims, and John R. Shaw are in Rhodesia. In "The Linguistic Work and Mss. of R. D. Mac-Minn," *African Studies*, xviii (1959), 180-189, Clement Doke discusses the papers of a missionary of the United Free Church of Scotland.

In addition to the various missionary archives and papers, there is a wealth of important information in the Public Records of Southern Rhodesia and Northern Rhodesia (including the separate Public Records of both Northwestern and Northeastern Rhodesia). These sources are particularly valuable since the files of the London office of the British South Africa Company were largely destroyed in 1941. A detailed catalogue of the Southern Rhodesian records is contained in V. W. Hiller, et al., *A Guide to the Public Records of Southern Rhodesia* (Cape Town, 1956). Within this collection, the papers of the Resident Commissioner, of the High Commissioner, of the Cape Town office of the Company, and the outgoing letters from the Administrator, are significant for the historian of Northern Rhodesia. The Public Records of Northeastern Rhodesia contain outgoing letters from the Administrator and incoming letters from the High Commissioner and the Company's London office. The earliest correspondence is dated 1896, but most of the relevant letters were written after 1902. The Public Records of Northwestern Rhodesia contain similar material, departmental and district reports, judicial files, and the papers of the Secretary for Native Affairs. The Public Records of Northern Rhodesia comprise a wide range of files emanating both from the secretariat and from the various centers of district administration. Microfilms of many district notebooks are also found in the Lusaka archives, the originals of which are usually available individually at the respective *bomas*. These notebooks, depending upon the way in which they were kept, are a further historical source. A list of the more important notebooks is included in this Appendix.

Of the Foreign Office papers, housed in the Public Record Office, London, both the Slave Trade (FO 84) and the Africa (FO 2) series deal primarily with the British Central Africa Protectorate and refer only occasionally, but often significantly, to the affairs of Northeastern Rhodesia, and rarely to Northwestern Rhodesia. The Cawston Papers, in Rhodes House, Oxford, relate to plans for and explorations of Northern Rhodesia, particularly during the years 1890-1892. The bound volume entitled British South Africa Company, Misc. II is especially valuable.

A List of the Author's Interviews with Missionaries[1]

Botes, Ella M. (DRC) 13 April 1959, Magwero.
Buckley, Mrs. S. E. (PMMS) 29 Oct 1958, Motherwell.
Carter, Herbert (WMMS) 27 Nov 1959, Salisbury, S.R.
Cronjé, J. M. (DRC) 20 April 1959, Madzimoyo.
Doke, Olive C. (SAB) 8 July 1959, Kafulafuta.
Etienne, L. (WF) 2 Sept 1959, Chilubula.

[1] For a key to the abbreviations used on these pages see footnote 1, 163.

APPENDIX IV: SOURCES

Fisher, Charles (PB) 20 June 1959, Kitwe.

Fisher, Ffolliot (PB) 23 June 1959, Hillwood.

Fisher, Wilfrid (PB) 20 June 1959, Luanshya.

Foster, Charles S. (SAGM) 3, 4 July 1959, Mukinge Hill.

Freshwater, Bruce B. (LMS) 30 Oct 1958, Darlington.

Freshwater, Mrs. Nancy S. (LMS) 30 Oct 1958, Darlington.

Geddes, Charles (PB) 27 June 1959, Loloma.

Gerrard, Herbert S. (PMMS) 31 Oct 1958, Hazel Grove.

Green-Wilkinson, Bishop Oliver (UMCA) 9 Aug 1958, London.

Hewitt, George Herbert (UMCA) 21 March 1959, Lusaka.

Houghton, John C. (UMCA) 21 Jan 1959, Lusaka.

Icely, Bernard (UMCA) 15 Aug 1958, Northolt.

Kabilinde, Joseph (LMS) 18 Sept 1959, Mbereshi.

Kawandami, William (LMS) 19 Sept 1959, Mbereshi.

Lammond, William (PB) 16, 17 Sept 1959, Johnston Falls.

Mackenzie, Kenneth (CS) 29 Oct 1958, Edinburgh.

McFarlane, Graham J. (LMS) 25 March 1960, Oxford.

Musgrove, Peter (MMS) 20 Feb 1959, Lusaka.

Mutakasha, Jonathan (UMCA) 8 Sept 1959, Fiŵila.

Mwanakube, Wellington (LMS) 19 Sept 1959, Mbereshi.

Nightingale, Edward G. (MMS) 21 Jan 1959, Lusaka.

Nkole, Joshua (LMS) 19 Sept 1959, Mbereshi.

Pirouet, Herbert Geffrand (SAGM) 24 Oct 1958, Wimbledon.

Price, John R. (PMMS) 7 May 1958, Wolverhampton.

Prokoph, M. A. (SJ) 11 Sept 1958, London; 19 Feb 1959, Broken Hill.

Pulley, Gerrard Todd (UMCA) 25 April 1960, Oxford.

Rodgers, A. G. (UMCA) 11 April 1959, Fort Jameson.

Roebuck, Oliver (WMMS) 7 Dec 1959, Salisbury, S.R.

Shaw, John R. (PMMS) 22 Jan 1959, Lusaka.

Shaw, Mabel (LMS) 17 Nov 1958, London.

Short, W. N. (CC) 12 March 1959, Namwianga.

Sims, Edwin Herbert (PB) 28 June 1959, Lukolwe.

Sims, George (PB) 15 Sept 1959, Fort Rosebery.

Siwale, Donald (UFCS) 25 Aug 1959, near Tunduma.

Suckling, Mrs. George (PB) 30 June 1959, Chitokoloki.

Wareham, Monica (LMS) 19 Sept 1959, Mbereshi.

Whyman, Elsie (PB) 25 June 1959, Kamapanda.

A List of the Author's Interviews with Chiefs

Chitimukulu (Bemba) 3 Sept 1959, near Kasama.
Ikalenge (Ndembu) 24 June 1959, near Mwinilunga.
Kanganja (Ovimbundu) 24 June 1959, near Kaleñe Hill.
Kazembe (Lunda) 18 Sept 1959, near Kawambwa.
Magodi (Tumbuka) 18 April 1959, near Lundazi.
Mpeseni (Ngoni) 21 April 1959, near Fort Jameson.
Mwamba (Bemba) 4 Sept 1959, near Kasama.
Sir Mwanawina Lewanika III (Lozi) 24 July 1959, Lealui.
Mwase Lundazi (Cewa) 17 April 1959, Nthembe.
Nyanje (Nsenga) 25 April 1959, near Petauke.

Written Communications to the Author

Abel, Mrs. Hope (LMS) 5 Oct 1958, Hayling Island.
Arnot, Robert S. (son of F. S. Arnot) 25 July 1959, Kitwe.
Clark, Ernest H. (LMS) 13 Aug 1958, Seaton, Devon.
Gray, S. Douglas (WMMS) 30 Nov 1959, Knysna, C.P., South Africa.
Kittler, Glenn (author) 21 March 1959, New York.
Lyon, John T. (PMMS) 23 Nov 1958, Tockwith, Yorks.
McFarlane, Wilfrid (LMS) 24 March, 21 April 1960, Bournemouth.
Pearce, M. J. (UFCS) 15 Nov 1958, London.
Ranger, A. Sidney B. (UMCA) 22 April 1960, Calne, Wilts.
Sims, E. Herbert (PB) 21 March 1960, Lukolwe.
Slater, Arthur F. (PMMS) 15 Sept 1958, Tarporley, Cheshire.
Ter Maat, Frederic (WF) 25 May 1959, Oss, Holland.
Tuden, Arthur (anthropologist) 15 Sept 1958, Pittsburgh.
Watson, William (anthropologist) 17 March 1960, Gatley, Cheshire.
Wilson, Hubert F. (UFCS) 26 Dec 1959, St. Fillans, Perthshire.
Wingert, Mrs. Ruth Taylor (BC) 6 April 1960, Mechanicsburg, Pa.

Unpublished Manuscript Sources

Baxter, Thomas William, "Bibliography of Northern Rhodesia History," unpub. typescript (1949) in National Archives of Rhodesia, Salisbury.

Bonner, N. N., "The Pilgrim Holiness Church in Northern Rhodesia," unpub. typescript (1956), lent by the Church.

Bruce-Miller, F. V., "Central African Spiritualism," unpub. typescript (nd).

——, "The Eternal 'Native Question,'" unpub. typescript (nd), lent by Mrs. Bruce-Miller, Lusaka.

Chilver, Mrs. E. M., "Origins of the Society" (Jehovah's Witnesses) unpub. typescript (1952), lent by Mrs. Chilver.

Coxhead, John Charles Codrington, "The Natives of Northern Rhodesia and the War" (World War I), unpub. mss. (1920), UMCA files, Lusaka.

Doke, Clement M., "Notes on the Lambas of Northern Rhodesia," unpub. typescript (1937), lent by Miss Olive Doke.

Doke, Olive C., "Beginnings of the Lambaland Mission," unpub. mss. (1959), lent by Miss Doke.

Icely, Bernard, "A Life of Bishop May and a History of the Northern Rhodesia Diocese," unpub. typescript and mss., and notes (1941-1950), lent by Rev. Icely.

Jones, David Picton, "After Livingstone," unpub. typescript (1936), London Missionary Society archives.

Melland, Frank Hulme, "The Missionary Conference of 1922," unpub. typescript (1922).

——, "Testimony on Native Reserves," unpub. typescript (1936).

——, "Rabinek," unpub. typescript (1937); in the Rhodes-Livingstone Museum.

Mitchell, J. Clyde, "Social Change and the New Towns of Bantu Africa," unpub. typescript (1959), lent by Professor Mitchell.

Moreau, Joseph, "The Chikuni Mission, How it Came to be

Started in 1905," unpub. typescript (c. 1940), at Chikuni Mission.

———, "Removing Natives from the Chikuni Mission," unpub. typescript (1948), at Chikuni Mission.

Nketsia iv, Nana Kobina, "The Effect of Christian Missionary Activities on Some Akan Social Institutions from the Portuguese Settlement on the Mina Coast, 1482-1916," unpub. D. Phil. thesis (Oxford), 1959.

Nkumbula, Harry, "The Watch-Tower Movement in Namwala District, Northern Rhodesia," unpub. typescript (1935), lent by John Shaw.

O'Reilly, J. P., "A History of the Zambesi Mission," (SJ) unpub. typescript (1938), in Campion Papers, Salisbury.

Procter, John C., "Under the Southern Cross," unpub. typescript (1943), lent by Rev. Procter. [A History of the South Africa General Mission.]

Robertson, W. Govan, "Missions in Africa," unpub. typescript (c. 1920).

———, "On the Character and Influence of Islam," unpub. mss. (1897).

———, "The Use of Native Tradition and Superstition in Bible Teaching Among Africans," unpub. mss. (1898), in Abel Papers.

Searle, Scott, "History of the South Africa General Mission," unpub. typescript (c. 1914), in Cape Town office, South Africa General Mission.

Shaw, John R., "The History of the Nanzela Mission," unpub. typescript (1920).

———, "The Mobilization of our Forces for the Efficient Occupation of our Mission Field," unpub. typescript (c. 1918), lent by Rev. Shaw.

Sims, E. Herbert, "The Valwena" unpub. typescript (1929), lent by Rev. Sims.

Wareham, Harold E., "The Central African Mission in 1902," unpub. typescript (c. 1944), lent by Winifred Wareham.

Watch Tower Bible and Tract Society, "History of Jehovah's Witnesses in Northern Rhodesia," unpub. typescript (1959), lent by the Society.

A List of District Notebooks of Historical Value

Abercorn, incorporating Tanganyika district notebook, 1906-1960, at Abercorn.

Balovale, 1908-1960, at Balovale.

Broken Hill, incorporating Mwomboshi sub-district and Loangwa District, 1902-1960, at Broken Hill.

Chiengi, 1907-1933, at Kawambwa.

Chinsali, incorporating Mirongo division, 1904-1960, at Chinsali.

East Luangwa, 1911-1924, at Fort Jameson.

Feira, 1914-1960, at Feira. Particularly useful.

Fort Manning, 1921-1960, at Fort Manning, Nyasaland.

Fort Rosebery, 1904-1960, with useful accounts of earlier periods by Hubert Tyler Harrington, at Fort Rosebery.

Gwembe, incorporating Sijoba and Buni-Kariba districts, 1902-1960, at Gwembe.

Isoka, incorporating Fife, 1905-1960, at Isoka.

Kasama, 1908-1960, 2 v., at Kasama.

Kasempa, 1905-1960, at Kasempa.

Kawambwa, 1922-1960, at Kawambwa.

Luena, 1907-1915, at Luwingu, 2 v.

Lundazi, 1904-1960, at Lundazi.

Luwingu, 1924-1960, 2 v., at Luwingu (one volume missing).

Magoye, 1915-1925, at Mazabuka.

Mkushi, incorporating Old Mkushi, 1902-1960, at Mkushi.

Mongu, Resident Magistrate's Notebooks, 2 v., 1905-1960, at Mongu. Particularly useful.

Mpika, 1902-1960, 2 v., at Mpika.

Mporokoso, incorporating Katwe, 1904-1960, at Mporokoso.

Mumbwa, 1905-1960, at Mumbwa.

Mwenga, 1905-1921, at Mumbwa.

Mwinilunga, 1910-1960, at Mwinilunga.

Nalolo, 1907-1930, at Senanga.

Namwala, 1905-1960, at Namwala.

Nsumbu Islands, 1916-1924, at Luwingu.

Petauke, 1915-1960, at Petauke.

Rhodesia, 1895-1896, at Mporokoso.

Senanga, 1931-1960, at Senanga.

Serenje, 1908-1960, at Serenje.
Sesheke, 1911-1960, at Sesheke.
Solwezi, incorporating Kansanshi, 1909-1960, at Solwezi.

Periodicals Published by the Relevant Missionaries Societies

Advance, The (London), 1923-1932, Primitive Methodist Missionary Society.

Aurora, The (Livingstonia), 1897-1902, United Free Church of Scotland.

Bible Advocate, The (Birmingham), 1905-1916, Churches of Christ.

Catholic Teacher, The (Broken Hill), 1952-1956, Society of Jesus.

Central Africa (London), 1883-1926, Universities' Mission to Central Africa.

Echoes of Service (Bath), 1891-1931, Plymouth Brethren.

Foreign Field, The (London), 1904-1932, Wesleyan Methodist Missionary Society.

Journal des Missions Evangéliques (Paris), 1892-1925, Paris Missionary Society.

Lambaland (Johannesburg), 1916-1932, South African Baptist Missionary Society.

Missionary Echo, The (London), 1872-1890, Plymouth Brethren.

Missionary Herald, The (London), 1905-1922, Primitive Methodist Missionary Society.

Missionary Record, The (London), 1870-1904, Primitive Methodist Missionary Society.

Missionary Record of the United Free Church of Scotland, later *Record of the Home and Foreign Mission Work of the United Free Church of Scotland* (Edinburgh), 1897-1917.

News from Barotsi-Land (London), 1888-1921, Paris Missionary Society.

News from Basutoland and Barotseland (London), 1921-1935, Paris Missionary Society.

APPENDIX IV: SOURCES

Nouvelles du Zambèze (Genève), 1895-1924, Paris Missionary Society.

South African Pioneer (Wimbledon), 1909-1923, South Africa General Mission.

Star, The (Kafue), 1918-1926, Kafue Institute newspaper.

Appendix V. A Select Bibliography of Published Materials

I. Studies of the Missionaries of Northern Rhodesia

GENERAL

Mackintosh, Catherine Winkworth, *Some Pioneer Missions of Northern Rhodesia and Nyasaland* (Livingstone, 1950). A brief summary.

Proceedings of the General Missionary Conference of Northern Rhodesia, 1922 (Livingstonia, 1923).

————, *1924* (Lovedale, 1925).

————, *1927* (Lovedale, 1928).

Report of the Proceedings of the First Meeting of the North West Rhodesia Missionary Conference (Livingstone, 1914).

————, *Second Meeting* (Livingstone, 1919).

Smith, Edwin Williams, *The Way of the White Fields in Rhodesia* (London, 1928). The section on Northern Rhodesia is not very useful.

BRETHREN-IN-CHRIST

Davidson, H. Frances, *South and South Central Africa* (Elgin, Ill., 1915). An account of pioneering mission days in Northern and Southern Rhodesia.

Engle, Anna R.; Climenhaga, John A.; and Buckwalter, Leoda A. (eds.), *There Is No Difference* (Nappanee, Ind., 1950). Contains a section with a useful summary of the activities of the Brethren-in-Christ in Northern Rhodesia.

DUTCH REFORMED CHURCH (OFS)

Cronjé, J. M., *En Daar Was Lig* (Bloemfontein, 1958). The only summary of this mission's activities in Northern Rhodesia. Often misleading and somewhat superficial.

APPENDIX V: BIBLIOGRAPHY

Douglas, W. M., *Andrew Murray and His Message* (London, 1925).

Du Plessis, Johannes, *A Thousand Miles in the Heart of Africa, a record of a visit to the Boer Missions of Central Africa* (Edinburgh, 1905). Useful for a contemporary, sympathetic view of the first Dutch Reformed Church mission establishments in Northern Rhodesia.

——, *Life of Andrew Murray of South Africa* (London, 1920).

Retief, M. W., *William Murray of Nyasaland* (London, 1958).

Van der Merwe, W. J., *Development of Missionary Attitudes in the Dutch Reformed Church in South Africa* (Cape Town, 1934).

LONDON MISSIONARY SOCIETY

Goodall, Norman, *A History of the London Missionary Society* (London, 1954).

Hanna, A. J., "The Role of the London Missionary Society in the Opening up of East Central Africa," *Transactions of the Royal Historical Society*, v (1955), 41-59.

Hore, Mrs. Anne B., *To Lake Tanganyika in a Bath-Chair* (London, 1886). Informal, but a commentary upon early mission activity.

Hore, Edward Coode, *Tanganyika, Eleven Years in Central Africa* (London, 1892). Not detailed, but still useful for this pioneer period.

Johnson, Harry, *Night and Morning in Dark Africa* (London, 1903). Written for the mission's supporters.

Lovett, Richard, *History of the London Missionary Society, 1795-1895* (London, 1899). 2v.

Shaw, Mabel, *God's Candlelights* (London, 1932). An expression of personal philosophy by the woman responsible for the beginnings of modern girls' education in Northern Rhodesia. She also wrote *Children of the Chief* (London, 1921), *Dawn in Africa* (London, 1927), and *Treasure of Darkness* (London, 1930).

Swann, Alfred James, *Fighting the Slave-Hunters in Central Africa* (London, 1910). Interesting, and valuable for one missionary's view of imperialism.

APPENDIX V: BIBLIOGRAPHY

METHODIST MISSIONARY SOCIETY (PRIMITIVE AND WESLEYAN)

Church, L. F., *The Early Methodist People* (London, 1948).

———, *More About the Early Methodist People* (London, 1949).

Findlay, George G., and Holdsworth, William West, *The History of the Wesleyan Missionary Society* (London, 1921-1924), 5v.

Petty, John, *The History of the Primitive Methodist Connexion from its Origin to the Conference of 1859* (London, 1860).

Townsend, W. J.; Workman, H. B.; and Eayrs, George (eds.), *A New History of Methodism* (London, 1909), 2v.

Wearmouth, F. R., *Methodism and the Working Class Movements of England, 1800-1850* (London, 1837).

———

Andrews, Charles Fraser, *John White of Mashonaland* (London, 1935).

Baldwin, Arthur, *A Missionary Outpost in Central Africa* (London, 1914). A useful discussion from a pioneer's viewpoint.

———, *The Rev. Henry Buckenham* (London, c. 1907). A brief account of the leader of the first Primitive Methodist expedition to Northern Rhodesia.

Butt, George E., *My Travels in Northwest Rhodesia* (London, c. 1921). An account of a visit to Primitive Methodist missions by a fellow missionary from the Cape Colony.

Chapman, William, *A Pathfinder in Central Africa* (London, 1910). The best of the books by missionary pioneers.

Gray, S. Douglas, *Frontiers of the Kingdom in Rhodesia* (London, 1923). Written for supporters of Wesleyan Methodist missions in Northern Rhodesia.

Kerswell, Mrs. Kate L., *Romance and Reality of Missionary Life in Northern Rhodesia* (London, 1913). Life in the Zambezi Valley and the Mumbwa District from a missionary wife's point of view.

Nightingale, Edward G. (ed.), *The Widening Way* (London, 1952). A series of sketches about Methodist life.

Price, John R., *Building the Christian Community* (London,

1928). A short discussion of African customs and their relation to the Primitive Methodist mission by an experienced missionary.

Shaw, John R., *Our Central African Field* (London, 1926). Written for supporters, but useful for statistics and views on missionary life at that time.

————, "Nkala: An Abandoned Mission on the Kafue Flats," *The Northern Rhodesia Journal*, iv (1961), pp. 484-486.

Smith, Mrs. Julia A., *Sunshine and Shade in Central Africa* (London, 1908).

Taylor, Henry J., *Cape Town to Kafue* (London, 1915). Report of a visitation to Northern Rhodesia by a Primitive Methodist Missionary Society director.

Temple, Merfyn M., *Rain on the Earth* (London, 1955). Tonga tales and modern Methodist views.

ORDER OF FRANCISCAN MINOR, CAPUCHIN

James, Fr. A., *African Adventure: Irishmen on Safari* (Dublin, 1936). Irish Capuchins in South Africa and Northern Rhodesia.

PARIS MISSIONARY SOCIETY

Addison, James Thayer, *François Coillard* (Hartford, 1929).

Benoit, Daniel (ed.), *Lettres et Fragments de Jacques Liènard* (Cahors, 1902).

Bouchet, J., *Comment l'Évangile Agit au Zambèze* (Paris, 1922).

Casalis, Alfred, *Croquis du Zambèze* (Paris, 1919).

Coillard, François, *On the Threshold of Central Africa* (London, 1902). Tr. by Catherine Winkworth Mackintosh from *Sur le Haut-Zambèze* (Paris, 1899).

Dieterlen, H., *François Coillard* (Paris, 1921).

Dogimont, Rachel, *Dans La Brousse Zambèzienne* (Paris, 1923).

Favre, Édouard, *Un Combattant, Épisodes de la Vie de François Coillard* (Paris, 1936).

————, *François Coillard* (Paris, 1907, 1910, 1913), 3v.

Goy, Mme. Mathilda K., *Alone in Africa or Seven Years on*

the Zambezi (London, 1901). The vicissitudes of a missionary's wife at Sesheke.

Jalla, Adolphe, *Pionniers Parmi Les Ma-Rotse* (Florence, 1903).

Jousse, Theoph., *La Mission au Zambèze* (Paris, 1890). For supporters.

Kuntz, Marthe, *Ombre et Lumières* (Paris, 1921).

——, *Terre d'Afrique* (Paris, 1921). Stories about missionary life in Barotseland—for supporters.

Lambert, John C., *Missionary Heroes in Africa* (London, 1923). Contains a section on Coillard.

Liènard, Jacques, *Notre Voyage au Zambèze* (Paris, 1900).

MacConnachie, John, *An Artisan Missionary on the Zambesi* (London, 1910). Biography of William T. Waddell.

Mackintosh, Catherine Winkworth, *Coillard of the Zambesi* (London, 1907). The standard biography.

——, *The New Zambesi Trail* (London, 1922).

Malan, C. H., *La Mission Française du Sud de l'Afrique* (Paris, 1878). Mostly about Basutoland, with a discussion of Coillard's plans for Barotseland, by an important supporter of the mission.

Peyer, G., *François Coillard de Apostel der Sambesi-mission* (Basle, 1905).

Rey, Mme. C., *Une Femme Missionaire* (Paris, 1892). By one who lived briefly in Barotseland.

Shillito, Edward, *François Coillard: A Wayfaring Man* (London, 1923).

PILGRIM HOLINESS CHURCH

Strickland, R. E., *Over Livingstone's Trail in Northern Rhodesia* (Indianapolis, 1948). The only published work about this mission.

PLYMOUTH BRETHREN

Beattie, David J., *Brethren* (Kilmarnock, 1939). Popular, but useful, history of the movement.

Broadbent, Edmund Hamer, *The Pilgrim Church* (London, 1931). Also popular.

Neatby, William Blair, *A History of the Plymouth Brethren* (London, 1901). Although outdated, probably the best source for Brethren beginnings.

Pickering, Henry (ed.), *Are "Brethren" a Sect?* (London, 1934).

————, *Chief Men Among the Brethren* (London, 1931).

Veitch, Thomas Stewart, *The Story of the Brethren Movement* (London, 1933).

Vine, William Edward, *The Divine Plan of Missions* (London, 1946).

———

Arnot, Frederick Stanley, *Bihé and Garenganze, or Four Years Further Work and Travel in Central Africa* (London, 1893).

————, *Garenganze; or Seven Years' Pioneer Mission Work in Central Africa* (London, 1889).

————, *From Natal to the Upper Zambezi* (London, 1883). Discussion of his first trip to Africa.

————, *Missionary Travels in Central Africa* (Bath, 1914).

Baker, Ernest, *The Life and Explorations of Frederick Stanley Arnot* (London, 1921). The official biography. Baker intrudes only occasionally, and confines himself, for the most part, to excerpts from Arnot's diaries.

Campbell, Dugald, *In the Heart of Bantuland* (Philadelphia, 1922). Mostly about the Congo; a missionary reminiscence.

————, *Blazing Trails in Bantuland* (London, 1930).

Crawford, Daniel, *Thinking Black: Twenty-two Years Without a Break in the Long Grass of Central Africa* (London, 1913). A readable statement of personal missionary philosophy.

————, *Back to the Long Grass: My Link with Livingstone* (London, 1923).

Fisher, W. Singleton, and Hoyte, Julian, *Africa Looks Ahead* (London, 1948). Popular history of the Brethren in Northwestern Rhodesia and the Katanga, but more laudatory than accurate.

Lammond, William, "An 88-year-old Missionary Looks Back,"

East Africa and Rhodesia (22 October 1964), pp. 141-143.

Lawman, Tony, *From the Hands of the Wicked* (London, 1960). [A popular biography of Arnot.]

Suckling, George, *Chitokoloki on the Zambezi* (np. nd., but c. 1941). A useful fund-raising pamphlet. Discusses the history of the Chitokoloki station; by its founder.

————, *Mission Work in the Kabompo Valley* (np., 1915). Fund-raising pamphlet; gives reasons for starting the Chitokoloki station.

Tilsley, G. E., *Dan Crawford, Missionary and Pioneer in Central Africa* (London, 1921). The official biography.

SEVENTH-DAY ADVENTISTS

Anderson, W. H., *On the Trail of Livingstone* (Mountain View, Calif., 1919). Mission work among the Tonga.

Olsen, M. Ellsworth, *A History of the Origin and Progress of Seventh-day Adventists* (Washington, D.C., 1925).

SOUTH AFRICAN BAPTIST MISSIONARY SOCIETY

Batts, H. J., *Story of 100 years, 1820-1920, being the history of the Baptist Church in South Africa* (Cape Town, 1923).

Cross, Arthur J., *Twenty Years in Lambaland* (London, 1925). A short summary of the mission's development.

Cursons, William E., *Joseph Doke, the Missionary Hearted* (Johannesburg, 1929). The official biography of the man responsible for this mission's activity in Northern Rhodesia. It contains a section about his trip to Northern Rhodesia in 1913 and about the events which led to the South African Baptist Missionary Society's assumption of responsibility for Kafulafuta station.

Masters, Henry, *Go Ye!* (London, 1908). Written for supporters.

———— and Masters, Walter, *In Wild Rhodesia* (London, 1920). Rather overdrawn account of activities in Lambaland, but useful for an expression of personal views.

214

APPENDIX V: BIBLIOGRAPHY

SOCIETY OF JESUS

Depelchin, H., and Croonenberghs, Ch., *Trois ans dans l'Afrique Australe* (Bruxelles, 1883). It is useful only for the first expeditions across the Zambezi River. It has recently been translated as *Diaries of the Jesuit Missionaries at Bulawayo, 1879-1881*, by M. Lloyd. (Publication No. 4 of The Rhodesiana Society, Salisbury.)

Verwimp, W. E., *Thirty Years in the African Wilds* (London, 1938). (tr. from *Dreissig Jahre in der Afrikanischen Wildnis* [Saarbrücken, 1936].)

Weld, F., *Mission of the Zambesi* (London, 1880). Fundraising pamphlet. Useful for expressions of intent about Northern Rhodesia.

UNITED FREE CHURCH OF SCOTLAND

Doke, Clement M., "The Linguistic Work and Mss. of R. D. MacMinn," *African Studies*, xviii (1959), 180-189.

Jack, James W., *Daybreak in Livingstonia, The Story of the Livingstonia Mission, British Central Africa* (Edinburgh, 1901).

Laws, Robert, *Reminiscences of Livingstonia* (London, 1934).

Livingstone, William P., *Laws of Livingstonia* (London, 1921).

Morrison, J. H., *Streams in the Desert: A Picture of Life in Livingstonia* (London, 1919).

UNIVERSITIES' MISSION TO CENTRAL AFRICA

Anderson-Morshead, A. E. M., *The History of the Universities' Mission to Central Africa, 1859-1909* (London, 1909), 2v.

Blood, A. G., *The History of the Universities' Mission to Central Africa, 1907-1932* (London, 1957), 2v.

Hine, John Edward, *Days Gone By, Being Some Account of Past Years Chiefly in Central Africa* (London, 1924). The first Bishop of Northern Rhodesia devotes pp. 251-282 to his experiences in Northern Rhodesia.

Smith, A. H., *An Appeal for Northern Rhodesia* (Mapanza,

1929). Summary of the mission and its problems, by a priest.

Universities' Mission to Central Africa, *Beyond the Waters that Thunder* (London, 1928). Popular history of the Northern Rhodesia diocese.

Wilson, George Herbert, *The History of the Universities' Mission to Central Africa* (London, 1936).

WHITE FATHERS

Attwater, Donald, *The White Fathers in Africa* (London, 1937).

Bouniol, J., *The White Fathers and their Missions* (London, 1929). Two short sections refer to Northern Rhodesia.

Clarke, R. F., *Cardinal Lavigerie and the African Slave Trade* (London, 1889).

Goyau, Georges, *Un Grand Missionnaire: Le Cardinal Lavigerie* (Paris, 1925).

Kittler, Glenn D., *The White Fathers* (London, 1957). Romantic popular account.

Pineau, Henri, *Évêque—Roi des Brigands, Mgr. Dupont* (Quebec, 1949). This book has been abridged and partially translated by A. E. Howell, *Bishop-King of the Brigands* (Franklin, Pa., 1949).

Tanguy, François, (trans. Clifford Green), "Kayambi: The First White Father Mission in Northern Rhodesia," *The Northern Rhodesia Journal*, iv, 2 (1954), 73-78.

II. Northern Rhodesian Missionary Ethnological Writings

Burner, Th., *Âmes Primitives* (Paris, 1922).

Campbell, Dugald, "Notes on Butwa—A Secret Society in the Bangweulu Batwa," *Man*, xiv (1914), 76-81.

Fisher, W. Singleton, "Black Magic Feuds," *African Studies*, viii (1949), 20-22.

———, "Burning the Bush for Game," *African Studies*, vii (1948), 36-38.

Hopgood, Cyril R., "Conceptions of God among the Tonga of Northern Rhodesia," in Smith, Edwin Williams, ed., *African Ideas of God* (London, 1950), 61-67.

Jalla, Adolphe, *Litaba za Sicaba sa Malozi* (Sefula, 1909).

Jalla, Louis, *Sur les Rives du Zambèze: Notes Ethnographiques* (Paris, 1928).

Labrèque Édouard, "Accidents de la Naissance chez les Babemba," *Anthropos*, xxv (1930), 730-731.

———, "Mariage chez les Babemba," *Africa*, iv (1931), 209-221.

———, "Le Tribu des Babemba," *Anthropos*, xxviii (1933), xxxi (1936), 633-648.

———, "La Sorcellerie chez les Babemba," *Anthropos*, xxxii (1938), 260-265.

Molinier, Lud., "Croyances Superstitieuses chez les Babemba," *Journal of the African Society*, iii (1903), 74-82.

Munday, J. T., "Some Traditions of the Nyendwa Clan," *Bantu Studies*, xiv (1940), 435-454.

———, *Kankomba: A Folk History of the Lala* (Lusaka, 1961).

Robertson, William Govan, "Kasembe and the Bemba (Awemba) Nation," *Journal of the African Society*, iii (1903), 183-193.

Smith, Edwin Williams, "Addendum to the 'Ila-Speaking Peoples of Northern Rhodesia,'" *African Studies*, viii (1949), 1-9, 53-61.

———, and Dale, A. M., *The Ila Speaking Peoples of Northern Rhodesia* (London, 1920), 2v.

Torrend, Julius, *Specimens of Bantu Folklore* (London, 1921).

III. Some Other Relevant Publications

Bertrand, Alfred, *En Afrique avec le Missionaire Coillard* (Genève, 1898).

Coillard, François, "Voyage au Pays des Banyais et au Zambèze," *Bulletin de la Société de Géographie* (November 1880), 385-401.

Decle, Lionel, *Three Years in Savage Africa* (London, 1898).

Drummond, Henry, *Tropical Africa* (London, 1889).

Gann, Lewis H., *The Birth of a Plural Society: The Develop-*

ment of Northern Rhodesia under the British South Africa Company, 1894-1914 (Manchester, 1958).

—————, *A History of Northern Rhodesia: Early Days to 1953* (London, 1964).

Gelfand Michael, *Northern Rhodesia in the Days of the Charter* (Oxford, 1961).

Gibbons, A. St. Hill, "A Journey in the Marotse and Mashikolumbwe Countries," *The Geographical Journal*, ix (1897), 121-143.

—————, "Marotseland and the Tribes of the Upper Zambezi," *Proceedings of Royal Colonial Institute*, xxix (1897-1898), 260-276.

Gouldsbury, Cullen and Sheane, Hubert, *The Great Plateau of Northern Rhodesia* (London, 1911).

Hanna, Alexander John, *The Beginnings of Nyasaland and North-Eastern Rhodesia, 1859-1895* (Oxford, 1956).

Harding, Colin, *In Remotest Barotseland* (London, 1905).

Holub, Emil, *Seven Years in South Africa* (London, 1881), 2v.

—————, *Von der Capstadt ins Land der Mashukulumbe* (Wien, 1890), 2v.

Hore, Edward Coode, "Lake Tanganyika," *Proceedings of the Royal Geographic Society*, iv (1882), 1-27.

Johnston, James, *Reality versus Romance in South Central Africa* (London, 1893).

Knowles Jordan, E., "Early Days in Kalomo and Livingstone," *The Northern Rhodesia Journal*, i, 4 (1951), 16-23.

—————, "Namwala in 1906," *The Northern Rhodesia Journal*, ii, 1 (1953), 24-36.

Moir, Fred L. M., *After Livingstone: An African Trade Romance* (London, 1932).

Moubray, J. M., *In South Central Africa* (London, 1912).

Nicholls, George Heaton, *South Africa in My Time* (London, 1961).

Oliver, Roland, *Sir Harry Johnston & the Scramble for Africa* (London, 1957).

Rotberg, Robert I., "The Emergence of Northern Rhodesia: The Missionary Contribution, 1885-1924," *St. Antony's Papers* (London, 1963), xv, 101-129.

————, "Missionaries as Chiefs and Entrepreneurs: Northern Rhodesia, 1882-1924," in Jeffrey Butler, ed., *Boston University Papers in African History* (Boston, 1964), i, 195-216.

————, "The Missionary Factor and the Occupation of Trans-Zambezia," *The Northern Rhodesia Journal*, v, 4 (1964), 330-338.

————, "Plymouth Brethren and the Occupation of Katanga, 1886-1907," *The Journal of African History*, IV (1964), 285-297.

Silva Porto, António F. F. da, *E Travessia do Continente Africano* (Lisboa, 1938).

Stewart, James, *Dawn in the Dark Continent* (London, 1903).

Thomson, J. B., "Memories of Abandoned Bomas: Chiengi," *The Northern Rhodesia Journal*, vi, 2 (1955), 67-77.

IV. Some Comparative Literature

Adelaja, B. A., "The Christian Faith and African Culture," *The East and West Review*, XXII (1956), 35-40.

Africa Committee on Foreign Missions, *Christian Action in Africa* (Westerville, O., 1942).

African Education Commission, *Education in Africa* (New York, 1922).

————, *Education in East Africa* (New York, 1924).

Allier, Raoul, *La Psychologie de la Conversion* (Paris, 1925), 3v.

Bascom, William, "African Culture and Missions," *Civilisations*, III (1953), 491-504.

Bates, M. Searle, *Data on the Distribution of the Missionary Enterprise* (London, 1943).

Beaver, R. Pierce, "Nationalism and Missions," *Church History*, XXVI (1957), 22-42.

————, "Recent Literature on Overseas Missionary Movements," *Journal of World History*, I (1953), 139-163.

Bowes, T. F. C., "The Work of the Christian Church Among the Kikuyu," *International Affairs*, XXIX (1953), 316-325.

Carpenter, George W., "Church and State in Africa Today," *Civilisations*, III (1953), 519-538.

Carrington, Philip, *The Early Christian Church* (Cambridge, 1957), 2v.

Cripps, A. S., *An Africa for the Africans* (London, 1927).

Culwick, A. T., *Good Out of Africa* (Livingstone, 1942).

Dougall, James W. C., "The Case for and against Mission Schools," *Journal of the African Society*, xxxviii (1939), 91-110.

———, *Christianity and the Sex Education of the African* (London, 1937).

Du Plessis, Johannes, *The Evangelisation of Pagan Africa* (Cape Town, 1929).

———, *A History of Christian Missions in South Africa* (London, 1911).

———, "Missions as a Sociological Factor," *South African Journal of Science*, xxix (1932), 84-97.

Foreign Missionary Conference of North America, *The Christian Occupation of Africa* (New York, 1917).

Gale, H. P., *Uganda and the Mill Hill Fathers* (London, 1959).

Gelfand, Michael, *Lakeside Pioneers* (Oxford, 1964).

Gibson, Alan G. S., "Christianity Among the Bantu," *The East and the West*, xi (1913), 383-396.

Goodall, Norman and Nielsen, Eric, *Survey of the Training of the Ministry in Africa* (iii) (London, 1954).

Gray, Ernest, "Some Present Day Problems for African Christian Marriage," *International Review of Missions*, xlv (1956), 267-277.

Hay, Hope, "Literacy Technique in Northern Rhodesia," *The Rhodes-Livingstone Journal*, ix (1950), 1-13.

———, "Mass Literacy in Northern Rhodesia," *Quarterly Bulletin of Fundamental Education*, i (1949), 11-17.

———, *Northern Rhodesia Learns to Read* (London, 1947).

Helander, Gunnar, *Must We Introduce Monogamy?* (Pietermaritzburg, 1958).

Herbert, Gabriel, *Fundamentalism and the Church of God* (London, 1957).

Hetherwick, Alexander, *The Gospel and the African* (Edinburgh, 1932).

Howell, W. H., " 'Functional' Social Anthropology and Christian Missionary Method," *International Review of Missions*, XXXVI (1947), 253-257.

Hutchinson, Bertram, "Some Social Consequences of Nineteenth Century Missionary Activity among the South African Bantu," *Africa*, XXVII (1957), 160-177.

Ibanez, P. Esteban, "Franciscanos Espanoles En Las Misiones de Marruecos," *Archivos del Instituto de Estudios Africanos*, XIII (1959).

International Missionary Council, *Treaties, Acts and Regulations Relating to Missionary Freedom* (London, 1923).

James, E. O., "The Christianization of Native Rites," in W. G. de Lara Wilson (ed.), *Christianity and Native Rites* (London, 1950), 41-51.

Joyce, George Hayward, *Christian Marriage* (London, 1948).

Junod, Henri Ph., "Bantu Marriage and Christian Society," *Bantu Studies*, XI (1941), 26-29.

Kale, S. I., "Polygamy and the Church in Africa," *International Review of Missions*, XXXI (1942), 220-223.

King, E. R. G., "On Educating African Girls in Northern Rhodesia," *Rhodes-Livingstone Journal*, X (1950), 65-74.

Knak, Siegfried, *Zwischen Nil und Tafelbai—Eine Studie über Evangelium, Volkstum und Zwilsation am Beispiel der Missionsproblem ünter den Bantu* (Berlin, 1931).

Koskinen, Aarne A., *Missionary Influence as a Political Factor in the Pacific Islands* (Helsinki, 1953).

Kraemer, Hendrik, *The Christian Message in a Non-Christian World* (New York, 1947).

Kuper, Hilda, "The Swazi Reaction to Missions," *African Studies*, V (1946), 176-188.

Laws, Robert, "Native Education in Nyasaland," *Journal of the African Society*, XXVIII (1929), 347-367.

Long, Norman, "Bandawe Mission Station & Local Politics, 1878-1886," *The Rhodes-Livingstone Journal*, XXXII (1962), 1-22.

Loram, C. T., *The Education of the South African Native* (London, 1917).

Lucas, William Vincent, "The Christian Approach to Non-

Christian Customs," in W. G. de Lara Wilson, ed., *Christianity and Native Rites* (London, 1950), 3-38.

MacGregor, J. K., "Christian Missions and Marriage Usage in Africa," *The International Review of Missions*, XXIV (1935), 184-191.

Miller, Walter R., *Have We Failed in Nigeria?* (London, 1947).

———, *Success in Nigeria* (London, 1948).

Morris, William Dale, *The Christian Origins of Social Revolt* (London, 1949).

Northern Rhodesia Government, *Jeanes and Agricultural Schools* (Livingstone, 1929).

Olangua, Augusto, "Cien Años de Historia en Las Misiones Expañolas en Guinea," *Archivos del Instituto de Estudios*, XIII (1959).

Oliver, Roland, *The Missionary Factor in East Africa* (London, 1952).

Parsons, Robert T., "The Missionary and the Cultures of Man," *The International Review of Missions*, XLV (1956), 161-168.

———, "Missions-African Relations," *Civilisations*, III (1953), 505-518.

Phillips, Arthur, ed., *Survey of African Marriage and Family Life* (London, 1953).

Price, Maurice T., *Christian Missions and Oriental Civilizations* (Shanghai, 1924).

Price, Thomas, "The Task of Mission Schools in Africa," *The International Review of Missions*, XXVII (1938), 223-228.

Ross, Emory, "Christianity in Africa," *Annals of the American Academy of Political and Social Sciences*, CCXCVIII (1955), 161-169.

Rousseau, M. H., *A Bibliography of African Education in the Federation of Rhodesia and Nyasaland (1890-1958)* (Cape Town, 1958).

Rowling, R. and Wilson, C. E., *Bibliography of African Christian Literature* (London, 1923).

Sarvis, Guy W., "The Missionary as a Social Changer," *Christendom*, VI (1936), 826-838.

Schapera, Isaac, "Christianity and the Tswana," *The Journal of the Royal Anthropological Institute*, LXXXVIII (1958), 1-10.

Shepperson, George, "Church and Sect in Central Africa," *The Rhodes-Livingstone Journal*, XXIII (1963), 82-94.

———, "Nyasaland and the Millennium," in Sylvia Thrupp, ed., *Millennial Dreams in Action, Essays in Comparative Study* (The Hague, 1962).

———, and Thomas Price, *Independent African: John Chilembwe and the Origins, Setting and Significance of the Nyasaland Native Rising of 1915* (Edinburgh, 1958).

Shropshire, Denys W. T., *The Church and Primitive Peoples* (London, 1938).

———, *Primitive Marriage and European Law* (London, 1946).

Slade, Ruth M., *English-Speaking Missions in the Congo Independent State (1878-1908)* (Bruxelles, 1959).

Smith, Edwin Williams, *Great Lion of Bechuanaland: The Life and Times of Roger Price, Missionary* (London, 1957).

Springer, John McKendree, *The Heart of Central Africa, Mineral Wealth and Missionary Opportunity* (Cincinnati, 1900).

Sundkler, Bengt, *The Christian Ministry in Africa* (Uppsala, 1960).

———, "Marriage Problems in the Church in Tanganyika," *International Review of Missions*, XXXIV (1945), 253-266.

Taylor, John V., *The Growth of the Church in Buganda* (London, 1958).

———, and Lehmann, Dorothea A., *Christians of the Copperbelt: the Growth of the Church in Northern Rhodesia* (London, 1961).

Trowell, H. C., *The Passing of Polygamy* (London, 1940).

Tucker, John T., "Fifty Years in Angola," *International Review of Missions*, XIX (1930), 256-265.

Velsen, Jaap van, "The Missionary Factor among the Lakeside Tonga of Nyasaland," *Rhodes-Livingstone Journal*, XXVI (1960), 1-22.

Warneck, Gustav, *Die Apostolische und die Moderne Mission* (Gütersloh, 1876).

Willoughby, W. C., *The Soul of the Bantu* (London, 1928).

Wilson, Monica, "An African Christian Morality," *Africa*, x (1937), 265-291.

Winterbottom, J. M., "Africans, European Culture, and the English Language," *The Rhodes-Livingstone Journal*, ii (1944), 1-7.

Wrigley, C. C., "The Christian Revolution in Buganda," *Comparative Studies in Society and History*, ii (1959), 33-48.

Young, T. Cullen, *African Ways and Wisdom* (London, 1937).

―――, and Banda, Hastings Kamuzu, eds., *Our African Way of Life* (London, 1946).

Zwemer, Samuel M., *The Unoccupied Fields of Africa and Asia* (London, 1911).

Index

Material in the biographical appendix is contained herein only insofar as it bears directly upon the history of Northern Rhodesia. Names of missionaries are included only if they appear in the body of the text and Appendices I, II, and IV. The entries in the bibliography are not repeated in the index. For abbreviations, see 163.

South African Baptist Missionary Society, the: 75, 77, 108-
109, 112-113, 139, 154, 157;
representatives of, 170; papers
of, 198-199; see also Kafulafuta
South-East Africa Evangelistic
Mission, the, 76
Southwark, the Bishop of, 79
Speke, John Hanning, explorer,
7
spheres of influence, missionary,
UMCA, 81-82, general, 86-
89; see also rivalry between
denominations
Springer, John M., missionary,
43n
Stanley, Henry Morton, journal-
ist and explorer, 7
Stanley, Governor Sir Herbert,
105
Stephen, James, British official,
quoted, 161-162
Stevenson Road, the, 18
Stewart, Dr. James, missionary,
quoted, 10
stockades, the use of by missionaries, 56-57; by others, 62
Suckling, George, missionary,
quoted, 117-118, 132; wife,
201
Swann, Alfred James, missionary, 32, 37

Tafuna, Chief of the Lungu, 33,
61
Tamanda, DRCM station, 155,
163, 168, 175, 190
Tanganyika, 7, 174, 185
Tanganyika, Lake: 7, 17-19, 31,
32, 33, 44, 55, 159, 176
taxation of Africans, 52, 100-
101, 117
Taylor, Robert Selby Bishop,
106
temperance, efforts to promote,

40, 41, 60, 64, 77, 116, 120,
132, 136, 139, 140-141
Teroerde, Anthony, missionary,
151, 197
Ter Maat, Frederic, missionary,
202
Tete, Moçambique, 5
Thompson, R. Wardlaw, LMS
secretary: 39n, 47n; quoted,
45-46, 65-66, 100, 111, 130,
158, 160
Toka, the, people, 14, 75
Tonga, the, people, 5, 14, 21n,
48, 71, 74, 75, 82, 87, 123
Torday, Emil, quoted, 127-128
Torrend, Julius, missionary, 156;
quoted, 97-98; diary of, 197
traders, the missionaries as; see
entreprenurial initiative
translation into African languages, 46-49, 77, 135-136,
169, 174, 184, 186, 188, 193
Trent, Council of, 128
trials by ordeal, 15, 60, 132
Trower, Gerald Bishop, 79, 81
Tuden, Professor Arthur, 202
Tuskegee Normal and Industrial
Institute, the, 124
Twingi, WF station, 169, 174,
186

Ujiji, Tanganyika, 7, 17, 32
Universities' Mission to Central
Africa, the, founding of, 6;
mission to Nyasaland, 6; enters Northern Rhodesia, 78-
86, 153; spheres of influence,
86-87; acts on behalf of Africans, 104-106; educational
work, 115-117, 121; and social change, 130-131, 133,
140; evangelism, 138-139,
140n; stations, 154-155; organization of, 156-157, 161;
representatives of, 164-193;
papers of, 197-199